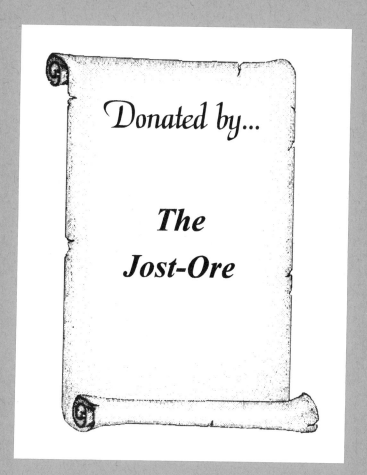

PRACTICAL POLITICS

E.F. Root
Richmond
11/19/76

BERNARD SHAW

PRACTICAL POLITICS

Twentieth-Century Views on
Politics and Economics

EDITED BY
Lloyd J. Hubenka

UNIVERSITY OF NEBRASKA PRESS · LINCOLN and LONDON

To Dan H. Laurence with gratitude

Publishers on the Plains
UNP

Introduction copyright © 1976 by the University
of Nebraska Press
Shaw texts copyright © 1976 by The Trustees of
The British Museum, The Governors and
Guardians of The National Gallery of Ireland,
and Royal Academy of Dramatic Art; reprinted
by arrangement with the Society of Authors,
London

Library of Congress Cataloging in Publication Data

Shaw, George Bernard, 1856–1950.
    Practical politics.

Includes bibliographical references and index.
    CONTENTS: Life, literature, and political economy.—The solidarity of
social-democracy.—The bitter cry of the middle classes. [etc.]
    1. Socialism—Collected Works. I. Title.
HX241.S53 1976   335   75–3571
ISBN 0–8032–0856–1

Contents

Introduction

I   The essays and lectures in this collection date primarily from the first three decades of the present century, a time when Shaw wrote the majority of his plays, established the drama of ideas as a vital force in twentieth-century theater, and captured the 1925 Nobel prize for literature for his achievements in theater. Two of the pieces are hitherto unpublished lectures: one delivered before the Liverpool Fabian Society in 1908, the other delivered before the London Fabian Society in 1931 after Shaw's celebrated trip to Russia. Why the first, "Socialist Politics," was not published is not known; nor can we be altogether sure that it is an accurate transcription. The second, "What Indeed?" was not published because, after examining the verbatim report, Shaw decided that he wished to write a book about developments in Russia, a book which he never completed but which was published in 1964 bearing the title which Shaw gave it—*The Rationalization of Russia*.

The remaining pieces in the collection are evenly divided between newspaper reports of lectures and newspaper articles, most of them having appeared in socialist or radical journals owned or edited by Shaw's friends. He was a frequent contributor to *The Clarion*, edited by Robert Blatchford, which was in its day the most widely circulated socialist newspaper in England. He also contributed articles and money to sustain fledgling radical publications, such as the *New Age*, edited by Holbrook Jackson and A. R. Orage. Yet, his support of such radical publications was not solely inspired by a longing for the "cause." Actually, except for letters to editors, animated debates with men like G. K. Chesterton and W. H. Mallock, and rejoinders such as his retort to G. R. Sims in "The Bitter Cry of the Middle Classes," Shaw and other socialists found it difficult to publish their views and activities in London daily newspapers. As Shaw notes in the 1908 reprint of the *Fabian Essays*, the press waged an effective conspiracy of silence against socialism in England. Not a word about his or others' lectures on socialism, he says, were "allowed to leak through to the public through the ordinary channels of newspaper reporting." Thus Shaw's audience, from the beginning of his career until well into the first decade of this century, consisted of a very small circle of people.

Such boycotting, however, ended with the success of *John Bull's Other Island* in 1904 and the enormous popularity of *Man and Superman* at the Court Theatre a year later. Aware that his reputation as a playwright was established, Shaw, being as shrewd a businessman as he was a controversialist, hired a legal stenographer to make verbatim transcriptions of his lectures and began placing these reports in some of the smaller nonsocialist British newspapers. A few years later, in 1911, beginning with a debate between Chesterton and himself, Shaw and the Webbs started the famous Fabian Lecture Series which for the next twenty years became not only a vital source of revenue for the society but also a valuable instrument of propaganda. Each year Shaw took the "star turn" at the annual series of six lectures, giving the audiences—now including an occasional Rothschild or a member of royalty—his views on a range of subjects from jingoism to the League of Nations. With each passing year, Shaw's audience widened until it no longer consisted merely of English intellectuals but comprised virtually the entire English-speaking world; as early as 1914 Shaw had become an international figure, equipped, as Beatrice Webb said, with a fascinating personality which he presented to the world as G.B.S.

He became, after a fashion, a sort of international syndicated columnist. He found it financially and politically advantageous to have his plays as well as his polemic essays published in America. After 1920, especially with his yearly contribution to the Fabian lectures, Shaw would first cable either the full text of his lecture or, more often, an important excerpt of it to the United States for copyright and publication in a large metropolitan newspaper like the *New York Times* and then a few days or weeks later, he would publish a revised, corrected, or entirely rewritten version of the same lecture in a British newspaper.

Yet, ironically, as Shaw's audiences increased both in the lecture halls and in the press, his political utterances became more and more disturbing to those who considered him a spokesman for social democracy. Beginning with his stand on the equality of income—an idea which most contemporary socialists viewed as utterly impossible—many Fabians, although aware that he was the society's most profitable spokesman, grew apprehensive about his political views. Shaw the Fabian agitator was dead. No longer, as he once said in another context, would his character be "smirched by compromise, rotted with opportunism, mildewed by expediency, blackened by ink contributed to Tory and Liberal papers, dragged through the mud of borough councils, stretched out of shape with wire pulling, putrified by permeation, worn out by 25 years pushing to gain an inch here or straining to stem back a rush there." From the date of his resignation from the Fabian Executive Committee in 1911 to the end of his life, Shaw stood as a solitary prophet. Liberals who felt that he was drifting to the right were horrified by his denunciations of parliamentary government and his approval of Mussolini's reference to democracy as a "putrefying corpse"; trade unionists were outraged by his insistence on compulsory labor as a necessary complement to equality of income; and socialists were shocked when he told them to seek a dictator. To many it seemed that Shaw had rejected much of what he previously had held or, like his own Roebuck Ramsden, had come to be a man with advanced ideas whom time had passed. As William Irvine observed, Shaw's later political record seemed "to consist chiefly in a bitter and impatient theoretical marching up and down before the daily facts of history"; and Julian Kaye has remarked that Shaw's reputation must stand on the work of his youth and his middle age, not on that of his old age, for with regard to politics and economics, Shaw did not understand the Zeitgeist of the twentieth century.

II Yet a close examination of Shaw's later political writings shows that many ideas which critics find repugnant either lie latent in Shaw's earlier political thought or naturally grow out of it. Shaw was a man of single vision, but a man flexible enough to adjust his focus to stress a truth to which he thought his contemporaries blind. It is also an error to dismiss him as an outdated prophet—an advanced thinker of the nineteenth century utterly overwhelmed by the catastrophic events of a new century. Certainly he is a nineteenth-century intellectual and therefore perhaps to many contemporary minds a bit old-fashioned. Yet he is a nineteenth-century intellectual nurtured in the faith that given the opportunity, men would demonstrate sufficient capacity to master modern industrial civilization. This faith, of course, proved hollow. To read Shaw is to explore the reactions of one of the keenest minds of that age as it watched European civilization descend into civil war, or so one might label the years 1914–45. This period saw Europe endure two world wars, a world wide depression, and the rise of fascism, and, equally important, saw socialist hopes for social democratic government shattered by feeble Labor governments in the West and Bolshevik dictatorship in the East. Accordingly, if there is any truth to Ezra Pound's claim that artists are the antennae of the race, these latter-day pronouncements by Shaw are a valuable commentary on our time.

It is in part the complexity of Shaw's thought that prevents us from seeing how his latter-day opinions evolve out of his earlier views. Shaw differs from most nineteenth-century reformers in that he draws his ideas for the reconstruction of society from two philosophical strands rather than one. One, the utilitarian tradition of Bentham and Mill, essentially political in nature, represented an attempt to reform society from without by giving it a more just and efficient social, economic, and political structure; most of the progressive and radical movements of the age were related to it in some way. The other, the transcendental tradition of Carlyle and Ruskin, was fundamentally moral and conservative; its apologists scoffed at any hope for progress through parliamentary legislation, insisting instead that until each human heart reformed itself there was little hope for the amelioration of the human condition. Thus, to use Koestler's terms, Shaw is part Yogi and part Commissar. For Shaw's readers, the disturbing thing is, of course, that Shaw does not choose between these two traditions: he uses ideas and principles from one or both—whenever it serves his purpose.

It is unquestionably the progressive or radical aspect of Shaw's thought which has made him popular with the general reader. This side of Shaw is omnipresent in the pages of *The Quintessence of Ibsenism, The Fabian Essays*, and *The Common Sense of Municipal Trading*, where assaults on slum dwellings and private enterprise are juxtaposed with ideas on free thought, unorthodox medicine, and the transformation of the family. That socialist and progressive concerns are mixed in Shaw's works is not incongruous, for in the nineteenth and early twentieth centuries the causes of socialism and progressivism ran a parallel course. Both ideologies were opposed to what Marxists call the "privilegentsia." The utilitarians, the political wing of nineteenth-century progressivism, for example, believed that institutions of British society promoted the happiness of the few at the expense of the happiness of the many; hence they advocated the abolition of outworn institutions and the repudiation of confining traditions and customs. Being constitutionalists, they argued for radical reforms in the political and social order as the only alternative to revolution. The utilitarians conceived a society which could work automatically through the operation of human nature if certain basic conditions were enforced. To them, human character was molded by circumstances. Evil did not reside in man but in his environment; and environment could be controlled by law. The purpose of law was to regulate the state, to prevent the operation of unfair advantage in human affairs. Although Bentham and other early utilitarians believed that the state should be nothing more than a policeman, later utilitarians, like John Stuart Mill, advocated more government rather than less in order to bring about a more just society. In politics, Mill reasoned, when any element of the population is excluded from suffrage, its interests may be disregarded. In economics, he repudiated laissez faire and advocated state intervention as necessary and legitimate in order to bring about an equitable distribution of wealth.

In an appendix to Pease's *The History of the Fabian Society*, Shaw denies that Mill and the utilitarians directly influenced him or any Fabian other than Sidney Webb. In all probability, there was no direct influence, but whether through Webb, their own reading, or the Zeitgeist, the Fabians were saturated in the Millite tradition. Like the latter-day Mill, the Fabians regarded the state as a necessary good rather than a necessary evil. They did not see the individual as an isolated unit. They conceived of society as a living organism of mutually dependent units and believed that society partially creates value by its actions. Thus they thought it appropriate that society should control and enjoy that value. The means to achieve this end was the state, for it was the organ by which society expressed its will. The state, therefore, became the indispensable factor in social progress. No revolution was needed to achieve this progress; reform could be achieved by parliamentary means and in progressive stages. As Shaw himself says, socialism would come through "the gradual extension of the franchise and the transfer of rent and interest to the State." The latter point, perhaps more than any other, establishes the connection with Mill, for Mill opposed rent as the "unearned increment" of land which the propertied class had stolen from the nation to whom, by right, it belonged. The Fabians advocated the socialization of every kind of rent, since that would give the state the funds necessary to achieve the vast range of reforms that were needed. To replace the selfish and grossly incompetent capitalist state, the Fabians advocated the creation of a collectivist state, one in which the wealth generated by society would be owned and managed by society and one in which questions of management and policy would be handled by experts rather than by businessmen turned politicians.

Yet while Shaw subscribed to most of these ideas, he never entirely embraced utilitarianism—or any other "ism." While he was willing to accept the means by which the utilitarians intended to achieve their ends, he could not accept the ends themselves. In brief, democracy was acceptable, but the ends of freedom and happiness were not. Shaw was not particularly interested in whether the poor were happier, he simply wanted them "better." He believed that the working classes could become "better"—cleaner, better housed, better educated, wealthier, in short more middle-class—by using the power they already possessed. He told them that if they wanted social reform—better housing, old-age pensions, a minimum wage—the way was not through a passive waiting for the millenium that the anarchists and utopians were suggesting nor the anticipated class war and the inevitable triumph of socialism which Marxists were forecasting but through the political activity of electing representatives to Parliament who would look after their interests.

Likewise, Shaw never entirely adopted the Fabian line. He recognized that he differed from his fellow Fabians on essential points. The majority of Fabians, he says, were "inveterate Philistines"—efficient, self-disciplined, hard-working citizens whose lives were consumed with political business. They were social engineers, who, Shaw says, "I could not interest . . . in art and metaphysics." Perhaps more than any others, the Webbs, who spent their honeymoon investigating trade societies in Dublin, typified the mentality of the Fabian membership. As Beatrice Webb put it, they had, owing to the concentration and constant attention which their work required, simply no time or energy to expend on appreciation of the arts. One is brought to feel, however, that, even had time permitted, they would still have regarded the arts as essentially frivolous activities. There is a good measure of truth in Max Beerbohm's caricature of Sidney Webb treating human beings as toy soldiers.

Shaw's concern for art and metaphysics distinguishes him from the majority of Fabians and links him to transcendentalists like Carlyle and Ruskin. Although as fascinated by economics and politics as were the Webbs, Shaw did not come to socialism, as they did, by way of the sociological survey or political tract. As he says in his lecture "Ruskin's Politics," his interest in economics and politics grew out of concern for art: like Ruskin, he began "as an artist interested in art . . . and was inevitably driven back to economics, and to the conviction that your art would never come right whilst your economics were wrong." Thus, as Shaw sees it, modern civilization requires aesthetic as well as economic reform; and the only hope for achieving these reforms is the artist-prophet who recognizes that social reform is the necessary first step to artistic health. Clearly, Shaw insisted, the capitalist era needed a Ruskin rather than a Yeats.

Undoubtedly the transcendentalists—the romantic essayists and poets of the nineteenth century from Coleridge to Morris—had a considerable influence on Shaw's thought; yet the influence is not immediately apparent. The transcendentalists tried to awaken the consciences of the Victorians and to apply, however imperfectly, the Christian ethic to modern conditions. They denounced the ethical foundations of the industrial civilization of the nineteenth century and its conception of wealth, while at the same time condemning the ugliness and vulgarity of Victorian life. Some of them, in short, combined the artist's longing for beauty with the moralist's passion for social justice. Shaw follows only the moralist line. In his political writings, he exhibits a utilitarian indifference to aesthetic values and seems unconcerned with physical beauty or ugliness. It is moral ugliness—the cheating, the swindling, and the deception which capitalism engenders in human conduct—that concerns him, not the ugliness and vulgarity which the machines create.

Although the transcendentalists were not socialists there were socialistic strands in their thought. In the main they were intuitionalists, rather than doctrinaire philosophers, their criticism humanitarian rather than scientific. They stressed the ideals of cooperation and human solidarity and rejected unrestricted competition. They denounced capitalism as a wicked system because it encouraged men to seek something for nothing, encouraged tradesmen to cheat the poor by buying cheap and selling dear. They condemned capitalist democracy because they believed that for most men its promise of freedom was hollow and because they did not believe that parliamentary legislation achieved lasting results.

The socialism of the transcendentalists was aristocratic. They had little faith in the common man. What they did believe in was the "gentleman": the synthesis, as Eric Bentley says, of the democrat and the aristocrat. The concept of the gentleman is central to Shaw's thought; it is one of the key links between his political and religious thought and between the thought of his early and late years. Like Ruskin, Shaw believes that honor or conscience should be at the root of social relationships. It is a keen sense of honor that distinguishes the gentleman from ordinary men in human activities. The gentleman makes certain claims on his country for subsistence and a full life, in return for which he willingly gives his country the very best service of which he is capable. Equally important, he scorns the idea of a monetary value being put on his services. The problem, as Shaw sees it, is that there is no place in modern society for this kind of human being, for in a capitalistic society any man who does more than any other man without being paid extra for it is a fool.

The Shavian gentleman is also a deeply religious person, but not in the conventional sense. For Shaw, both a higher and a lower morality are at work in the world, each serving useful purposes. These two moralities are in some respects analogous to Christian grace and law; the unconscious knowers are under grace and follow a higher morality; the conscious knowers are under the law and follow a lower morality. The mass of common men need law, the rules of conventional morality, to guide their conduct. Without grace or the happiness within yourself, as Mrs. Knox says in *Fanny's First Play*, "youd best be respectable and stick to the ways that are marked out for you; for youve nothing else to keep you straight." But the uncommon gentleman follows the higher morality; he belongs to that small minority of people who apprehend by an inner

light the purpose of a universal power with such clarity that they
can disregard the rules of conventional morality. These people are
often considered troublemakers by their contemporaries; sometimes in fact they are murdered by them. It is often difficult to sort
out the great saints and supermen from the criminals or charlatans,
the murderer from the patriotic hero, their actions often being the
same. As in the case of Jesus, Socrates, or Saint Joan, as Shaw says,
we must wait to see whether in the final analysis the action of the
person in question is good for society or not. Thus saints and sin-
ners alike await the judgment of history.

III It is not until the first decade of this century that Shaw's
transcendentalism gradually comes into prominence.
While we cannot be absolutely certain what prompted this change,
is was probably the reaction of progressives to a series of political
events—the Boer War, the Balfour Education Act, and Chamberlain's proposed tariff reforms—which led Shaw to reevaluate some
of his earlier political positions. On each of these issues, Shaw and
his fellow Fabians took stands which put them at variance with
radical opinion. Instead of leading other radical groups in protest-
ing against imperialist Britain's bullying a small nation, which was
what one might expect from a society claiming leadership of the
constructive left wing of British thought, the Fabians voted not to
make an official pronouncement on imperialism in relation to the
war. In a lengthy pamphlet drafted by Shaw in 1899 for the society
entitled *Fabianism and the Empire*, the Fabians took the very illiberal
view that a great power "must govern in the interest of civilization
as a whole." In the same year, they further alienated radicals and
Labourites when they promoted the conservative-sponsored but
Fabian-inspired Education Act, which was intended to provide assistance out of the rates to Anglican schools. Later, in 1903, the
Fabians again irritated Liberals and Labour men when they supported Chamberlain's tariff reforms calling for taxes on food and
allowing preferential duty systems.

Clearly the society as a whole and its members as individual
socialists seemed out of step with left-wing British opinion; and the
controversies, coming as they did one directly after another, made
plain that it was perhaps time for Fabians to reassess their aims and
directions. Such a reassessment was in part H. G. Wells's objective

in his ill-executed attempt in 1906 to enlarge and invigorate the society by making it more active politically; and although the society rejected the future he envisaged for it, it did admit that the time for "more cordial cooperation with the Labour Party" had come.

This was a puny concession at best, for the Fabians had little choice but to cooperate with Labour if they wished to play any part in leftist politics. For in the very year that Wells was conducting his reform movement within the society, the Labour party emerged as a force in British politics and became established as the intellectual left. Labour's success produced an upsurge of interest in socialism, and a somewhat astonished society, whose membership had never exceeded 750, now experienced a substantial influx of new members. The new members, however, were a different breed from the old guard to which Shaw belonged; they were young and more sympathetic to trade unionism and to the new winds blowing in that movement—syndicalism, industrial unionism, and guild socialism.

While the spirits of the young were buoyed by Labour's success, Shaw thought that with Labour's victory the dream of socialism was now further away than ever. While he did not admit to pessimism, there can be little doubt that he was growing increasingly disillusioned about the prospects for political change. Though some contend that this disillusionment was only a momentary lapse, certainly the old enthusiasm did not return, or, if it did, it returned considerably altered. To Shaw, the problems of society appeared more and more to be human rather than architectural. Twenty years of socialist agitation had been spent telling the laboring class to use their vote to achieve the collectivist state, only to find that the British working man was not only anticatastrophic, even worse he was antisocialist. Ironically, the aspirations of the working class were the same as those of the people who were exploiting them. The Labour movement, then, was among the first of the radical groups to feel the bite of Shavian criticism. Although, as Shaw observes, the Labour party had both the money and the opportunity to create the socialist state, the "labor men were all for seats in Parliament and State regulation of employers (not of trade unions) by means of factory legislation . . . they were out to exploit capitalism not to abolish it."

Viewing the Liberals' support of the underdog in the South African war as mere sentimentality and their opposition to religious education as largely a reflex action, Shaw also dismisses the Progressives as a constructive force in contemporary politics. The ideology of the Progressives and socialists is, in Shaw's estimation, a collection of time-worn slogans and catchwords which its proponents do not really understand. In "The Solidarity of Socialist Democracy," Shaw contends that even Marx was not a socialist, but was instead an antibourgeois-humanitarian-individualist who could never abide the bureaucracy and vast public revenues which socialism would require. So, he reasons, if such confusion and misunderstanding is present in the political thought of the most advanced thinkers, what hope is there in the political wisdom of the mass of men? Shaw finds no justification for hope in man as he is. The species, he says, has not evolved perceptibly within historic time. With the theories of Flinders Petrie concerning the decay of civilizations in mind, Shaw views the contemporary scene from a broad philosophical perspective and goes on to argue that "we [presumably the English] have just reached that point in civilization at which empires have always broken down: that point at which our social organization over-taxes the political capacity of its human units requiring from them a magnanimity both of character and intellect which the average man not only does not possess himself but which he will not tolerate in a statesman."

Thus, during this decade, while he continues to insist on the abolition of private property and to stress the importance of using the franchise to assure passage of socialistic legislation in Parliament, Shaw begins with equal vehemence to insist that human material has to be improved. In *Man and Superman*, he declares that men are cowards if they have not a cause which will unite them; and, given the state of modern civilization with its variety of sects and beliefs, Shaw says that the only religious cause with which all men are likely to identify and to which they will give credence is the religion of Creative Evolution, that is, to the continual ascent in the organization, power, and extension of life. Depending on the audience and the circumstances, one or both topics—socialism and Creative Evolution—received attention in his lectures and essays; and it is only gradually that we come to see how his political and religious views fit together to form a synthetic philosophy.

The essays in this collection which date from the first decade of the present century reflect these dual interests. The majority of them are concerned with purely political matters. "Socialist Politics," for example, emphasizes that Fabianism is constitutional rather than revolutionary and that the road to socialism is through increased taxation and municipalization. Since the Fabians were among the first to support woman suffrage, it is not surprising that in "The Unmentionable Case for Women's Suffrage" we find Shaw calling for the presence of women on public councils, paradoxically, not because they have a "human" right to be there, but because their presence is a means of keeping English decency in line. In "On Driving Capital Out of the Country," Shaw responds to the charge that socialism is driving investment capital out of the country by asserting that it is not socialism but the enormous profits derived from that form of parasitic capitalism known as absentee ownership which makes investment in developing nations attractive.

Other essays and lectures, however, while concerned with domestic political issues, reveal a change in Shavian strategy. Disheartened by the prejudice, ignorance, and bourgeois respectability of the working classes, Shaw turns away from labor and overtly tries to attract the middle class to socialism. His reasons are both political and practical. For one thing, he is trying to generate interest among the middle classes to form a socialist party. For another, as he says in "What about the Middle Class?" his success as a playwright changed his audience from laborers to middle-class ladies and gentlemen. Shaw thus sets out to persuade this new audience to adopt socialism by giving them a sympathetic appraisal of their complaints against both the idle rich and the working classes, by indicating how vital middle-class "brains" are to industrial society, and finally by insisting that modern society is indebted to middle-class artists for its ideas.

Three of the collected pieces from the pre–World War I era establish the connection between Shaw's political and religious thought. In "Life, Literature, and Political Economy," Shaw declares that man, because of his brain, is the means by which the Life Force *economizes* life—records the use of resources so that a higher, more comprehesive consciousness may eventually be achieved. How an optimum relationship between subsistence and a more abundant life may be achieved is the topic of "The Case for Equality" and "The Case for Socialism." Both provide insight into the chief tenet of Shaw's socialist thought—the question of equality of income. Shaw first gives his views on the equality of income in a lecture entitled "Equality" before the Fabian Society on December 9, 1910. The date is significant, for the lecture was delivered at the very height of the agitation over Lloyd George's pension plan and "monster" budget which called for a tax on unearned income. This attack on property gave Shaw the opportunity he was seeking. Believing that the socialist movement embodies too much principle and too little action, he thinks that Lloyd George has opened a door which will allow socialists, rather than the trade unionists, to assume the leadership of the left. To achieve this end, however, will require a change in tactics. Intimidated by the violence of the anarchists and dynamitards, socialists were eager to prove to the public that they were reasonable people, not in the least dangerous to anyone. But Shaw feels that it is time to show that there is still a spark of daring in socialism: for socialism to mean what the man in the street has always meant by it—a system where all the income of the country is divided up into exactly equal portions. Thus where Lloyd George was uncertain regarding the amount which should be granted to the aged as a pension, Shaw argues that now is the time to reject mere half-measures and to enlist the support of all men on behalf of a life pension.

Interestingly enough, Shaw's conception of a life pension bears a striking similarity to the one presented by Ruskin in "Unto This Last." Both Shaw and Ruskin insist that it is by the work or service which they render to society as adults that men should reimburse society for the education which they received as children and the pension which they receive in old age. This service men owe, as a matter of honor, to the commonwealth. With Shaw, a motive of social service in human actions is consciously being substituted for the motive of private profit; and the motive of social service, as we have seen, is one of the distinguishing characteristics of the Shavian gentleman.

To Shaw, the life pension would give men a cause which they could understand and which would unite them. Mankind, he contends, should be made to see that equality of income can be the keystone of a new social order. Equality of income would benefit the race politically by making real democracy possible, economically by equalizing purchasing power so that the needs and desires of people would be satisfied according to their order of importance, and personally or sexually by widening the prospects for intermarriageability. By solving the problem of subsistence, it would make all men better, more virtuous in the Shavian sense; that is, all men would have the opportunity to be "fully fed, presentably clothed, decently housed, fairly literate and cultivated and gently mannered." For Shaw, however, this is not enough. Civilization, as he sees it, will not be saved if only these changes take place. The political act of achieving equality of income would only make possible the next step, one proffered by transcendental prophets—the reformation of man, the improvement of human stock through greater freedom in the selection of mating partners.

In addition to providing an alternative to the pension plan proposed by Lloyd George and his Liberal government, Shaw also reproves socialists who reject the idea of equality of income. The British Labourite Ramsay MacDonald, for example, in his book *The Socialist Movement*, written in 1911, argues that equality of income is incidental to the problem of collectivism or nationalization. In a sense Shaw's article "The Case for Socialism" is a rebuttal of MacDonald. To Shaw, equality of income is fundamental; nationalization without equality of income, he says, is perfectly compatible with capitalism: collectivism is not socialism, for the income derived, say, from nationalizing the railways will be distributed, not equally to all people, but unequally to shareholders.

To the very end of his life, equality of income remained the chief tenet of Shavian socialism. In "Cultural Internationalism," he proposes it as a belief which can unite the peoples of the world; and in both *The Intelligent Woman's Guide to Socialism* and *Everybody's Political What's What?*, the idea is presented as the political and economic panacea for modern civilization. The article "How Much Money Do We Need?" which appears in this collection, shows the extent to which Shaw came to modify his views on equality of income, particularly after his visit to the Soviet Union. While continuing to insist that equal distribution is the best possible distribution of national income, he admits that if society is to have the experts and administrators it needs in order to function effectively, equal distribution cannot be implemented immediately upon the advent of socialism.

But although Shaw continues to present his case for equality of income whenever circumstances permit, the distressing events of the 1920s and '30s induced him to use the lecture hall and the newspaper article as a rostrum from which to give his speculations on the general health of world civilization. For him the picture is grim. Although he has given the socialists—floundering after the demise of the Second International's dream of social democracy— the idea of equality, which is both a religious and political panacea, politics in the West are out of control; civilization is going bankrupt. Uncertain that anyone can govern, he feels that Western politicians are trying to placate the people with bread and circuses, much as the Romans did. The West needs the order and direction of socialism; and the time, he insists, is ripe for it. These speculations lead Shaw to criticize Labour from yet another vantage point. This time his attack focuses on its leadership. As Shaw sees it, the Labour party is either unwilling or unable to overthrow capitalism. Having been given the opportunity to create the socialist state, labour leaders have been content to develop the trade union consciousness instead. Nonsensically to his mind, Labour leaders, in 1926, advocated a general strike—the ultimate weapon of anarchistic Proudhonian syndicalism—which is nothing but general suicide for the laborer, when, regardless of how unpopular the idea, the Labour leaders should have advocated the Ruskinian dogma of compulsory labor for all.

Shaw also denounces liberal democracy, contending, as in the case of Labor, that it is in the hands of politically inept party heads. In "Follies, Fallacies, and Facts," he deplores the trust which the early Fabians placed in parliamentarianism. Yet even if capable men were to control Parliament, parliamentary government, Shaw maintains, would prove inadequate as an instrument of governance. As a political form, parliamentary democracy is clearly beaten by the enormity of the problems confronting modern states. The machinery of modern government needs a complete overhaul. The volume of business—political, economic, and social—makes necessary not one but several parliaments, organized not like the House of Commons into hostile parties but like municipal councils into cooperating committees. These parliaments, he argues, should advise, not obstruct the executive. People, moreover, should qualify for the franchise by examination, and more important, for political candidacy by a very severe examination. "Government," he concludes, "presents only one problem: the discovery of a trustworthy anthropometric method."

Ultimately Shaw is driven to a more elitist view of political action. According to Shaw, it is because liberal democracy is so clearly a failure that people are looking around wildly for a savior and are greeting demagogic dictators with enthusiasm. These circumstances plus the success of Russian Communism lead Shaw to preach drastic action—armed insurrection. Because people are disgusted with liberal democracy, a socialist victory is obtainable, he contends, if men move quickly. But what men? As Shaw sees it, revolutionary changes are the work of minorities. A mere five percent of the population is capable of leadership. It is their capacity for leadership and their ability to see through the sham of liberal democracy that temporarily leads Shaw to admire fascist adventurers like Hitler and Mussolini. He decides finally that the governments of Hitler and Mussolini cannot produce lasting results because they proceed from a faulty intellectual basis, fascism, and because ultimately they are dependent on a man, not on a constitution. With a world desperately in need of strong leaders who can effect change, Shaw asks that the intellectual aristocracy, what he calls C-1 people in "Cultural Internationalism," be given a chance to rule. In his mind, this group represents a sort of priesthood, at once similar to Plato's natural aristocracy and Carlyle's "aristocracy of talent." This intellectual aristocracy is a kind of voluntary nobility; they are gentlemen driven entirely by the motive of social service. They are not elected to positions of leadership, although they should constitute the executive branch of government. The authority and continuance in power of this natural "called" minority rests solely on their ability and efficiency. But these powers will corrupt them as they were to corrupt Hitler and Mussolini, unless, as Shaw says, they have a religious vocation, unless they feel that they are the instrument of a purpose in the universe which is a high purpose and is the native power of evolution itself. Their common faith will ensure that they are likely to arrive at a unanimous decision. Finally this "aristocracy of talent" which is to run the country must live like the poor so that they can raise themselves up only by raising their people.

The government which Shaw describes is what he perceives to have been the government of the Catholic Church in the Middle Ages: a hierarchical government ruled by an official priesthood which was bound together by a common faith. This form of government, he contends, has reappeared in the twentieth century in Bolshevik Russia as the only alternative to capitalist democracy. Ironically, the U.S.S.R., as he sees it, swept away the Church, only to reproduce its hierarchy in the Communist party. The parallels which Shaw sees between his own socialism and Bolshevism are worthy of notice. The Communist party in its dedication and elitism is similar to Shaw's own fraternity of gentleman technicians or, more precisely, of what he and Beatrice Webb considered the perfect Fabian. However, this Shavian elite or fraternity of technicians differs fundamentally from Lenin's conception of a party member. For Shaw the gentleman technician is both a man of honor and a man of ability whose chief concern is working for the welfare of mankind. On the other hand, while Lenin believed that the party member should be a man of ability, devotion to the party was a more important consideration with him than devotion to conscience. Once when someone pointed out that a certain party member was a scoundrel, Lenin is reported to have said: "Sometimes a scoundrel is useful to our party, precisely because he is a scoundrel."

There is little doubt that Shaw had deep admiration for the Bolshevik society; there is also little doubt that he wished to see the same planned structure in Western governments. The party members in Russia and the expert or technicians in the Shavian state determine the laws, politics, and regulations; the only task left for the multitudes is apparently to do their bidding. However, such political architecturing reveals a defect in Marxist and possibly in Shavian socialism, that is, the absence of a theory of political liberty. As Milovan Djilas (and before him Rosa Luxemburg) makes clear, in the Communist states, where only party members are free (some being freer than others), there is no freedom at all. The important question remains: How free is the individual who thinks differently?

As we saw earlier, Shaw believes that the "called" minority, or natural aristocracy who follow the higher morality, are free and may even on occasion invent their own ethic; equally important, he seems to be saying that the mass of men who follow the lower morality need laws and codes. On the surface, then, it would appear that there is little real freedom in Shavian socialism, that the Shaw who preached a laissez faire ethic as a young man has turned full circle. Shaw would probably respond by saying, first, that liberty is a puzzle since it is best achieved through its opposite, restriction, and, second, that liberty or freedom turns not on the number of laws a man must obey but on his sphere of action outside of those laws. For Shaw, as he makes clear in "The Impossibilities of Freedom," individual liberty has only one reality—leisure. If a man may do everything except what the law expressly forbids him to do, he is free. It is his residual rights, not his legal obligation, that are the test of his freedom.

What is true of his view on liberty is also true of many of his other ideas: in the 1930s, for example, his call for a revolutionary violence to overthrow capitalism. This seems to contradict the ideas he held on revolution as a young Fabian. There is, however, no contradiction in his thinking at all. In "The Transition to Social Democracy," written in 1888, Shaw rejects revolution not because he believes violence is wrong but because he believes revolution, at that time, an inappropriate means to socialism. Since by 1930 parliamentary government, in his view, had proved a failure, Shaw declares that armed insurrection is now the only way to achieve socialism. In short, he talks approvingly of Bolshevik Communism as a philosophy of method, which is essentially what it is. He had learned that the Bolsheviks as an organized political elite had proved that a party is a stronger motivating force for revolution than class. It is for this reason, then, that Shaw calls the intellectual elite to act in the West. Thus with regard to all questions, Shaw remained intellectually supple, rarely adopting any objective principle as a guide. In all things, he was prepared to work, like the Life Force, by trial and error. And it is precisely this quality which he admires in the Russians. As he says in "What Indeed?" the Russian experience has shown that by force of circumstance the party (or priesthood) has systematically abandoned all the shibboleths and ideals of conventional socialist thought—syndicalism, the class war, anarchism, and social democracy—just as he was forced to do in his work as a socialist. The residue, he is proud to proclaim, is Fabianism.

NOTE ON THE EDITING

Although the lectures and articles comprising this collection are taken from many sources and thus reflect the practices of numerous editors, I have tried to make them conform to the typographical and grammatical practices that prevail in the Constable Edition of Shaw's works. Here are the rules of Shavian usage that govern in my text: *shew* for *show*; *-or* for *-our* (as in *honor, labor,* *glamor*); the American *z* for the British *s* (as in *recognize, organization, advertizing*); and the omission of the apostrophe from most verbal contractions (*dont, isnt, wernt*), of the italics or quotation marks from book titles and titles of periodicals and newspapers, and of period from abbreviations such as *Mr* and *Dr*. The capitalization and hyphenization practices as well as the spelling of *laisser-faire* used in *Everybody's Political What's What?* have been followed in the text. Editorial emandations have been inserted in square brackets.

Notes to the lectures and articles appear at the end of the collection. They are not intended to be comprehensive, but are intended instead to provide information on events, persons, etc., which figure importantly in the lecture or essay in question but which may not be familiar to the reader.

PRACTICAL POLITICS

Verbatim "Notes to an Address" delivered to the Students' Union at the London School of Economics and Political Science on Wednesday, 13 December 1905. Revised by Shaw for publication in the Clare Market Review, January 1906.

Life, Literature,
and Political Economy

MR. CHAIRMAN, LADIES AND GENTLEMEN,

I believe that I have undertaken to speak this evening on Life, Literature and Political Economy. Those of you who have had any experience of public life will perfectly understand that as I foresaw that I should have no time to prepare anything, I chose my title so that it would be very difficult for me to say anything that could possibly fall outside it.

I am speaking tonight mainly to students, to those whose intention it is to study, especially to students of Political Economy. Possibly some of you have mistaken your profession. You will find quite a number of professional economists who know nothing of political economy, and never will. They are attracted to it by their natural incapacity for it, just as, on the stage, the man who is naturally a comedian craves for the tragedian's part. If you can find, at a University, a man who is by nature utterly incapable of abstract thought, you will generally find him going in for philosophy and metaphysics. If you want a man who is thoroughly unhygienic in his habits, go to a doctor. If you want to consult a man who not only has no legal knowledge but who has no conception of the nature of law, consult your solicitor. And if you want to find the man who is weak in conduct, go to a clergyman. So remember that you must finally learn Political Economy from life, and not from your professors.

Life is a thing of which it is important to have a theory; yet most
people take it for granted, and go on living for no better reason than
that they find themselves alive. But why should you persist in living?
You are not compelled to: there is always the river and plenty of
chemists' shops. Why should you go on living in spite of all these
resources, and so cause youself and other people a great deal of
anxiety? If you test life by striking a balance between the pleasures
and the pains of living, you will go straight from this lecture and
commit suicide. Probably very few will do that. Nevertheless if you
dont, you will commit yourself to the very serious course of continuing to live. Surely you should not take so grave a step as that as a mere
matter of course without knowing why? Well, you will never know
exactly why. There is a force behind you driving you to do it: that is
all you can say. It drives us to do many things, including a number
that we dont want to do. You are studying, and studying with great
difficulty, because the implement you use, your brain, is very imperfectly contrived for that purpose. We are here wearing absurd
costumes, and in many ways behaving ourselves like lunatics. Clearly
the force behind us is neither reasonable in our sense of the word,
nor concerned with our individual ease and happiness.

Please note that this unaccountable force is not in man alone: we
find it, for instance, in black beetles. The men who have studied
black beetles (and some of our most able scientists have spent their
lives i doing this) have an enormous respect for black beetles—a sort
of fellow feeling. Black beetles behave very much as you behave; for
they live in the most uncomfortable places and keep up a feverish
activity with no discoverable prospect of being any the better for it.
Why do they do it? Why do we do it? What is the point of life? That is
what I, like all other philosophic persons, am continually trying to
find out. But I cannot make much of the inquiry, because I have only
my brains and my senses to work with; and the brains are very
imperfect, the senses very deceptive. How deceptive, you will see if
you set yourself to cheat other people; for then you will realize how
easy it is to cheat yourself. Let me recommend you to practise
cheating. It is a most valuable and instructive exercise; only you must
do it in the spirit of an artist, and not for irrelevant pecuniary gain. If
you cheat vulgarly for the sake of five shillings, you will learn
nothing, because you will concentrate your attention on the money
and miss the real point. But do it in the right spirit, and it will teach
you, by the ease with which you can cheat others, how easy it is for

others to cheat you, and, above all, how easy it is for your own senses and your own brains to cheat you.

I suggest to you that the reason why we go on striving to understand life better instead of confining ourselves to mere pleasure hunting, is that this mysterious force behind us—I will call it the Life Force—is itself in desperate need of an organ of intelligent consciousness; and that the human mind is its most elaborate experiment in the evolution of such an organ. It is certainly not as yet anything near a successful contrivance; and it may prove only a provisional one to be abandoned later on; but so far, it is the best attempt we know of. In its absence the Life Force, though excessively active and fecund, is inconceivably wasteful and destructive—that is, suicidal—whereas in its presence some beginnings of intelligent order and providence are apparent. Intelligence and providence are what the Life Force drives at above all things at present. Beauty it seems to have abandoned as it grew older. Some lower forms of life are extraordinarily beautiful: they almost completely satisfy the senses; and yet higher up the scale of organism ugly things are produced. Man, the supreme organism, is an extremely dangerous and ugly animal. Aristophanes and Swift represent him, quite rationally, as being physically despised by birds and morally loathed by horses. He is not even wise in his own individual affairs; for no man manages his affairs as well as a tree does. But he speaks, he writes, he records, stores, and accumulates philosophic observations; he *economizes* the Life Force; and for that all his sins are forgiven him: his ugliness, his cruelty, his inferiority to the other animals in many points of temperance, decency, and beauty. Proving the moral superiority of birds, beasts, fishes, and plants to men is easy and sometimes salutary; but it is just like proving the superiority of the New Zealand football players to Ibsen: the Life Force absolutely forbids us to believe anything of the sort: it sets the grimmest philosopher above the comeliest athlete as inexorably as it sets the most brutal athlete above the most amiable dog.

Now do you begin to understand the importance and dignity of your own position as students of those departments of philosophy called Economics and Political Science? Do you see that the reason you will decide to continue living is that you have in hand the pressing business of conquering for the Life Force a larger, higher, more intelligent, more comprehensive consciousness: in short to enable it to economize?

Now, whatever you conquer in this way you must record and store up. The most important method of doing this is writing books; for speeches from the platform, as some of you may already have had occasion to reflect, are not always too intelligible! Literature is the recorded expression of the former consciousness of the race; and in contributing anything new to literature you are adding to that consciousness. Few people realize how much of our consciousness—of our conscience in fact—is of literary origin. Larochefoucauld said truly that very few people would fall in love romantically if they had never read anything about it; and this saying of his, like all deep sayings, applies to everything as well as to love. There is, of course, a great danger in this. Most of our worst mistakes arise from false consciousness: that is to say, from books which are not true. We do an enormous number of things as a matter of course which nobody would ever dream of doing were it not for this factitious world consciousness, called literature, with its alloy of false pathos, false sentiment, romance and imaginary heroism. You should ask yourselves the question, "How much of my conscience is founded on my own nature and observation, and how much—for instance—on the plays at the Court Theatre?" Until you have formed a philosophy of your own, you must always be in the characteristic youthful attitude of constant and vigilant suspicion, never believing anything you are told or anything you read. At the same time you had better remember that nothing you hear and nothing you read is a *genuine* lie. There are very few genuine lies in the world. There are often profoundly moral necessities at the back of a lie; and it is often well to give a false consciousness to another person. Illusions play a large and often beneficial part in human conduct; and truth may mean falsehood to people incapable of it: a nurse's reason to a child may be of more use to the child than the reason Socrates would have given to Plato on the same point. In fact, parents are always telling their children lies, or keeping from them a knowledge of the truth. And the tragedy of family life is that when the children grow up and get some knowledge of the truth, they resent the deception and regard their parents as detected impostors. The estrangement is not got over until the child takes on the responsibility and lie-telling of maturer age, and realizes that after all its parents could not help themselves.

Political Economy is the specific department of the Life Force's consciousness in which you are engaged. As it was much preoccupied with wheat in the last century, it got the reputation of being dry; but it is really most momentously interesting. Even wheat is not dry, philosophically considered. If the highest aim of Life is the perfection of its conscience, its first aim is the production of the means of life. Think what happens if you abstain from food. During the first two hours or so the intellect gets brighter, and occupies itself with thinking about higher things than eating. But as the hours go on the subject of food recurs, at first as a slight whim. Then gradually the subject becomes pressing, and finally so pressing that at last all the larger concerns of life retreat into the background, and every other consideration gives way to the necessity of having something to eat. But does the act of abstaining from the study of political economy produce a similar result? Will the subject become more and more pressing as the time goes on, so that in the end you will be prepared to kill anyone who attempts to stand between you and political economy? I fear not. In fact, the contrary is rather apt to take place: abstention from the study of political economy is a habit that grows on you.

One of the charms of the subject is that it lays a great deal of emphasis on the fact that although "man doth not live by bread only," yet until he lives by bread he cannot live by anything else. Political economy teaches the great lesson of the basic importance of the economic man and of money. Money, food, clothes, houses: these are the lowest things, but only in the honorable sense that they form the basis on which stand the higher things that mankind requires. The lazy, parasitic people protest against this doctrine as materialistic, and accuse its teachers of taking all the romance out of life, because unless the working majority accept it as a sacred duty to live on sixpence a day, or, if possible, fourpence, it will not be possible for the parasites to enjoy the romance of living on other people's labor with no occupation but reveries and pleasures. Political economy exposes this hypocrisy. It reveals the importance of money, and shows it to be the most poetical thing in the world. Indeed the imagination of the world has always felt the magical appeal of money. Alnaschar dreamt of having unlimited money.[1] The ideal world asked for on the stage is one in which everyone, even the villain, is never in want of money. The heroes and heroines have all plenty of money, nice houses, and good food. The demand, in fact, is for a comfortable world.

Now, what has been the history of political economy? I may

remind you that political economy has the name of being bad literature; for when it is good literature it is not recognized as political
economy, but classified as something else. The Bible, for instance,
contains much political economy; but who recognizes the Bible as a
text book on the subject? Take another example, the subject of Free
Trade. The first and conclusive criticism of the Manchester School
of Free Trade was made before it was born by John Bunyan in The
Life and Death of Mr Badman. The title, of course, begs the question
of Mr Badman's character; but nevertheless that book ought to be
one of the text books on political economy. Of course it is not; for a
school text book is, by definition, one which no human being would
read except under compulsion. Bunyan tells you how a man can
become rich by a succession of bankruptcies: a method well known
and much practised today. He also says that Mr Badman's theory of
trade was to buy in the cheapest and to sell in the dearest market,
which, of course, is the essential doctrine of the Manchester School.
Bunyan condemns this as "trading without conscience." If Bunyan
had been read by the rationalists who were so delighted with Adam
Smith and Ricardo, they would have seen that the Manchester
School was not only a school of Free Trade, but a school of Protestant-
ism, of Anarchism, of Nietzschianism, of moral revolution, of dozens
of religious, political, and moral doctrines of which Ricardo never
dreamed. Is it right to trade without conscience? Answer that in the
affirmative as the propagandists of Free Trade, "natural liberty,"
and *laisser-faire* practically did; and you have affirmed something for
which you may one day have to go to prison or the scaffold. You can
specialize on political economy as a teacher; but you cannot isolate it
as a philosopher. Every economic problem will be found to rest on a
moral problem: you cannot get away from it. The moment you touch
life at any point you raise numbers of moral problems of all kinds. In
a University you may divide the conscience of the world into faculties, and group the faculties into triposes; but in the universe the Life
Force makes short work of such distinctions. As Major Barbara says,
"Life is all one."

Adam Smith was a literary artist as well as an economist. You can
read him for pleasure. He did not produce a finished theory of rent,
value, exchange, or even Free Trade; but he made it quite easy for
very inferior men to complete his work for him. He was, of course, a
Scotchman, which reminds me that our three nationalities exhibit
very interesting differences in their attitude towards philosophy. My

theory of life never appeals to Englishmen, because an Englishman never asks what he is doing or why he is doing it. He prefers not to know, as he suspects that whatever it is, it is something wrong. The Scotchman, nurtured on the Shorter Catechism, is able to use his brains, and therefore likes using them. He attacks the problem of life with an appetite. The Irishman, on the other hand, knows what he is doing without any study of the subject whatever. The result is that he often gets there before the reflective Scotchman or the recalcitrant Englishman.

To return to Adam Smith. As I said before he handled certain theories of political economy so suggestively that men like Ricardo were able to complete the argument for him. Ricardo was not a literary artist. He had a most remarkable knack of saying the very opposite to what he meant; and yet he generally contrived to make you understand his meaning. No doubt this is partly because we have found out what Ricardo means from other writers; but he certainly had a telepathic quality in his style that defied mere logic and syntax. His main contribution to the consciousness of the world was the law of rent. If you want to read the most lucid explanation of that law, you should read an article by myself in Fabian Essays; but if you have conscientious scruples about reading a Socialist book, then read De Quincey's Logic of Political Economy. De Quincey was a consummate literary artist, and, being fascinated by the study of political economy, he puts its one sound discovery up to that date, the law of rent, in lucid literary form.

This law of rent has played a great part in the consciousness of mankind. Modern civilization is reduced to absurdity by obvious and monstrous inequalities and injustices in the distribution of wealth and the encouragement of labor. The well-to-do man ascribes these to inequalities of character, to improvidence, intemperance and laziness being beaten in the race by thrift, sobriety and industry. The poor man pleads that he is unlucky. Both will tell you that if an equal distribution of goods were made now, all the present inequalities would presently reappear. This is quite true, and would be equally true if the equal distribution of goods were accompanied by an equal and permanent distribution of character. Character is a negligible factor in the business. The real importance of the law of rent is that it shows how the governing factor in the distribution of wealth is not the individual human producer, but the material at his disposal and the place in which he works. Faculty is tolerably equally divided; but soils and situations vary enormously. And so in the course of time the proprietors of the better soils and the masters of the better situations become rich without working at all and accumulate spare money. And spare money, according to the terse and perfect definition of Jevons, is capital: the most important of all the factors in production nowadays. This is the foundation of modern economic socialism, the greatest revolutionary force of your time.

Other economists continued the elaboration of the law of rent, and the muddling of the law of value, which had beaten Adam Smith completely. John Stuart Mill was not a good economist. This is because he wrote a tremendously long treatise, in the first half of which he was teaching himself political economy—and if you want to teach yourself anything the best way is to write a book on the subject—and so his conclusions are shallow, timid, and mostly erroneous. By the time he reached the second half of the book he had taught himself some political economy, and so was in a position to contradict everything important in the first half. Unfortunately, very few people ever get further than the first part; and those who do, think it wiser to hold their tongues about it.

Henry Fawcett did not add anything to the science.[2] He was a popular exponent of other men's results. Then came Ruskin, who refused to concern himself with abstract laws of rent and exchange, and never took the trouble to understand them, having more important business in hand. Hitherto the economists had always treated wealth as though it could be measured by exchange value. Ruskin exposed this as a fundamental error: a profound religious, social and philosophical error: in short, a damnable heresy. He asked whether Tintoretto's irremovable, unexchangeable, and consequently commercially worthless ceiling in the School of St Roche, in Venice, was of less value than an obscene French lithograph exchangeable for two francs fifty in the Rue de Rivoli, and produced expressly for sale to English tourists. This is but one illustration of Ruskin's method of argument. By it he succeeded in making an end of the folly of measuring social need by commercial demand or wealth by exchange value. And he introduced the conception of "illth" as a positive thing to be measured and dealt with as urgently as "wellth."

Ruskin's advance was reduced to pure economics by Stanley Jevons, who treated Ruskin's wealth and illth as utility and disutility; raised anew the whole question of value; made an end of the theory that value is the result of labor instead of being the cause of it; abolished the old distinction between use value and exchange value; and formulated a law founded on the comparison of abstract desirabilities, which gave new life to academic economics by bringing it into direct relation with human passion.

I am perhaps wrong in assuming that you are all too well acquainted with the views of Ruskin and the formulae of Jevons to tolerate a demonstration of them from me; but I must make that assumption for want of time. I must conclude by saying that since Ruskin and Jevons showed that economic science is concerned with nothing less than a calculus of human welfare and human desires, the old purely industrial economists have become obsolete; and such treatises as they wrote must rate for the future as mere compilations, like Fenn on The Funds, or Whitaker's Almanack, useful, but not part of the great game of economics.[3] The players of that great game in future will have to be philosophers dealing with human conduct and destiny in the largest sense, international as well as national. The field of the political economist will be life; and his instrument will be literature. The prophet of the race and the organizer of the race will be a political economist. I hold that out as the possible future for each of the students in this room.

The English version of an article written for the 1 May 1906 "Labor Day" issue of the German newspaper Vorwärts *but not published. It was rejected by that Social Democratic publication because, as Shaw says, the article was too radical for a party filled with "the spirit of anarchistic sectarianism."*

The Solidarity
of Social-Democracy

The first of May is the Festival of Labor. What is a Festival? It is an occasion on which men take a holiday from the realities of life, and delight themselves by declaring to all the world that things are, not as they really are, but as they would like them to be. In other words, a Festival is a day set apart for telling agreeable lies.

Let us compare the festivals of two great causes to which men are devoted in Germany, Christianity and Social-Democracy. On Christmas day it is proclaimed that Christianity established peace on earth and goodwill towards men. Next day the Christian, with refreshed soul, goes back to the manufacture of submarines and torpedoes. On the first of May Social-Democracy proclaims the solidarity of Socialism; and the next day the Socialists go back to their quarrels as enthusiastic Liberals, Conservatives, Radicals, Freethinkers, Marxists, Revisionists, Nationalists, Possibilitists, Impossibilists, Imperialists, Republicans, Nationalists, Internationalists, and what not? We have, as a matter of fact, no solidarity. In the Reichstag we seem to have it because we are in Opposition. But all parties seem solid in Opposition, because they are all agreed on the main thing they have to do: namely, to oppose. The moment we go into office the party will fall asunder into a Liberal–Individualist–Protestant–anti-State party and a State-Socialist party as surely as the sun will rise tomorrow.

Nay, long before this can happen in Germany, a section of the party, though still in opposition, will abandon the barren formula that the sole business of an opposition is to oppose. They will seize on whatever makes for Socialism in the measures of Government, and help the government to carry such measures against the opposition of the bourgeoisie to all state activity. They will form combinations which must necessarily be combinations with imperialistic State-Socialism against 1848 Liberalism. They will throw themselves energetically into reforms which are not specifically socialistic at all, but are none the less socially needed. They will claim all the official positions to which the members of the party entitle them, and swallow whatever ceremonial at court or elsewhere may be indispensable to such positions for the moment.

Where will the solidarity of Social-Democracy be then? It will instantly appear that many of our so-called Social-Democrats are not really Socialists at all, but simply what we in England should call radicals. They want Peace, Retrenchment, and Reform: they hate the Church, the Army, and the Crown; they are bitterly opposed to the huge budgets, the multiplication of public officials, and the growing interference of the State without which Socialism is a clear impossibility. Like all men, they want the millennium; but they expect to get it for nothing; the moment you ask them to pay an extra penny in the pound for it, they repudiate it in the name of Liberty, Equality, Democracy, Socialism, and any other battle cry that they may have picked up in the street without a thought as to what it means. In England they do not call themselves Socialists, because they find their opinions sufficiently voiced by the Radical party. Bebel[1] can point to two million votes cast for "Social-Democracy" in Germany at the last election. But if Social-Democracy means nothing but Free Trade and reduction of military expenditure, Mr Lloyd George will get ten million votes for it in England. The comparative backwardness of Socialism in England is an illusion produced by the forwardness of radicalism.

Let me suppose an imaginary case. Suppose the present relations between parliamentary liberalism and the Crown produce the same result as they did in England in the seventeenth century: that is, a civil war between the Kaiser and the Reichstag. On which side will the Social-Democrats fight? Monstrous question! your readers will exclaim, rank Social-Democratiebeleidigung! The Social-Democrat will fight on the side of the Reichstag (if he may say so without being sent to prison for it). But why should he? The victory of the English parliament, which, in spite of the Restoration, broke the power of the Crown for two centuries, also made England a capitalistic anarchic hell for these two centuries, because the principles of the English Revolution were violently anti-socialist; and the same thing is true of the principles of the French Revolution, the American Revolution, and the 1848 Revolutions in Germany. Marx has made his readers conscious of this by his history of Capital. Unfortunately the readers of Marx do not amount to one per cent of the German Social-Democrats: you are not a nation of Kautskys.[2] In England the percentage is so small as to be negligible. Marxism means in both countries a tradition of Marx's personal political opinions.

Now, in practical politics Marx was not a Socialist at all: he was simply an anti-bourgeois humanitarian Individualist, whose sole quarrel with the Liberals of 1848 was that they exempted Mehrwerth from their crusade against State Churches, political class privileges, and autocracy. The moment Napoleon III or Bismarck began to meddle with Socialism, he attacked Socialism as bureaucratic "State Socialism" (as if Socialism could ever be anything but a huge bureaucracy) and began pushing his disciples backwards in the direction of anti-State Liberalism, a direction in which they have now retreated so far that the last general election in Germany was fought on a manifesto which the Fabian Society of London would smile at as a typical proclamation of the English Liberal principles of Free Trade, Peace, Retrenchment, and Reform by a radical Labor Party. Every forward step taken by Socialism has been taken in the teeth of the Marx tradition. Fortunately Marx's own works have made Marxism impossible for the real leaders of Socialist thought in England. Just as Herbert Spencer, the arch-individualist of England, made Socialists of his most intelligent pupils by teaching them to regard society as an organism; so Karl Marx, by his demonstration of the industrial basis of political history, made it impossible for the younger generations to tolerate such superstitions as his class war of a heroic proletariat against a villainous bourgeoisie, his childish seventeenth-century theory of value, and his brilliantly written by insufferably pharisaic Jeremiads against Napoleon III, Thiers,[3] etc., who were according to his own theory, the merest flies on the wheel of capitalist production. In fact, Marx, like his ancestor

Moses, brought us up out of the land of Egypt only to have us wandering for forty years in the wilderness. To him the whole world consisted of himself and Engels, surrounded by an invisible angelic choir called the proletariat, persecuted by a body of police spies disguised as anarchists and organized by Bakunin,[4] and several million scoundrels, plagiarists, and exploiters, including all the Socialists who were turning his own ideas to any practical account in real administration.

Now let us go back to our supposition. Suppose Marx had been a Socialist in administrative practice as well as on paper. Suppose he had taken part in public life in his own country instead of being a refugee spending his days among the books in the British Museum. Suppose he had at last succeeded in getting his idealized portrait emancipated by popular suffrage, only to find that their prejudices, their ignorance, and their intense bourgeois respectability were more than all the greed of the Liberal manufacturers and all the exclusiveness of the aristocratic Conservatives. Suppose he had found that every blow dealt by the Liberals and Radicals to the supremacy of the State and the rapacity of the Exchequer was a blow dealt at the growth of the huge bureaucracy and vast public revenue which Socialism needs. Suppose he had realized that the President of a Liberal Republic is always given far more power than a hereditary monarch enjoys, and that in the present condition of public opinion hereditary monarchy is one of the most effective political devices for preventing the titular head of the State from becoming a tyrant. Suppose, finally, that whilst all these lessons and disillusions were fresh in his mind, the German parliament had revolted against the German crown; and declared civil war in the Empire. Is it quite clear that Marx would not have rallied to the Kaiser and the Chancellor as Falkland rallied to Charles, Strafford, and Laud?

I confess I should be sorry to be placed in any such dilemma. If you ask me to fight for Bernstein against Bebel, I can see some socialism in that. But to risk my skin to substitute a President for a Kaiser and Pierpont Morgan and Carnegie for Count von Bülow is another matter.[5] As a Socialist, I am on the side of the German conception of the organized State as against the American conception of individual "freedom." So, I take it, is the Kaiser. My quarrel with the revenue is that it is too small, not too large; and my quarrel with the official departments is that they are not powerful enough, and allow individuals far too much liberty. I am, of course, a thorough Protectionist, and agree with Carlyle that Free Trade is heartbreaking nonsense. As to the working classes, I believe neither in their virtue nor their intelligence: on the contrary, my objection to the existing order is precisely that it inevitably produces this wretched, idolatrous, sentimental, servile, anti-Socialist mass of spoiled humanity which we call the proletariat, and which neither understands us, believes in us, nor likes us. I am not the friend of the working class: I am its enemy to the extent of ardently desiring its extermination; and the one ray of hope it sheds on me is the approval with which it invariably receives these sentiments of mine when I utter them on the platform. It may not understand Socialism; but at least it knows that it is not fit to govern, and despises Democracy accordingly.

Please observe that I, who write all this, am a Socialist, converted to Socialism by reading Das Kapital in 1883, and ever since then an active worker for the cause. And Bebel is a Socialist too. I wonder is there any line of this article with which he agrees! And Millerand is a Socialist. Also Guesde. And Singer. And Bernstein. And Hyndman.[6] And Sidney Webb. How touching, this rocklike Solidarity! Hail, thou glorious first of May! Proletarians of all lands, follow the example of your leaders, and Unite.

Seriously, is it not time for us to face our Socialism as Bismarck would have faced it: that is, to begin building up a Socialist administration, instead of leaving that work to be done by Conservative Chancellors and Prime Ministers, and confirming our followers in the Liberal habit of opposing and denouncing them. For we are essentially State-Socialists, aiming at the rescue of State Socialism from its present exploitation and restriction by Capitalism; and if we lose sight of that fact for a moment we relapse at once into the old revolutionary insurrectionism in which we can be nothing but the catspaws of republican Liberalism.

An article published in two installments in The Tribune *(London), on 14 and 15 August 1906. Shaw is responding to a series of articles submitted to* The Tribune *by George R. Sims (1847–1922). Sims was a poet, playwright, and novelist; he also contributed a column to* The Referee *under the pseudonym of "Dagonet," beginning with the first issue of the paper in 1877. His letters to the* Daily News *on the condition of the London poor led to the formation of a Royal Commission to investigate and remedy the horrors he revealed. In the* Tribune *articles, Sims says that, while his earlier work stands as proof of his sympathy for the poor, he contends that the poor are today faced "not with the peril of neglect but with the peril of pampering," and that the middle classes are being crushed between the tyranny of capital on the one hand and the demands of labor on the other.*

The Bitter Cry
of the Middle Classes

I Mr Sim's Bitter Cry of the Middle Classes may be read with perfect safety if the reader fixes the following facts firmly in his mind before he begins:—

1. The middle class is at present the richest, most powerful, most courted class in the world. Only by forming alliances with it can our aristocracy avoid bankruptcy, or, at best, what Mr Stead calls "splendid pauperism."[1] Modern millionairism has become billionairism in the United States of America, an exclusively middle-class state. An income of ten thousand a year is now thought less of than an income of one thousand fifty years ago. The country is dotted with hotels—Metropoles, Granvilles, Ritzes, and the like —where the main purpose is to organize middle-class daily life in such a way as to gratify the sense of having money, and to affirm that fact publicly at every possible moment by changes of dress and elaborate meals.

2. The middle class is the brain of private property. Its function is to employ land, capital, and labor, by organizing and conducting

industry with them, paying out of the proceeds rent, interest, and wages, to the landlords, capitalists, and workers, and retaining what is left as its own profit. It is thus master of the industrial situation, both property and labor being dependent on its employing ability.

3. When the Government and the municipalities socialize industries, they take them out of the hands of the middle class, paying rent, interest, and wages just as the middle class does, but cutting off the profit and presenting it either to the whole public in cheaper services or to the ratepayers in relief of rates. Hence the bitter cry of the private employer for his lost opportunity, and the delight (expressed by Progressive voting) of the public at large.

4. If all our municipal works departments, tramlines, gasworks, yards, and factories were closed, the plant sold as scrap, and the staffs discharged (which appears to be what Mr Sims means by getting rid of the burden of municipal debt), the debt would remain just as before; the ratepayers would have to pay interest on the capital and maintain the sinking fund at a dead loss instead of providing for both painlessly out of municipal profits; rates would go up with a bound when the contractors' rings had no longer to fear the competition of the works departments and there were no more pennies in the pound or more coming in to the ratepayer from municipal electric light factories and the like; tram-fares and the price of gas and electric light would go up at once under Protection from municipal competition; all those public services which pay for themselves but leave no margin of profit would be discontinued (because commercial companies attract investors for dividend only, and not for the incidental public good); thousands of persons would be thrown out of employment, and those who belonged to the middle class and got re-engaged by private companies would be in a less secure position, involving higher salaries and later marriages; the City would float a multitude of new joint-stock companies, of which only a small percentage would prove anything but traps to catch middle-class savings; the survivors of the boom would conduct their businesses without the slightest regard to the effect of their operations or of their treatment of labor (casual labor, for instance) on the police rate, or on the poor rate and the sanitary rates, which would go up in consequence; we should return to the state of things that existed in the eighteenth century before municipal Socialism was invented by Mr Chamberlain and the hard-headed business men (mostly Tories) of the

boroughs (rates were sometimes 18 shillings in the pound then); the "independent" middle class would secure more openings for their spare cash, on the interest of which they would live more idly and extravagantly than ever; the bitter cry of the poor ratepayer would become a howl of despair, which would nevertheless be inaudible because no surviving newspaper would be independent enough to publish it; and Mr Sims would receive a peerage.

That, I think, is enough for the readers of The Tribune to go on with until the County Council election is over.

The middle class suffers from a double share of that burden of incompetence and unemployableness which hangs like a millstone round the neck of the whole world today, mostly in the shape of poor relations. The aristocracy dumps its younger sons and their penniless descendants on the middle class from above, infecting it with parasitic, expensive, and pretentious habits, with snobbishness, shabby gentility, and unfitness for practical life. The working classes snatch at its opportunities from below, pushing up into it all those who dislike manual labor and are literate enough to be useful in offices or capable of entering a profession. Meanwhile the middle class has to keep all its own weaklings; for though a carpenter will make his son a clerk, or his daughter a school teacher, a clerk will condemn his son to the desk or his daughter to become a domestic fellow struggler and household slave of another clerk sooner than make the one a carpenter and the other a dairymaid, a factory hand, a domestic servant, or even a shop assistant. True, he will make his daughter a duchess; but the dukes will not fall in with his views, and prefer Chicago to Tottenham as a field for matrimonial adventure. Thus the middle class is continually precipitating a sediment of underfed, under-trained, under-educated, helpless people, who insist on being middle-class ladies and gentlemen without either the energy or the capital to go into the business of their class as employers of labor. They are too genteel to learn or practise trades, too genteel to go to public elementary schools, too genteel to speak to anybody except the rich middle-class people who will not speak to them; and they are too ignorant, too weak, too infatuated with their social points of honor to do anything but the unskilled labor of the counting-house, sharing oneanother's poverty in a harassed and narrowing domesticity, and spending their lives in what is popularly called pulling the devil by the tail. They are despised by the working class, which nevertheless extorts tips from them, whilst the unhappy donors are too genteel to accept tips from the aristocracy. Life is with them a long agony in which every quarter's rent, every knock of the rate collector, every tradesman's bill, every hole torn in a child's knickers or hole worn in its boots is a fresh turn of the rack.

In short, the middle class has a proletariat of its own, which is perhaps the most harassed class in the community; and it is the Bitter Cry of this proletariat which Mr Sims is now raising. And the case he has made for it is all the more representative of the unteachableness of his clients because everything he demands would make their position still more wretched, putting up their rates, gas bills, and travelling fares; abolishing that municipal bureaucracy which is their only means of access to the security of public service; destroying their sole hope of escape from the jerry builder and rack renter; and still further enriching that already too rich millionaire class whose outrageous standard of expenditure makes the struggle to keep up appearances continually more desperate, and the price of common civility from the retainers of the rich continually more exorbitant.

II The notion that Socialists have never concerned themselves for the sufferings of the middle-class proletariat is one of its own delusions. The middle-class proletarians do not know how repeatedly their cause has been pleaded, because they are too genteel to go to Socialist meetings. Socialism has brought me into contact with the peerage, the Privy Council, the leaders of the professions, and the millionaires; but it has cut me off completely from the middle-class proletariat. The Socialists have urged the wrongs and miseries of that proletariat at every opportunity. The most obvious works on the subject, apart from books of reference like the Municipal Year Book, are Mr R. B. Suthers's Mind Your Own Business, my own Common Sense of Municipal Trading, and Mr Sidney Webb's London Programme, all full of the ratepayer and his grievances and the remedies for them. The Fabian Society has been bitterly reproached for its "middle-class Socialism," for its "gas-and-water" policy, for its pamphlets appealing to the ratepayer to save his pockets and use his municipal and parliamentary vote to save himself from being crushed between the remorseless grinding of private capital and land on the one hand, and the revolt of the working classes on the other. But it is of no use. Your middle-class proletarian would rather let a judgment summons into his house than a Socialist tract. Somebody might see it and conclude that he was not in the best society. He would rather send his general servant to the pawnbroker's than go to a Socialist meeting. Somebody might see him and suspect him of being a Liberal, like the Duke of Devonshire and other second-rate persons.[2] As to combining with his fellow clerks, can you expect a gentleman with a pound a week to degrade himself by Trade Unionism to the level of a common carpenter, or mason, or fitter, with thirty-eight? If he let himself down to that, no one knows what might happen to him: the next thing would be Mr John Burns speaking to him in the street, or something equally dreadful.[3]

I am not in the habit of giving counsels of despair; but my feeling towards Mr Sims personally is too friendly to allow him to flatter himself with false hopes of rousing these unlucky people to help themselves. After all, they are not so unhappy as they seem. Their dream of gentility is sweet to them; and they get used to being wakened two or three times a day by a money worry or the scolding of their dreaded employer. And as they never think, but only dream and drift along in their half-alive way, they probably perform a useful physiological function in providing a fallow for the energy-harvest of the race. Their children often rebel mightily, the eternal spirit rising in the son and daughter refreshed by its spell of listless idleness in the father and mother.

Whether there be anything in this speculation or not, of one thing Mr Sims may be quite certain. If The Times and the Municipal Freedom League and all the forces of private capitalism failed in their attempt to induce the late Government, with its huge anti-Progressive majority, to dare lay a hand on the imposing edifice of municipal enterprise, Mr Sims will not succeed any better with a Government that is identified with Progressivism. Whether the Conservatives or Liberals are in power, the boroughs will not stand any wrecking; so Mr Sims may just as well spare his breath to cool his mustard and cress.

If he still doubts the soundness of the municipal position, I ask him, as a personal favor, to get me some municipal stock at panic prices, as I am on the look out for cheap gilt-edged investments. A brief search will show him that the very people who have been stuffing him with all this nonsense about municipal bankruptcy will lend money to a municipal corporation on terms that they would not entertain for a moment from a private company. The London County Council is at present in financial despair because the actual scarcity of money caused by the burning up of hundreds of millions of pounds in South Africa, Manchuria, Russia, and other seats of war, prevents it from raising capital at 3 per cent. The County Council has to pay extra for scarcity, as everyone else has; but will anyone be so hardy as to pretend that it has now, or ever has had, to pay a farthing for risk? And yet if a private company had been financially written down by the Moderate Press and the anti-Progressive Alliances and Leagues and Ratepayer's Associations for twenty years as the Council has, it would not be able to raise a shilling at 50 per cent.

However, I do not want Mr Sims to throw up his clients' case as hopeless. Having smashed his program, I now offer him a better one. His grievance is a simple one: the burden of the rates. The Progressive remedy is equally simple: abolish rates altogether. Give the middle-class Bittercrier every public service that he now enjoys, and a good deal more into the bargain, without levying a farthing of rates on him, and without reducing a single pauper below the Poplar standard.[4] Mr Sims will, perhaps, think this Utopian; but if he would like to see it actually done, let him take a trip to Monte Carlo. There he will find a town in which rates are unknown, and which is nevertheless better kept than London. There is no secret about it, no miracle, no difficulty. All that happens is that the principal industry is the property of the Government; and the town is maintained out of the profits of that industry.

The chief industry of Monaco is the organization of gambling for the rest of Europe. Monaco itself does not gamble, except in the sense in which an insurance company or a bank gambles. No citizen is allowed to enter the gaming-house; and the bankers of the gaming tables play at odds which secure a steady percentage of profits. Much of the money they take is paid by the London Bittercrier as rent and interest—apparently with enthusiasm, since his bitter cry is to be compelled to pay more of it.

What is the moral for London?

The moral for London is simply, Go and do likewise. "What!" our Nonconformist friends will exclaim: "Set up a gambling-house?" Not at all: we have two already at Capel-court and Tattersall's. Besides, gambling is not the chief industry of London. Our chief industry is building and landholding. Municipalize that industry, which is just as practicable as the municipalization of the tramway or the electric lighting industry, and its rents and profits will provide a fund out of which London can be made the healthiest, happiest, and cheapest-to-live-in city in the world. The cost of the operation need not alarm the Bittercrier. To him it will be just exactly nothing except the trouble of understanding and voting for it. No doubt this will involve a severe and unaccustomed exercise of a long-disused organ in his head. The uniform narrowness and stupidity, not always free from dull malice, which mark the letters elicited from him by Mr Sims would be depressing but for the irresistibly funny superfluousness of his anxiety lest we should think that his mind is at all like Mr Chesterton's.[5] But he can think if he likes, and he can hardly be such a fool as not to suspect that his own ignorance and the cheap vulgarity of the rag heap of political catchwords and second-hand newspaper phrases which constitute his political and sociological equipment, are at the bottom of his daily defeats in the struggle for life.

In short, what we want at present is not a restriction but an energetic extension of municipal enterprise. The housing question is still the most important one in our towns, after the feeding question. It cannot possibly be solved as long as our municipalities are restricted to the building jobs that private enterprise rejects as not worth while. The rents of our County Council and Borough Council dwellings are ridiculously high, although they do not really pay their way. As long as the squares are reserved for the private builder and landlord, and the slums left to the unfortunate ratepayer, municipal housing can never pay its bare expenses; and until it does that at least it can never pretend to overtake the evil of insanitary housing. Give the Council power to acquire London land and build or rebuild the whole metropolis, slums and squares, mews and avenues, courts and King's ways alike; and we shall at last be able to make a fair start for the time when London will belong to her citizens and not to the speculators and landholders who now create and maintain her poverty by draining her of monstrous sums of "unearned increment" (very hardly earned by other people, by the way) every year, every quarter, every month, every day.

So far from municipal Socialism being excessive, we have not half enough of it. The London Progressive councillors have been getting sleepier and elderlier of late years; and if they do not wake up it will become as necessary to abolish the County Council and get a new broom as it was to sweep away that intolerable old School Board which some misguided elders among us are now infatuatedly proposing to restore, at the risk or a defeat at the approaching municipal election.

Corrected verbatim reports of a lecture delivered before the Fabian Society at Essex Hall, London, on Friday, 23 November 1906, and published as a series of five articles in the New York Evening Journal on 22, 24, 25, 26, and 27 December 1906.

Socialism
and the Artistic Professions

I The function of the middle class in modern society is to organize the industry of the country. At the present time you have a class of persons in possession of land and capital of which they are incapable of making any use: and you have also another—much larger—class of persons who have the brain power and labor, which they dont know how to employ.

Both parties, at opposite ends of the scale in society, are altogether helpless.

The landlord, with all his acres, is in a pitiable condition by himself, because, he says, "What is the good of these acres to me?"

He is told that, having land, he can grow wheat and produce bread. "But," replies the landlord, "I can do nothing—I cannot dig and I cannot bake."

On the other hand, you have the workman who is skilled, and he says: "There are certain jobs which I can do. If somebody wanted to build a house I could put the bricks together, but you cannot expect me to provide all the bricks and materials. I am entirely helpless unless materials are provided."

What is wanted, therefore, in order to keep our society alive is clearly some class of persons who will step in between these two extremes and who will take the land and the capital from the landlord and capitalist class, and who, in taking it from them, will undertake to pay them sufficient to live in a very handsome manner, without expecting them to use their brains.

That is what the landlord and the capitalist want.

On the other hand there is wanted somebody who will take the laborer and in return for his labor will give him enough to live on.

All this requires a man with sufficient intelligence, sufficient education and sufficient monetary power to be able to judge what businesses will pay: be able to buy raw materials, construct factories, choose markets and do the whole routine which we know generally as business. That is, of course, the function of the middle class in modern society, and that is the reason why some economists have said that both the labor class and the proprietary class are entirely dependent on the middle class.

This middle class is continually propagating itself, and is continually bringing into the world a number of persons who are good for nothing at all; who cannot use land, who cannot employ labor and have therefore to find some other occupation. Some of them go into the professions, become doctors, lawyers, and clergymen, according to the degree of mental ability that they happen to possess; and there are others who think that these regular professions—these ordinary, utilitarian professions—have no charms for them.

They are persons who were born with a congenital dislike for honest work. I was born in that particular way myself.

I wanted to do what I liked. A great many persons are born in the middle class who are in this position. They generally take up the fine arts for their living.

That is really the way you get the artist occurring in modern society, and one of the consequences of that is that the modern artist is, in the most extraordinary degree, an amateur. You notice that very especially in painting.

If you compare modern paintings with the old paintings from the sixteenth century and earlier without going into the general question of the artistic merit of the pictures—you will see that there is one very remarkable difference; the painting of the earlier period is a painting by a man who was what the working classes now call a "real tradesman"—who had passed through a long apprenticeship, and was able to give to his work what is called "trade finish."

If you engage a man to paint your hall door he is perhaps not a

Royal Academician, but an ordinary painter; still your hall door will be turned out with an extraordinary degree of trade finish.

If you go back to the paintings of Van Dyck you will find this particular kind of trade finish. If you look at the Royal Academician's pictures you will see a great deal of very clever work, but no trade skill or trade finish.

Almost the last painter who had that trade finish was Hogarth. From Hogarth to Sir Joshua Reynolds trade finish was gone. You see lots of very clever modern painting which has all sorts of qualities about it, but it has not that professional quality which you get used to in the Old World.

You get almost all your painting done by a sort of general amateur, who really is a man born into the middle class, who has no natural aptitude or taste for the specific economic function of the middle class.

A remarkable result of that is that all classes in society have now got middle-class ideas. I dont know anything more pathetic than some public affair, usually a divorce case, which gives you an insight into the upper class, and when you see the letters they write and which are read in court you will be immediately struck with a sort of disappointment, because you discover that these glorified creatures of the upper classes have really got middle-class ideas, jealousies, and disappointments.

The middle class, in fact, paints all the pictures, and middle-class writers write all the books, and in the end it gives consequently all the ideals and ideas to the world.

II   The artist is a man who forms the human mind.

You see people who set to work quite seriously to write books to form the human mind who are not artists, and who never succeed in forming the human mind, and who never can write a book which anybody would read.

It always rests in the hands of the man who will write a readable book, and that man is the artist. The artists who are really furthest from nature and furthest from reality finally manage to impose their code on mankind until it becomes a real thing, and people begin to have romantic ideas and instincts.

You see the same thing in religion. The instinct to which people's religious ideas are turned from the first goes very far beyond what most people are conscious of.

If you take the most sacred visions which are given to you by your religion it is worth while considering where you get them. Take all the people of this country who are really devoted Christians, to whom the most sacred picture in the whole universe is the picture of Jesus Christ.

You will find that almost all of these people have a pretty definite idea of Christ as being a man whose personal appearance is like that of Lord Battersea, a very handsome young man, with a touch of Mr Keir Hardie about him.[1]

That is only the middle-class idea, which, of course, did not prevail in the old Flemish school of painting, although there is no doubt whatever as to the sincerity of their Christianity.

It is really worth considering for a moment why it is that you have got that vision of Christ.

The answer to the question is that artists have adopted that type and made it familiar to you. If you went to your Bible to try to find out the type, and really tried to imagine it from that, I really dont know who is the person to whom you would most liken Christ.

The artist is too much for you.

A most remarkable example—in England, at least—of the enormous influence of art on people and the reason why you get your religious ideas is the extraordinary susceptibility of English people to art.

I have come to the conclusion myself that they are probably more susceptible to art than any other nation in the world, and the reason of that is that the Englishman, having always been a relatively prosperous person, is not a critical person or an analytical person, and there is nothing but the faculty of intellectual analysis that could enable a man to discriminate between an idea which is fantastic or fanciful and the real idea.

The English, therefore, being weak on the critical side, dont know the difference between art and reality.

The Englishman is so susceptible to art that to a very great extent the one thing he will not bear to be told is that a work of art has affected him at all. Englishmen are more affected by art and literature and more affected by words than any other nation in the world.

One of the greatest monuments of thought that you have in this world is the authorized translation of the Bible.

The artistic character of that version is the explanation of that very curious fact which must have struck all of you who have travelled—that the Bible plays such an enormous part in English thought and life and religion as compared with the Bible on the Continent, the trouble being that the French and German Bibles are not at all comparable as works of literary art to our English Bible, and therefore they have never taken hold of the imagination of the people to the extent that the English Bible has.

That is, of course, not altogether confined to the Bible. You have Shakespear as another case.

The ordinary Englishman will not regard Shakespear as literature; he regards him as omniscient and infallible. This opinion of two books that the ordinary Englishman hardly ever reads—Shakespear and the Bible—is strange to us; nevertheless he has heard enough of their phraseology to get more or less captivated by it.

The art of music is very closely allied to literature, because the fascination of literature lies very largely in the music of words, which is almost the whole secret of Shakespear or of anybody who makes a great success in literature.

There is only one country in the world where people pay open worship to a piece of music, and that is England. In Handel's Messiah when the Hallelujah Chorus is sung the people stand up, and there is a tradition in England that when you come to that particular passage you should stand up.

When the Messiah was performed for the first time no sooner had the lady who sang "He Shall Feed His Flock" finished than a clergyman in the audience got up and said: "Woman, for this shall all thy sins be forgiven thee!"

Fletcher, of Saltoun, said that he did not care who made the laws of the country so long as he made its songs.[2] The reason why all clever rulers like Napoleon have been careful to get control of the art and literature of the country is because art forms our ideas, and finally forms our ambitions and the human conscience.

III   I want to look at the economic side of art and see how Socialism proposes to deal with art.

Property is an institution which has only been applied to art in recent times. If you compare the creation of a work of art with the production of a loaf of bread you come across some rather remarkable differences. The consumer, after buying a loaf of bread, eats it, and thus destroys it.

Compare that with what happens when I produce a book. You devour that book with the greatest avidity, and, although you have devoured that book, it is not destroyed, and it can be eaten over and over again.

At least, that is the way I want my books read.

It is the same way in admiring a picture. We go and look at the pictures in the National Gallery, and we dont wear them out; on the contrary, many pictures get the better with age. That, of course, puts the artist who produces new work in a very peculiar position. You cannot arrange for his remuneration exactly in the same way as the remuneration of the baker.

If you, for instance, take a modern writer and give him copyright all over the world—and it really is a very extensive copyright—under the modern Berne Convention, one consequence if he produces an enormously popular book is that instead of producing more books, he may simply sit down and wallow in the proceeds of that book and thus produce a most grotesque injustice in his remuneration as compared with other people.

Even in literature you still have these strange inequalities. I remember when I was a journalist, when I was in active work, writing every week, I used to work exceedingly hard, and I used to produce very good work, but I got so many guineas for what I produced in the week, and then I was not done, as then a new number had to be produced, and I had to produce new articles for the next week, instead of continually living on the proceeds of the old articles.

It was only when I escaped from journalism and became a writer of books, and could live on a continual tax, that I dared to become a capitalist. I found that I could write a play in the same time in which as a journalist I would have earned at the outside forty guineas; but in writing a play I find myself the possessor of the sum of £2,500, which, by the way, is still being added to.

In fact, I am in the position of a landlord. I bear no malice for that observation: I endeavor to submit to my fate.

What is very interesting to Socialists is the fact that this particular sort of property, which enables a man to levy a tax in this way, is quite a recent institution. It is a very much younger thing in the world than property in land and houses.

They might be said to be natural growths out of the conditions of society. It is found necessary that what a man produces by his labor or by the force of his arms shall be secured to him, and it is recognized that he has a right to it.

These earlier rights have now become the very grossest superstition; we find ourselves maintaining them in the greatest jealousy and sanctity.

Property in land was instituted in order to secure to the tiller of the soil the reward of his labor. Property on the land has the effect of entirely preventing the tiller of the soil getting anything out of it; he gives all the rest to absolute idlers.

We go on in the old way and we dont revise it.

It is perfectly evident to me that if we, by some means or other, could be thrown into a state of chaos, and if tomorrow we could sit down and work out new institutions, we would not dare to institute property in land at the present time. It would be the act of madmen.

Property in books, however, is a matter of recent institution, and we find this property strictly limited. You dont say to a man who has written a particular book: "This book shall be yours and your heirs forever." What you say, very sensibly, is, "We will allow you to have that privilege for fortytwo years, or, if you live longer, for seven years after your death, or rather, whichever period shall be the longest."

It is quite useful for Socialists who are engaged in propaganda to remind people that in this very important department of production, the production of works of art, they have actually applied the strictly Socialistic method of settling property, that instead of giving a man an unlimited period, they only give him a limited period, and then throw the book into the common stock.

At the end of that period all these extraordinary works of a man will be thrown into the common stock and another person will be at liberty to print his books. I then shall occupy the position that Shakespear holds at the present time—a most intolerable blackleg.

IV It is a rather nice question what the Socialistic solution would be, as to how the artist would be paid under Socialism.

I really think that the very best solution is the simple solution —that they should not be paid at all. There is a great deal to be said for it, and yet I am convinced that it would not work.

I think on the whole, we should get rather too much amateurishness. You will always have a class of men producing works of art, and you must either give them a copyright, such as they have at the present time and enable them to extort from the rest of the community money payments for enjoying that work of art, either that, or you will have to endow them in some particular way.

The procedure of a Socialistic state in that case would be, when a man produced a book, to purchase that book and thereby make it public property, and to give the producer of that book a pension, with the object of making him produce more books, or preventing him producing more books, whichever was the better thing.

I do not know any solution myself—the copyright solution is a most extraordinarily unsatisfactory one. It leads to the most grotesque inequalities.

You find a man at the present day who will write a novel of adventure, and will slosh it all over, and yet have an enormous sale and get a great deal of money.

Then you get another work, like a French dictionary; a monumental work, a thing which will take the whole lifetime of a most careful vegetarian to produce, a thing which must have required the most amazing patience, coupled with the most astonishing endurance and the most revolting drudgery.

Then he will get very little indeed for it when it is done.

That is the sort of equality and justice which is produced by the copyright system.

I do not know any other way of doing it; I have often tried to find out.

A copyright also involves this question—it gives an artist a power over his own work which is sometimes a very questionable power; it gives him the power of suppressing his own work, which is sometimes very undesirable.

I have always felt there are some things in my earlier writings of which I am beginning to disapprove. I am becoming an old fogy; I am also beginning to get more and more conservative.

I am bound in honor to refute myself at a previous period in my existence just as much as I am bound to refute anybody else. When a book has once gone forth I think it is an open question as to whether the author should have the power of suppressing it.

If a man has changed his mind, let him say he has changed his mind, rather than suppress the article, and say he was more intelligent than he was at an earlier time.

That is one of the advantages of the State buying the copyright of a book—the State would then prevent the author of a book from suppressing any portion of it afterward.

V   With reference to the present remuneration of artists and their possible remuneration under Socialism, there is no doubt that when we have got society into something like the order into which we have been striving to get it a great many of the incomes which some artists at present enjoy would practically disappear.

Our present plan throws into the hands of a relatively small class an enormous mass of wealth, and you have a sort of millionaire class, or "thousandaire" class, who have nothing to do and still have a tremendous lot of money—so much money that any particular sum is of no value whatever, and consequently the expenditure of a thousand pounds to people who ride in carriages involves very much less privation than the expenditure of sixpence does to many persons of the working class.

In this way the artists whose work happens to please the fancy or to flatter a particular rich class can, under existing circumstances, get most enormous payments for it, and the fashionable portrait painter of the day in London will get about two thousand pounds for a portrait.

On the other hand, you can get a portrait of yourself, the only objection to which is that it is far too faithful, in the form of what is called tintype for anything from one penny to sixpence, according to the bargaining.

Tintypes involve a much greater sacrifice on the part of the people who buy them than the payment of two thousand pounds to the fashionable artist.

The artist, by the revival of Socialism and the much greater equalization of purchasing power, would be affected in this way—I do not think he would find anybody who would give him two thousand pounds for a portrait.

There would be, of course, an immense opportunity for multiplication in the number of artists.

You would even find art growing among the very poor class, and you must nourish the production of the artistic faculty.

The great majority of artists who keep art going almost always come from the well-to-do class and not from the working class.

I think I might assume that with the greater spread of comfort and education, and when everybody was decently fed, clothed, and housed, and when everybody was really artistically cultured, to a great extent you would have a much larger material from which to draw.

The question to decide is that since there would not only be a larger artistic production, but also a larger artistic demand, what would be the effect on the prices of works of art? I do not think artists would be able to make much more money.

All improvements must necessarily take the form of making men more fastidious. You would have a larger demand for art and a much greater equalization of purchasing power and a much greater increase in production.

But, taken altogether, the economic problem of art is still most imperfectly solved.

A series of articles which appeared in The Clarion *on 9, 16, and 23 August 1907. The first two articles were entitled "Fabian Notes–Unauthorized." The third and final article was given the title which is being used here.*

A Socialist Program:
The Gentle Art of Unpleasantness

I What I like about Blatchford is that he really does consider Socialism a matter of some importance.[1] Of late this view has fallen into discredit in the movement, which consequently doesnt move much. The first item in the Socialist program today is "Do not hurt the feelings of the Labor Party." And the first item in the program of the Labor Party is "Be gentlemen."

Now, the essence of gentility is that you should never exploit your views (which may be of the highest Platonic or Christian kind—the higher the better) for political purposes, or allow them to make you socially disagreeable to other gentlemen. Everybody knows that the rich live by robbing the poor. That is why no gentleman ever mentions it. To call a man of independent means a thief is, argumentatively, to hit a man when he is down: it is like mentioning the facts concerning a lady's inside to prove that she is not an angel. Realism in art or conversation is felt to be dastardly. Social intercourse with Bluebeard being decently possible only on the assumption that he is an excellent husband, and Bluebeard being a desirable social acquaintance, you make the assumption and the thing is done. You dine with Judge Jeffries on the assumption that he is an impartial and benevolent lawyer; with Archbishop Laud on the assumption that he is a humane Christian; with Sir ———— ————, notorious vivisector and champion liar of his profession, on the assumption that he is a fountain of healing and a soother of fevered brows; and with openly bought and sold men and women of all the professions, from journalism to marriage, on the assumption that they are engaged in the free and independent pursuit of their holiest ideals.[2] When you can be depended on to make all these assumptions you are a gentleman eligible for all dinner tables.

Now please to remark that there is a fine side to all this as well as a silly and cowardly side, and that, as usual, it is by keeping on the fine side of it and ignoring the silly and cowardly one that men contrive to behave as gentlemen, not only without injury to their selfrespect, but even with considerable inflation to their sense of superiority. For the assumptions, being all assumptions of noble ideals—of the ideal husband, warrior, churchman, lawyer, healer, etc., etc.—show that your nature is noble enough and your perceptions lofty enough to grasp and aspire to these ideals. It sets you apart from the sordid cavillers who have no imagination and throw mud at the idols of the hour just as they would throw mud at Goethe or Dante or anybody else above their comprehension. There is even something fine in being duped by idealism; better be Don Quixote than Sancho Panza. And so idealism gets hold of the gentleman by his loftier imaginative side and makes him a humbug and a member of the Conspiracy of Silence on the highest principles.

Take as an example the debate in the House of Commons the other day on the proposal to grant £50,000 to Lord Cromer, known ironically in the Egyptian Nationalist Press as the Duke of Denshawai.[3] The money part of the proposal was reasonable. Lord Cromer will not get more than £2,000 a year on his £50,000, if he gets so much. His salary in Egypt, £6,000 a year, was obviously not enough for the position he had to maintain there. Put any Labor man on the job at that figure; and he will resign after eighteen months on the plea that he cannot afford it, and will spend the rest of his life trying to get out of debt. To the average supporter of the Labor Party, who feels generous when he subscribes to Mr Pete Curran's £200 a year,[4] this may be inconceivable; but Sir Henry Campbell-Bannerman and Mr Balfour know that it is true, and that the £6,000 was even less of a living wage than the £20,000 of the Lord Lieutenant of Ireland or the £15,000 of the Governor-General of India. Consequently when Lord Cromer said, in effect,

"I have outrun the constable; you must pay up," they could not honestly refuse, whatever they may have felt privately about Denshawai. So far, nobody who knows what it costs to be a pro-consul could reasonably object. No doubt Mr Victor Grayson[5] would have been more than human if he had resisted the opportunity of making the debut of Socialism in the British House of Commons by saying "Why is all this £50,000 not given to the poor?" but that is not permanent practical business: you cannot keep the country going even as it is, much less introduce Socialism by saying to your higher State officials, whenever they say they have not had enough to eat, "Nor shalt not, till Necessity be served," though Orlando pleases the gallery in As You Like It by saying that to the Duke. No doubt the disciples who said "To what purpose is this waste? This ointment might have been sold for much, and given to the poor," also make a strong point from the general Socialist point of view; but it is clear that when Mr Grayson is a responsible member of a Socialist Government he will not find it possible to treat immediate questions of ways and means in that fashion. He, too, will reply, "Ye have the poor always with you; but Lord Cromer ye have not always."

But though it was right and reasonable to give Lord Cromer his £2,000 a year, yet the way it was done was financially and morally foolish. The £2,000 a year should have been given as a terminable annuity for Lord Cromer's life and that of his widow, or until his children were all of age; for there is no sort of reason why our great grandchildren should support Lord Cromer's grandchildren to the tune of £2,000 a year, or whatever the £50,000 may then produce. But that is by the way: what I am concerned with here is the moral folly of the debate.

The ground on which the Right Honorables on both sides took that stand in supporting the grant was that Lord Cromer had restored the finances and enormously increased the prosperity of Egypt.

Let us see. Suppose a hard-working woman has a drunken, violent, idle, spendthrift husband. Suppose that the moment she earns a shilling he extorts it from her with threats, and if she refuses, takes it from her by force. Suppose that when she hides it, he beats her until she confesses where it is hidden. Suppose he finally beats her continually on the chance of her having money hidden somewhere. Suppose she loses all strength and selfrespect under his treatment, and cares no longer to do anything but suffer hopelessly.

Now, suppose the husband has borrowed money from a money-lender on the security of what he can beat out of his wife. Suppose the moneylender is quite content to pocket his interest without concerning himself as to the sufferings of the wife. Suppose when the wife is beaten and trampled into unproductiveness, and the payment of interest stops, the moneylender suddenly wakes up to the fact that the husband's methods are unbusinesslike; that he is killing the goose that lays the golden eggs; that he is himself an unproductive and superfluous nuisance; and that if the woman is protected from violence and extortion she will be able to pay the interest herself easily. The moneylender accordingly takes the hus-band into the police-court; gets him convicted; and saves the woman from him for ever by a magistrate's separation order.

The woman, freed from her tyrant, raises her head from the gutter; resumes her old industrious habits; pays the interest to the moneylender willingly, since it is only a tithe of what her black-guard of a husband used to extort from her; and presently, by dint of her own industry, becomes ten times as well off as she was during her married life.

And then the moneylender says, "This is my doing." And the magistrate says, "Excuse me: this is *my* doing." But the woman says, "If you please, gentlemen, my increased earnings are by my own doing; and though you set me free to do it, I cannot forget that you only did it to secure the interest on your money, and that whilst my husband paid it you never lifted a finger to protect me, no matter how cruelly he beat me."

The moneylender is England, the magistrate Lord Cromer, the woman the Egyptian fellahin, and the husband Ismail, the spend-thrift ruler whom we cleared out by military force. There is not a private soldier who charged at Tel el Kebir, not a gunner who pulled the string that sent a bomb into the hospital at Alexandria, who might not be put forward as the author of the increased pros-perity of Egypt as eligibly as Lord Cromer. What enabled Egypt to labor fruitfully instead of perishing in despair was the substitution of Western European law for tyranny and personal despotism. Lord Cromer did not make English law: on the contrary, he pleaded consistently for coercion, for trial without law, for flog-ging, for terrorism, for bureaucracy, for autocracy, for gagging the

Press, and finally for impressing Oriental peoples with the necessity of submission to us by deliberate exhibitions of sensational cruelty decreed by courts-martial. No sensible person who has read the Denshawai correspondence (to go no further back) can doubt that if he had not been restrained by the democratic and nationalist element in public opinion in Western Europe, and by the knowledge that Mr Wilfrid Scawen Blunt[6] was watching him as the policeman of that element, he would, in every respect except his sense of the need of making Egypt a paying concern from the capitalist point of view, have been a more complete tyrant than the thriftless and indifferent Ismail was ever capable of being. As it was, he disgraced us in the face of Europe by declaring that the culminating explosion of panic stricken cruelty and class rancor at Denshawai was "just and necessary"; and he created a bitterly anti-English national movement which has made Egypt into another Ireland standing right in the world-highway from west to east. His retirement is a relief so heartfelt both at home and abroad among those who either regard the Egyptians as fellow creatures or at least have to face the trouble made by the bad blood of which Lord Cromer was such a notable manufacturer, that £50,000 seems too little to pay for so signal a mercy.

And yet the House of Commons could not give him his money and let him go without lying and pretending about him for hours in a desperate attempt to persuade itself and the nation that Lord Cromer was Egypt's sunshine; that he has been the Nile, the seed, the labor, the harvest, the animals, the vegetables, the minerals, the commerce, the law, the peace, the prosperity, the energy, the enthusiasm, the prayer, the joy, the religion, in a word, the life of Egypt for 25 years past, and that without him the country would have become as the shore of the Dead Sea. Now even if Lord Cromer had been as conspicuously large-minded and humane as he was conspicuously the opposite, it would still be a sort of blasphemy to attribute to one man the benefits conferred by the freedom and law that have arisen from the struggles of thousands of generations of men towards the still invisible goal of humanity. If, when Lord Cromer carried that treasure in his hand to Egypt he had carried it willingly and understandingly, instead of reluctantly and with a determination to hold back as much of it as English public opinion would allow him to; if he had enshrined it and worshipped it instead of demanding the substitution for it of the lash, the gallows, and the court-martial; if he had left Egypt as satisfied with English institutions and English officials as the Carlton Club, we should still have to remind Sir Edward Grey and Mr Balfour that the praise due to a capable administrator is to be distinguished from the worship due to a creator. But when it is plain to all the world that the same increase in the yield of Egypt's industry would have followed the change from the Khedive Ismail's idiotic rapacity to Anglo-French institutions if any man of ordinary official ability had been the administrator, the farce is beyond human patience. Lord Cromer had his points, no doubt, notably the class prejudice that made him as unsympathetic to the financiers whom he looked on as cads and outsiders as to the fellahin, whom he regarded (when they were not absolutely submissive) as rebels and poachers. He liked keeping both in what he conceived to be their places; and as he could snub the financiers only by standing for public interests against them, it is possible that his arrogance may have been as useful in public business as it was disastrous in public justice. But for the rest, what can be said in defence of a man whose social prejudices are so inhuman that he thinks a young Egyptian peasant should be sent to penal servitude for life because he joins his fellow-villagers in throwing stones at a party of British officers who, in the course of a day's shooting for their private amusement, have just shot his wife, and, as he believes, killed her? I say nothing of the four men who were hanged or the seven who were flogged. That cannot be undone now. I also am quite ready to give the assaulted British officers the sympathy Sir Edward Grey asks for them when he tells me what is the matter with them. *They* were not hanged. *They* were not flogged. The gentleman who got the small bone of his arm broken has had it mended. If they had provoked an English crowd as they provoked the Egyptian one, they would hardly have escaped alive. Yet they are all alive and well except the one who ran away and died of sunstroke; and he cannot be recalled to life, nor can his representatives expect us to punish the sun. But Abdel Nebi, whose wife received the charge of one of the officers' guns in that part of her person which, were she accustomed to use English furniture, would be frequently protected by a chair (if an English sportsman had shot a partridge or a rabbit that way Lord Cromer would never have forgiven him), was sentenced to lifelong imprisonment, and has already served more than a year of it. And though even Sir

Edward Grey has at last been shamed into admitting that the time may come for clemency (clemency!) when it can no longer be interpreted as a sign of weakness—which means never, as our supply of fools and cowards is not likely to run short in Abdel Nebi's lifetime—Lord Cromer's declaration that the sentence was "just and necessary" still stands to testify to his "intense love of justice, real sympathy with the weak and oppressed, and singular freedom from British insularity or narrow-mindedness." Such is the enthusiastic language of my old friend the Saturday Review.

Why does the Saturday Review utter such exceeding tosh under the shadow of the gallows and whipping post of Denshawai? Why does it pretend not to know why the Liberal Government could muster only half its usual majority in favor of the grant, and, in spite of Mr Balfour's support, had to face 107 votes against it?

I will answer the question, and draw the moral with its application to the Labor Party and to Blatchford's article on The Socialist Ideal next week.

II The answer to the question with which I broke off last week, namely, why the Saturday Review repeats in cold blood the polite romancings of the front benches about Lord Cromer, is simply that the Saturday Review is written by gentlemen for gentlemen, and would not, if it could divest itself of the habits of fashionable society. Such society would obviously be impracticable if realism and recrimination were not absolutely barred in it. If I myself could not go out to dinner without being reproached for all the disgraceful things I have done, I should never dare to go out at all; for I am no more an angel than Lord Cromer. The condition on which I take my part in idle social intercourse is that every person I meet shall assume that I am perfect saint and perfect hero, with a spotless past, an assured salvation, all my teeth real, all my clothes paid for, my marriage an ideal union: in short, absolutely nothing the matter with me morally or financially, and nothing the matter bodily either, except a limited range of genteel diseases, provided they are not associated with misconduct of any kind. And in return for this trifling concession I agree to make the same assumptions with regard to everybody else, Lord Cromer included. Any intelligent and sincere person who considers the matter for five minutes will admit that those conditions are unavoidable if we are to have any tolerable social intercourse at all. We are none of us perfect, not even the Fabians.

But it is equally obvious that unless these conditions are totally discarded, and replaced by an uncompromising adherence to facts the moment we come to the serious business of life, we can have no medical advice, no legal advice, no newspapers, no national defence, no political action that we can trust. In short, we can have nothing real, except what we produce automatically or stumble on by accident or natural selection. And as a matter of fact that is all we have at present, because we are all determined to be ladies and gentlemen. For my part I say that this state of things is too dangerous to be tolerable. I want gentility to be kept in its proper place, the drawing room, and sternly banished from the House of Commons. Whether a member be Conservative, Liberal, Irish Nationalist, Labor or Socialist, he will do no good there until he ceases to be a gentleman and becomes a shameless realist. When the strain becomes too great, he can go out on the Terrace and be a gentleman again for half an hour there. But when he returns to his work he must become as a little child again, utterly outspoken, just as when a judge goes on the bench he must discuss and deal with the most unmentionable crimes, no matter how strongly the prisoner may appeal to his sense of decency to have a disgusting subject dropped.

The House of Commons has never understood this. It is always trying to live up to its reputation as the best club in London. That is why it is so useless, so futile, so exasperating to anyone who wants to get something done or at least to hear the truth about it. That is what drove Mr Pete Curran and Mr Grayson the other day, before they had caught the tone of the House, to tell the naked truth about it in public. That is why, in spite of all our reporters and newspapers, nobody ever knows what Parliament is really doing. That is why all the laws that are popularly supposed to be unrepealed relics of the bad old times were actually passed in the reign of Queen Victoria, except in a few that are Edwardian.

But why do I use up The Clarion columns with this restatement of a case against Parliamentary gentility which every reader of The Clarion knows and admits? Because impatient reader, the class in which the hypocrisies of gentility are carried to the worst extremes is the working class. The reason I prefer a conversation with a duchess to a conversation with a charwomen—and I avow the preference impudently, having tried both—is that I can talk to the duchess much more frankly and with much less affectation and reserve, than to the charwoman. If I met the Queen, I dont know what she would talk to me about; but I should certainly try to get the benefit of her large experience and responsibility in the matter of country houses by asking her what system of drainage she had found best. If I were to betray to a charwoman the faintest consciousness that such a thing as a system of drainage exists, or that any lady or gentleman could possibly have any use for such things, she would conclude that I was behaving coarsely and disrespectfully to her, because she was a charwoman, and cut me dead.

The men are just as bad. When I was on St Pancras Borough Council I was engaged, not so much in preaching the class war as in a long and mostly fruitless struggle to obtain lavatory accommodation for women. The very men who were red in the face with suppressed laughter at the schoolboy jests they were exchanging on the subject in private would become ten times redder with open shame at having such "abominations" mentioned in public. Now, the pretence that a lady has no bowels is really part and parcel of the pretence that a gentleman has no vices or corrupt motives. In Dickens's Our Mutual Friend, Mr George Sampson tries to soften Mrs Wilfer's indignation at the mention of a petticoat by saying, "After all, ma'am, we know it's there." Such a betrayal shattered the whole convention on which social intercourse was possible between Mrs Wilfer and Mr Sampson; but it is evident that unless, when Mrs Wilfer is elected to the Borough Council and Mr Sampson goes into parliament, they reverse their attitude and make the unmentionable their first business, they might just as well remain in private life except for the mere maintenance of routine. Whilst public bodies consist of ladies and gentlemen, behaving as such, nothing will ever be done except supervising the routine. A useful work in its way, but not what the Socialists have organized the Labor Party for, and not what they will have to organize their own party for when the Labor men have all become perfect gentlemen.

When John Stuart Mill was standing for Westminster, an indignant representative of the working classes rose at one of his meetings and asked him whether he had dared to say that the British working man was addicted to lying. "Yes," said Mill: "havnt you noticed it?" Everybody was so stunned by this ungentlemanly realistic reply that Mill got into parliament before they recovered, and was not turned out until the next election. Feargus O'Connor,[7] the Chartist leader, idealized the honest horny-handed fustian-coated son of toil much more absurdly than Mr Balfour has just idealized the English country gentleman (East Coast, force-you-to-attend-your-brother's-hanging variety) in the person of Lord Cromer. All the aristocrats and cerebrocrats who have done the thinking and leading of the revolutionary movement have idealized the proletariat. They could not deny that the oppression of the capitalist had reduced the laborer to a condition in which he occasionally drank and even raised his hand to his wife otherwise than in the way of kindness; but it never seems to have occurred to any of them that a laborer could be a snob and a humbug, or that a parliament of Labor members might be one in which it would be harder to speak the truth than in the parliaments of Lords Melbourne and Palmerston.

And yet what Socialist who really knows the working class is not appalled by its capacity for snobbery and humbug? That the capacity is not yet realized is no comfort to the realist. You do not admire a drunken man in a dirty shirt for his freedom from the snobbery and make-believe of the idle rich: you know very well that Bohemianism, no matter what class it occurs in, is due much oftener to weakness and worthlessness than to the strength that sometimes leads to complete preoccupation with higher matters than clothes and soap. I have always, in spite of Dickens, admired Mrs Jellyby for taking a greater interest in the salvation of Borrioboola Gha than in the kitchen and nursery at Thavies Inn;[8] but the truth is that most of the women whose houses are as badly kept as Mrs Jellyby's are not interested in anything at all. If you could make snobs and humbugs of these women you would improve them enormously, just as you would elevate the drunkard in the dirty shirt beyond recognition if you could make him a respectable Conservative churchwarden.

When the Labor Party has secured for the English laborer a minimum standard wage of £78 a year, he will become more particular about his clothes and his skin. He will become more particular about his language, discarding one of his favorite adjectives wholly; replacing the other by "bally" or "blooming"; and taking, as to his pet substantive, the hint given to the British private soldier by Mr Rudyard Kipling in his famous euphemism The Absent

Minded Beggar as far as his means will allow, he will obliterate, one by one, the visible distinctions in personal habit between his class and the middle class, just as the middle class tries to obliterate, as far as *its* means will allow, the visible distinctions between it and the plutocracy. He will call his dinner lunch and his tea dinner. When he entertains, his wife will suppress his beer, and offer the guest his choice of red ink or vinegar, which she will call claret and hock. He will attend a place of worship regularly and compel his unfortunate children to accompany him. But above all he will begin to pick up the ideals, especially the Tory ideals, for which sentimental Socialism is such an excellent training: tho difference, indeed, being merely a sordid detail as to the distribution of the national income. With Sidney Webb's scholarship "ladder to the universities" at his son's foot, he will begin to understand the public school ideal, the Oxford ideal, and the Anglican ideal. He will say Hear Hear when orators tell him, not for the first time, that Waterloo was won on the playing fields of Eton; and he will get his boy an Eton collar and jacket for his next outfit. He will remember with shame that his father was so ignorant and degraded that he could see nothing in an aristocracy of English gentlemen and Churchmen but thieving swine. Or if he is too hardheaded and individualistic for this, he will catch the American plutocractic ideal, the efficiency ideal, the neo-Darwinian ideal. He will begin to see how childishly men who have never had a hundred a year over and above their bare living wage to invest and administer, think and and talk of administrators who have millions to handle daily, and who break down repeatedly from overwork and the starvation of the man whose nerves are so worried that he cannot eat. In the reaction from his old romantic ignorance, in his interest in and enthusiasm for the new world opening before him—the wonderful new world of gentlemanly ideals and cultivated intercourse—he will give slightly moralized plutocracy a new lease of life. He will drop The Clarion as vulgar and taboo Justice as undesirable; and The Times and The World and The Saturday Review and the rest, reduced to a penny, will be his regular papers. All of which will be an immense advance, a brilliant promotion for him and his prudently limited family; BUT—where do I, the Socialist, come in?

Readers who desire an answer to this important question should buy next week's Clarion.

I I I Last week I broke off on the momentous question "When the Labor Party becomes a party of gentlemen, where do I, the Socialist, come in?"

As the combed and brushed labor gentleman, with his minimum wage and his ideals, will certainly retort by asking "And pray who are you?" I reply, uppishly, that I am a gentleman of landed estate and an eminent cerebrocrat. Blatchford instinctively asks why I am not in Parliament, with Cunninghame Graham and Hyndman.[9] And a very proper question, too. For we three are none of your Labor riff-raff, we would have you to know. Your gentlemanly ideals have no illusions and no charm for us: we are in the position of the medieval cynic who stood unmoved in the frantic crowd of recruits for the Cross when Peter the Hermit had filled them all with enthusiasm by preaching the Crusade. "Why are you so cynical?" they said. "Are you deaf, or are you a follower of the accursed Mahound?" "Not at all," said the unmoved one: "I've been there, that's all." We, too, have been there. We have worn the tall hat; we have been washed and combed and taken to church; we have heard our sisters practising the Sonata Pathetique and damned Beethoven and all his works; we have eaten and drank (sometimes excessively) with public schoolboys and university graduates; we have discussed industrial questions with "captains of industry," religious questions with bishops, political questions with cabinet ministers, and social questions with peers and peeresses. We have been in the ideal business from our cradles; we have examined its books; we have discovered that it is a Long Firm Fraud; and we have been promptly kicked out for our pains. Instead of weeping and rubbing our booted posteriors, we have made such a row in the streets that the door has been opened again, and we have been begged to enter as amusing and talented eccentrics, and to slip in quickly so that the mob may have the door slammed in its face on our heels. But we cannot help wondering whether even that grace will be tolerated by the servants when their wages are doubled and there is a grand piano in the servants' hall.

For even as it is, Labor does not approve of us. When I became a Socialist, with some ability as a journalist to place at the service of the cause, it did not occur to me that my contributions would be as unwelcome to Justice, The Commonweal, and Vorwärts as to the Liberal-Radical papers, and that I should one day retire from journalism with a remarkable record for revolutionary utterances in

The Times, The Saturday Review, and The World, and practically no record at all as a contributor to Socialist and Labor papers. The same thing is true of Cunninghame Graham, and would be true of Hyndman if he had not virtually had a Hyndmanist paper of his own in Justice, of which Labor has never approved. Morris's Commonweal was even less popular than Justice, though ladies and gentlemen buy old numbers of it for five shillings and upwards. Kropotkin's works appear in The Nineteenth Century: Lloyd's Weekly would not touch them with a pair of tongs. Walter Crane's works are on the walls and bookshelves of the cultivated capitalists whom he denounces, and nowhere else.[10]

The fact is, the working classes, when they are not simply idolizing us for our reputation, as they idolize Gladstone and Shakespear, object to us because we scandalize them; and the more the Labor Party raises them to the level of middle-class and plutocratic ideals, the more they will object to us. Our quarrelsomeness and bad manners shock them even more than our cynicisms, our blasphemies, our irreverences and indecencies. Hyndman and I are the recognized obstacles to the sweet ideal of Socialist Unity, with its gentlemanly policy of never mentioning your differences. Cunninghame Graham's conduct may pass in West End drawing rooms; but it would not be tolerated in a public-house parlor; he actually damned the House of Commons to its face when he was in it; and his writings are so—shall I say, irreticent—that The Saturday Review is almost the only paper that will stand them. H. G. Wells, our latest eminent recruit from the villas, is so incapable of behaving himself in public life that his temper very nearly broke up the Fabian Society exactly as William Morris's temper broke up the Social Democratic Federation when he founded the Socialist League. R. J. Campbell, our latest recruit from the pulpit, shocks the masses by his New Theology and delights the middle-class City Temple.[11] Wilful, impatient, petulant, quarrelsome we have no sort of docility, no self-sacrifice, no humbleness, no modesty, none of the qualities that make it so easy to fleece the proletarian lamb. When we were against the workers we conquered them as we conquered the Maoris. The Maoris, you will remember, were not cynical enough to believe that Christian English troops would fight on Sunday, a delusion which did honor to their feelings, but which enabled us to massacre them when they had nothing but hymnbooks in their hands to defend them. And the Labor Man face to face with the Plutocrats will be in as great danger as the Maoris, all the greater because he will regard his gullibility as a moral superiority. He will turn on us—the cynics who have been clean through the genteel ideals and broken out on the other side of them—and, help his masters to muzzle us, the day after he has attained his moral minimum by our help.

Therefore I now solemnly abandon the Labor Party after doing my share of the work of setting it on its feet—or rather on its knees—in Parliament. I now want to get my own class—the disinherited poor relations and younger sons' progeny of the plutocrats and aristocrats—into parliament and into political array. I want a party of Socialists who have had enough of being gentlemen. No common working man need apply: his dissatisfaction with genteel life cannot be sincere, because he has never tried it. Poor people are always objectionable; and no poor person shall be admitted into my new party unless he can prove that his poverty is his own fault and that his parents were respectable. The children of atheists, who have never been to church, will be rigidly excluded; but those who were taken to church regularly every Sunday by their parents and broke loose later on will be welcome. All members over 30 must be married or at least domesticated: bachelors and libertines invariably idealize matrimony, and put forward impracticable plans of education. Drunkards, borrowers, amateur gamblers, and seducers will be excluded, not from moral prejudice, but because they are nuisances, and will find plenty of congenial company in the other parties; but disinterestedly irregular and insubordinate persons will be specially welcome, provided they are ladies and gentlemen. Various tests of gentility will be applied: for instance, candidates will be asked whether it has ever occurred to them to clean their own boots or go to bed in their dayshirts. An affirmative answer will be a decisive disqualification. The thing must be kept select at all costs. Keir Hardie, obviously the most ingrained gentleman in the House of Commons, will be admitted on his renouncing Labor and either publicly apologizing for having worked as a boy in a mine, or else confessing that the story of his having done so is as unfounded as it seems improbable; but as a rule only Socialists who are renegades from Capitalism will be tolerated. Professional men and gentlemen-employees will then have a society suited to their position, free from the red tape of the trade unions, and the aspirations of the working man to be "a gentleman in the true sense of the word"—that is, on the cheap.

I have great hopes of persuading the Fabian Society to adopt these regulations and to organize a real socialist party, openly bent on abolishing property, breaking up the family; annihilating militarism by refusing to renew the Mutiny Act; making our domesticity decent by stamping out marriage and all other legal forms of prostitution and chattel slavery; purifying religion from all forms of idolatry, including the idolatry of saviors, saints, prophets, prime ministers, playwrights and pianists; complicating life until nobody can live on less than several thousand a year, or earn it without practically continuous activity: abolishing all pleasures, holidays, and other agents of exhaustion and tedium; and (incidentally) criticizing the Labor Party on all possible occasions with studied arrogance and without the slightest regard for its feelings.*

In the meantime, what is the poor old Labor Party to do? Why, get a program from the Fabian Society, of course. Is there not the Minimum Wage Act to be forced on the House? Is there not the Poor Law to be utterly abolished, and proper provision made for the widow and orphan, for public health and public education, with a complete system of Labor Exchanges for the supply of unskilled labor to employers on conditions subversive of unemployment and casual employment? There is five years' work in these alone for any party. And what else, we may be asked, could a Socialist Party do if it were in parliament? I reply, lots of things of which the Labor Party would never dream. First, make a desperate resistance to the annual renewal of the Mutiny Act, and thereby make it possible for self-respecting free men to form a citizen army with the ultimate object of conquering their own country, now held up by genteel brigands. The Labor Party, with the eminently sensible exception of Will Thorne,[12] would of course not think of such a step, and would either blow Disarmament bubbles and sing carols out of season about Peace and Goodwill on Earth to an accompaniment of protests against "Tory extravagance," or else rally to the defence of

* Shaw's note: Will the Editor kindly send a copy of the Clarion, with the above paragraph conspicuously marked, to the editor of the Daily Express. That unfortunate gentleman is at present quoting my utterances of twenty years ago, and explaining to the chuckling public that the ideas of his paper are at least twenty years older again. He had better have something fresh. I owe him this kindly attention in return for his gratuitous reprint of the Fabian Society's appeal for funds. It elicited an immediate response greatly to the relief of our treasurer.

the British Army, the British Navy, the patriotic ideal, and the inspiring watchword "Kneel down, you dog, or take five years penal servitude." Then take in hand the abolition of absurd municipal boundaries that make public enterprise impossible, organizing your local governments into provinces, and coordinating them for inter-municipal trading.* Then demand an enormous increase in the income tax (graduated) to relieve the wretched ratepayer and improve our towns. Then push forward International Federation by organizing Imperial Federation on a democratic (*i.e.*, a Home Rule) basis, and insist that countries like India, which are alleged to be incapable of policing themselves efficiently, shall be placed under international control to secure person, property, and peaceful rights of way for foreigners in their territory, and thus knock the bottom out of the strong practical excuses for the exploitation and domination of Oriental and colored communities by powerful Western nations, armed to the teeth, and for such openly atrocious crimes as the bombardment of Casa Blanca.[13] Here we have much more than five years' work for a Socialist Party.

Meanwhile the Liberal Party could denounce the House of Lords, and flog, shoot, hang, imprison, bombard, muzzle the Press, and amuse itself generally after its manner, and that of its old friend, Russia, what time Mr Balfour would chivy it and make the Labor Party ashamed of not being well up in the ideals.

If any man idly inquire how the Labor Party and the Socialist Party can do these things without a majority, I reply that if, as is undoubtedly the case, thirty men who are in earnest can prevent any man in public assembly, no matter how large his majority, from wantonly wasting their time, by simply crying "Agreed," or "Divide," until he sits down, so the Labor Party and the Socialist Party, if the House of Commons persists in neglecting the business of the nation and plodding through its party game of croquet (old style), can do a great deal to spoil the genteel amenity of that fashionable sport. I will not say that if the House will not do our business it should at least be prevented from doing anything else, because it would like nothing better: but it might be prevented from enjoying its inactivity. There is no reason why the House should be made a comfortable place for the old bucks of the party world or the golden youth of the plutocracy. I do not suggest anything ill-mannered,

* Shaw's note: Please underline this heavily in the Daily Express copy, and warn the editor to break it to the investing classes by degrees.

anything noisy, anything violent, except when a bore has to be suppressed, or a time limit imposed on the front bench over the head of a Speaker or chairman who considers that time was not made for Right Honorables. I have great faith in patient common sense, good-humored implacability, superior knowledge of social problems, and really scientific criticism. They quite spoil the club atmosphere. Later on perhaps—but this article is already too long. Another time.

A series of articles which appeared in the New Age from 31 October 1907 through 25 January 1908.

On Driving Capital Out of the Country

I [SOCIALISM AND THE QUESTION OF CAPITAL LEAVING THE COUNTRY] Those who have done their share of Socialist oratory of late must have noticed how often, thanks to the Tariff Reform League, the dread of driving capital out of the country crops up in opposition to Socialism. It is, of course, easy to give the stock answer. You draw a derisive picture of our shareholders crossing the Channel with their pockets stuffed with locomotives, spinning-mules, and blast furnaces, carrying bundles of steel rails with their golfing clubs. You add, in a graver vein, that as long as we have land, labor, and intelligence, vitality and honesty, water to boil into steam, and coal and wood to boil it with, nitrogen in the soil, oxygen in the air, electricity everywhere, and a knowledge how to set it in motion, the fear that we can either be starved or even stinted by the sulking of our reactionaries is only a nightmare.

This is obviously true; yet it is not convincing. It silences your opponent; but it is not desirable to silence an opponent who is not convinced. He should be encouraged to pursue the subject until you have secured his vote: otherwise you only add him to that large and dangerous body of obstructives who say that Socialism is all very fine in theory, but that it would not work. Let us see, then, whether this alleged phenomenon of capital leaving the country can actually happen, and, if so, to what extent.

But before you try to find out how far the objector may be right, it is just as well to find out how far he may be wrong in the assumption on which he is arguing. It may be, for instance, that instead of being a thoughtful observer who believes that capital can leave the country for the excellent reason that he has seen the thing occur, and has perhaps been made bankrupt by it, he may be simply an ignorant man who believes that a capitalist is an earthy Providence who supplies the worker with wages, raw materials, and machinery out of a fund of which he is himself the original source. A man may believe this without being mad, absurd as his delusion is to an economist; for very few people look beyond the immediate source of the things that come to them; and the employer is undoubtedly the immediate source of all these things. As recently as October 24, a gentleman wrote to The Times a quite coherent, grammatical, and ordinarily sane letter in which he spoke of the landlords of London as "supplying" land for the use of the community just as miners supply coal and bakers supply bread. After this, it is not surprising that many honest tremblers for the safety of the country's capital sincerely believe that the capitalist is a man with the purse of Fortunatus, who continually supplies his employees with wages and salaries, and the public with commodities and services, at his own expense. It is no use losing patience, and declaring that a man who believes such a thing must be a fool. The fact remains that people of quite ordinary intelligence do believe it. Such people have before now taken shares in companies for the exploitation of perpetual motion and the transmutation of metals. Such people believe in sporting prophets with the fact staring them in the face that no sportsman who could foresee the results of our races would need to earn a precarious living as a journalist. There is nothing for it but patience and instructive explanations. Until you man understands, however roughly, that no employer would employ at all if he did not intend to get out of his business everything that he puts into it, with a substantial profit to boot, he will only bewilder himself over economic questions. If you were to put his own error to him in another way by claiming that when, for example, English capital is sent abroad to make a railway in South America instead of being kept at home to make a railway in Middlesex, England benefits by a great saving in railway fares at the expense of South America, he would be unable to confute you, and would perhaps even declare himself a Socialist, because Socialism, by, as he thinks, driving capital out of the country, would effect an enormous reduction in our national expenses.

It is, indeed, hardly possible to exaggerate the ignorance and confusion of mind which stands in the way of intelligent social organization. In spite of all the campaigning of Cobden, the present generation of Englishmen believes for the most part that if you buy foreign horseshoes, you take wages that might have been paid to an English workman and pay them to a foreign one instead. Mr Chamberlain himself began his Tariff Reform campaign by tumbling head over heels into this crudest of all popular economic blunders, and would probably be wallowing in it still if it were not that, with Mr Balfour at one elbow and Mr Hewins[1] at the other, even Mr Chamberlain may not violate the elementary decencies of economic discussion without a warning pull at his coattails. And if I were to advocate sending all contracts abroad on the ground that work is a curse, and that it would be far better for us to have a perpetual holiday and let other nations work for us, I have no doubt that the majority of the readers of The Daily Telegraph would think me an uncommonly sensible man. Before we can make any headway, we must knock into people's heads that workmen produce their own wages and would not be employed unless they did; that all sound businesses are necessarily self-supporting, and, in fact, a good deal more than self-supporting, since they at present have to carry a huge burden of extravagant and expensive idleness; and that it is silly to argue as if self-supporting industry in South America can disable self-supporting industry in England. On the contrary, if its products are imported into England, it actually provides employment for the English workman whose products are exported to pay for the imports. If its products are not consumed in England, it cannot directly affect English industry at all.

Nevertheless, we must not draw the comfortable Manchester School conclusion that all will be well with us as long as we do not interfere with trade. The existing system does permit a very great evil; and not only Socialism, but every improvement in the condition of our people, whether socialistic or individualistic, encourages that evil. It is an evil familiar to every Irishman. It is the evil of Absenteeism.

It may be remembered that one of the moral horrors of the Irish Famine was that at the very time when the people were starving;

when peasant women who had hit on the expedient of secretly
feeding themselves and their children on snails were accused of
witchcraft because their bones could not be seen through their
skin; when ignorant English sentimentalists were sending shiploads
of cheap food to Ireland, as if money had lost its purchasing power
there: at this very crisis of destitution, Ireland was steadily exporting food, and products which could be exchanged for food, in
payment of rent and interest to absentee landlords and capitalists.
If it had not done so, the landlords would have starved; and as we
all know, the landlords did not starve, and the people did. But this
phenomenon of absenteeism is not peculiar to Ireland. It is a universal one. Take my own case. I am an absentee Irish landlord. As
such, I have by no means an idle job, whatever my tenants may
think. I have to give a bit of my mind and a bit of my time to the
management of the estate. That is to say, I do five per cent of the
work and my agent does the other ninetyfive per cent, whilst I get
ninetyfive per cent of the rents and he gets five per cent. But by far
the greater part of my income comes to me as an absentee capitalist.
The last time I had any capital to spare it was "driven out of the
country": that is to say, I lent it to a Canadian municipality instead
of to an English one. I had already lent earlier accumulations to
local authorities in New Zealand. The fact is, I am entirely at one
with the opponents of Municipal Socialism in preferring municipal
and State securities for my private investments whenever I can get
them, because they are the most highly socialized and consequently
the safest securities available. I am, therefore, not only an Irish
absentee, but a Canadian absentee, and a New Zealand absentee. I
draw money regularly from all three countries which I do not
spend in them, and which I do not repay to them in any way. I am
also a Scotch absentee; for I have shares in the Caledonian Railway.
I am a Brazilian absentee: at least I have shares in the San Paulo
Railway Company; and I think San Paulo is in Brazil, though, to be
quite frank, it may be in Kamschatka or Van Diemen's Land for all
I know. I feel surer about the Argentine Republic: it must certainly
be in South America; and I am one of the proprietors of its Northern Central Railway. Buenos Ayres also pays me tribute. Japan
owes me the glory it has gained from a couple of thousand pounds'
worth of exploded gunpowder and the slaughter of sundry Russians; so I am entitled to sign myself an absentee of that much-
admired little State, and to levy *bushido* to the tune of 5 per cent.

II ABSENTEEISM AND TARIFF REFORM.   Last week I established two important points. First, that our present anti-
Socialist system has driven my capital out of the country, just as it
has for years driven millions of other people's capital out of it. So,
even if we admit that Socialism would drive capital out of the country, honors are easy as between Socialism and anti-Socialism. Second, the imports which represent the interest on my foreign capital
are not balanced by any exports, except the original export of the
capital sum. No doubt I sent out to the San Paulo Railway a brace of
locomotives or a few thousand tons of Welsh coal to start with; but
that contribution is long since consumed and done with, whereas
the revenue from it is being continually produced by the daily
renewed labor of the inhabitants of San Paulo, and is being exported to England and handed over to me and my fellow
shareholders without any daily renewal of production on our part.
Thus the Manchester School and its Free Trade optimism has no
locus standi in my case, because my case is a case of imports in
excess of exports: that is, unearned imports.

It is a conceivable thing that the entire country, in the ordinary
Manchester course of free exportation of capital, should finally
become a country of absentees, without any productive industry
whatever. This phenomenon already exists in sub-divisions of our
national area. I have shares in Brunner, Mond and Company.[2] I do
not know where their works are or what they work at; and, speaking as a private person, I do not want to know and I do not care so
long as they remain solvent. When I go to Barmouth or to Bour-
nemouth, I am not only an absentee as regards the dominion of
Brunner, Mond and Company, but I am practically one of a whole
community of absentees and their parasites. The Isle of Wight, the
Principality of Monaco, are examples of absentee communities:
they absorb and consume: they produce nothing, not even amusement for oneanother; for their efforts in that direction end on the
whole, in boredom, so that they are obliged to hire professional
entertainers to make life endurable. They appear to give employment to these entertainers and tradesmen; but clearly it is Messrs
Brunner, Mond and Company and the laborers and organizers of
South America and other places who give that employment. The
absentees only intercept a good deal of it for their own consump-
tion. The only exceptions are among the women, some of whom
are engaged in the important industry of producing children; but

as some of these children are not destined to become producers, they will be a burden to the nation instead of a reinforcement of it.

I do not see how any reasonable person can deny that absenteeism is, from the national point of view, a serious aggravation of the fundamental evil of parasitism. From an international point of view, it may not matter where the parasite is. But we have not yet come to industrial internationalism. If, for instance, America were to become a sort of industrial hell of mines, and factories, and sky-scraping working-class dwellings, whilst England became a magnified Eastbourne, in which all the natives who had not emigrated got an easy living by touching their hats and letting lodgings to a huge and opulent plutocracy of American absentees, the conditions of both nations would be as unwholesome, as the conditions of Wigan and Nice are at present. One of the reasons why Free Trade no longer holds intelligent individuals as it once did, and that Tariff Reform has been taken up by men who know all about the arguments of Cobden and Bastiat, is that they see in taxation of imports a discouragement to the export of capital.[3] They see that the logical consummation of Free Trade is as unbearable a horror as the logical consummation of Socialism, or anti-Socialism, or Christianity, or decency, or honesty, or anything else that is capable of a logical consummation. They see that as the consummation of Manchester Capitalism in the town is a division of the town into an East End and a West End; so the consummation of Manchester Capitalism in the World is a division of the world into East End nations and West End nations. They are ready to snatch at anything short of downright Socialism that promises to checkmate this; and as they see such a promise in Tariff Reform, they will probably try it before they allow us to convince them that Socialism is the only real alternative to Industrial Individualism. However zealous a Free Trader you are, you cannot get out of the fact that if all imports were taxed, that taxation would act finally as an additional income tax on my revenue from foreign investments, and would give me a solid reason for preferring English investments to foreign ones, instead of, as at present, preferring foreign investments to English ones. In vain will the Cobden Club demonstrate that this is an error, because the consumer would pay the tariff in heightened price. I reply that I myself am the consumer of my own dividends. And if this is too subtle for the rough and ready economists of the Club, they will at least admit that you cannot raise your price without restricting your market, and you cannot restrict your market without affecting your profits. If Tariff Reform would not damage me it would not damage anybody; and then what would become of all the arguments against it? If Free Trade does not benefit me, it does not benefit anybody; and then what becomes of the arguments in its favor?

The Socialists, of course, regard the Tariff Reform remedy for absenteeism as burning down the house to roast the pig. To tax directly all imports, both earned and unearned, in order to effect an indirect taxation of the unearned fraction of them is silly when you have the alternative of direct taxation of that fragment without interfering with the rest. It would be just as easy for Mr Asquith to levy five shillings in the pound on my San Paulo dividends as against one shilling on my Brunner-Mond ones as it is for him to tax them equally, as he does at present. But the Tariff Reformer prefers the clumsy, indirect method because it is one of the established expedients of capitalism, whereas the direct method is an open application of Socialist finance which would incidentally act as an education towards further applications. He does not want Socialism, and is willing to sacrifice a good deal to stave it off. Besides, it may be argued very plausibly that the discouragement of foreign investments is almost the only permanent change that Tariff Reform would make. The Cobdenite notion that we import only those commodities which can be made more cheaply in other countries than in our own, and that we export only the commodities which we ourselves can produce to a greater advantage than other countries, no longer holds good. The international division of labor that grew up when Germany and Italy had neither Manchesters nor Birminghams, and when Swiss and Italian waterfalls could not do the work of British coal mines, may be upset now without any commodity necessarily rising in price by a farthing. Other things being equal, the nearer your factory is to your market the cheaper your product will be; and nothing will persuade me, as I look down the long list of our actual imports and the black register of our sweated trades, that we import all these things because all our workers are better employed then in producing them. I cannot estimate what proportion of the world's navigation and transport is pure waste of time, or how far Tariff Reform would save it; but that the waste is going on, and that the possibility of saving it is one of the most plausible economic pretensions of the Tariff Reformer, had better be admitted as at least worth considering. I admit it the more readily because the more this point is understood the more it will become apparent that under our present system the proposed saving could not be introduced without an appalling financial crisis which no Government dare bring about intentionally. Not until Socialism makes an end of crises will wholesale transfers of industries from country to country be possible without colossal crashes, and all the bankruptcy and ruin they involve. Which leads neatly to the conclusion that Tariff Reform involves, as a preliminary step, Socialism.

Next week I shall consider how far the exportation of capital can go at present, and what it really means.

III   ABANDONED CAPITAL AND TRANSPORTED CAPITAL.   We have now got clear on a cardinal point. It is possible to drive income out of the country; and so, as all Capital begins as spare income, it is possible to put a stop to the application of fresh capital to British industry, and thereby reduce the country to stagnation.

What is more, the capital which has already been applied to our industry, though it cannot be carried away across the Channel in the Gladstone bags of our capitalists, can be abandoned by them. Abandoned capital is as common a spectacle in England as dead cities are in India. The ruins of a mill, the shaft of a disused mine, a pair of rotting lock-gates on a ditch full of weeds which was once a canal, an obsolete martello tower, a windmill without sails: these may be met with on most walking tours; and they are all cases of abandoned capital, skeletons of dead industries. The capital was not driven out of the country; but it was killed, which is a still graver matter. Capital, then, is mortal. In point of mere physical possibility, if one mill, one canal, one mine could be abandoned and left to perish, all our mills, all our railways, all our mines can be abandoned and left to perish. How far are we in danger of this happening?

The risk is obviously not so great as the risk of sending newly-accumulated capital abroad, because you can export spare income without losing any of it; but you cannot abandon your fixed capital and have it too. No man will turn a thousand pounds' worth of machinery into fifty shillings' worth of scrap iron as long as it will bring in its bare upkeep; but he will export fresh capital that might bring him in four per cent at home if he can get five per cent for it from Japan. Thus we see enterprises that have never paid— Thames Steamboats and Kentish railways—struggling on because the only alternative was to abandon the capital already irrecoverably sunk in them. Dividends are better than mere hope; but even hope is better than despair and dead loss; so the capitalists will struggle on without dividends as long as the concern will pay its working expenses. Not until a reduction of profit to zero is followed by an actual deficit on the working expenses, and the capitalist must either abandon the enterprise or throw good money after bad, does he leave his capital to perish. Indeed, he so seldom recognizes the situation at first that he generally does throw some good money after bad before he faces the fact that he is beaten.

Thus we see that there is a very effective check on the abandonment of fixed capital which does not apply to the export of floating capital. A very slight rise in wages or shortening of the working day beyond the point at which better conditions for labor mean greater efficiency and increased product may drive floating capital abroad, or drive it from the town to the country; but fixed capital is tied to the stake, and must put up with the worst that Socialism can do to it short of making its working expenses greater than its takings.

However, before dismissing the threats of exporting fixed capital from our minds as impracticable, let us make a note of the fact that the derisive picture of the capitalists taking the railways and mines across the Channel as part of their luggage had better not be drawn before a popular audience unless the orator is prepared for the retort that a good deal of modern industrial plant can be so exported. Much of our electric lighting plant has come from Germany; and there is no physical impossibility in its going to Jericho if its proprietors choose to take it there. Many of our internal explosion engines have come from France, and could drive themselves back there easily enough. The Lusitania could ply between Buenos Ayres and New York as easily as between Southampton and New York. Even buildings can be mobilized when it is worth while. Industrial plant, when it is movable at all, is sometimes more easily movable than men and women, because it has no sentimental local attachments. If it has been possible for capitalism to drive three-quarters of the population of Ireland to America, what is there, except the American tariff, to prevent Socialism from driving three-quarters of our power-looms, steam-hammers, and electro-motors thither?

We must admit, then, that there is no physical impossibility in taking movable industrial plant out of the country if the operation is worth while. But movable plant is small and short-lived com-pared to the capital sunk in preparing the actual earthly body of the country for its use. It is not much satisfaction to the makers of a dock that they can take their cranes to Peru, when they must per-force leave the pier on which the crane stands and the breakwater which protects it. Many costly enterprises result in nothing movable at all. Brooklands motor racecourse, for example, though it was made for the accommodation of the most movable form of machinery in the world, is itself immovable. Mines, roads, wa-terways, shipyards are all immovable; and this immovability in-volves the immovability of many other businesses which depend on them. You must either work them where they stand or abandon them.

Do not forget, by the way, that abandonment is a familiar com-mercial operation. Our manufacturers have been trained to face it in that form which them call scrapping. Machines are often ren-dered obsolete by improvements or new inventions before they are worn out—sometimes before they are even finished; and the aban-donment of plant is therefore by no means so unfamiliar and de-terrent a sacrifice as members of a popular audience can be led to believe. Plant, in short, is not only more easily transported, but more lightly abandoned nowadays than people think. The taking over to Holland of all the machinery in a woollen mill or the selling of it as scrap iron are both of them operations which the modern employer is quite prepared to consider and to carry out, if neces-sary, without turning a hair.

But all this leaves the Socialist withers unwrung. The capitalists cannot export more plant then we can replace; nor do they at present save one-third as much as they waste. Our actual saving of capital is about £200,000,000 a year; our unearned incomes amount to £630,000,000 a year. As far, therefore, as the question is merely one of capital, the country stands to gain by Socialism more than the capitalists can possibly take out of it. If the capitalists ship a machine to Holland, and the Socialist Administration which has driven them to do it buys another machine from Germany, or makes it at home—in either case at the capitalists' expense through an income-tax on their dividends—the laugh is clearly with the Socialists and not with the capitalists.

But when we throw off our pre-occupation with machinery and money, and come down to the actual realities of the export problem, all these arguments seem little better than quips. The real question is, what services are the employers rendering to the country? And can they take these services to Holland or South America? How far are they in a position to say to us: "You can keep our mines and yards and railways and all the land we have reclaimed from waste. You can replace every machine we take abroad with a newer machine paid for by the money you take out of our own pockets by confiscation disguised as taxation. Much good they will be to you without our brains and knowledge of business! Your Keir Hardies and Pete Currans[4] can manufacture talk on the largest scale, and produce gas enough to fill all the gasholders in Wandsworth twice over; but you cannot eat their talk or wear it; and their sort of gas will not burn anything except their neighbor's houses. Your Mr Sidney Webb knows all about how wealth is produced: can he produce it? He can employ a few secretaries; can he employ a thousand workmen? and if not, what is to become of the thousand workmen when we have all gone to countries where workmen are reasonable and are content to remain in that state of life to which it has pleased God to call them?"

The capitalist might refine a little on this. He might point out that though he employs a thousand men, he does not do so singlehanded, but through a system which involves the application of a great deal of slave labor of a very abject kind: labor of clerks, for instance. He might remind us that Socialism may not only deprive us of his services by driving him abroad, but of the services of all the men who are doing their daily drudgery now only because they are virtually his slaves, and who, once set free, will positively refuse to waste their lives and narrow their chests in making uninteresting memoranda of uninteresting transactions in uninteresting ledgers. Every year millions of separate entries are made in commercial books, not one of which separate entries will ever be required again. If one of them by chance were wanted, the inconvenience caused by its absence would be as nothing compared to the frightful waste of human life represented by its presence. Except for statistical and historical purposes, few accounts are worth keeping; and I am convinced that it will be as impossible under Socialism to find a man willing to undertake the work of an ordinary office bookkeeper as it is now for the sweep to find a climbing-boy. What, then, is to be the fate of England if her employers go abroad and her counting-house are left without clerks?

To some extent the two difficulties dispose of oneanother; and I have juxtaposed them purposely to bring out the fact that even if our employers all remain patriotically with us and help us to organize our industry socialistically, they will be more of a hindrance than a help, because the means of carrying on their old routine will no longer be available. They will be rather like that familiar and pathetic sight, the retired Indian Civil Servant struggling with English democratic insititutions, and discovering that his well-learnt art of autocratic government is useless and impracticable under home conditions. I am persuaded that if the hundred most successful English and American employers of the nineteenth century could be resuscitated in the twentyfirst and put into harness again, not one of them would be worth his salt, except perhaps as a park constable. Our feudal magnates on City Boards, our retired colonels in counting-houses, are less at sea than such ghosts would be. Many noted men of business who have been made railway directors and chairmen because of their experience and knowledge of the industrial world, are already so pitiably behind the times that if they left their country tomorrow they would leave it for their country's good much more than any criminal we ever sent to Botany Bay. Their experience is all to the bad: what is to the good is only what is left of their native wit and character; and England's fund of that cannot be exported. But the question remains, will the inheritors of that wit and character work for Socialism as they do for Unsocialism, when the bait of profits and dividends no longer dangles before them? That is the question I shall tackle next week.

IV WILL THE EMPLOYERS EMIGRATE?   Having now got the matter into something like a true Socialist perspective, let us consider what our employers actually do for us.

They take the land, capital, and labor of the country under their direction, and produce from them commodities which make life and civilization (such as it is) possible. That is not only a very considerable service, but an indispensable one. If we are dependent on them for that, we are dependent on them altogether, body and soul. The Social-Democratic Federation asks whether there is a single service performed by them which the people, organized, could not perform for themselves. This begs the question, because though the answer may be in the affirmative, the difficulty remains, who is to organize them? It is no use asking whether the people, if organized, could do without organizers. It is like asking whether a man can do without food if you give him a good dinner.

Nor is it any use to point out that the employers distribute the product unfairly. For the moment, that is not the point. Granted that they allow the landlords and capitalists to take a huge share of the product without helping to produce it, and that their reason for submitting to this apparently intolerable oppression is that they intend to become landlords and capitalists themselves, and quarter their descendants on future employers, which can only be done by keeping up the system of private property in land and capital. Granted also that the rest of the product is divided between the employer and his employees as unfairly as he can possibly divide it. That does not at all lighten his contention that he performs an indispensable service, and that if you drive him abroad without making other provision for that service, our industry will collapse like a cart when the linch-pin is pulled out.

Note also, if you please, that the employer not only claims that this service cannot be done without him, but that it cannot be done at all from Socialist motives. He tells you that though his particular incentive happens by a strange chance to be simply the golden rule of our Saviour, yet the incentive of all the other employers is a desire to make money, and that every mature man of the world knows this to be the only incentive that will nerve men to the strenuous effort of building up the large businesses on which the industry of our country depends. "Now," he continues, "I admit that up to a certain point—which is, curiously enough, the point we have just reached—Socialism has done good. Why? Because, up to a certain point, it pays to spend some money on the worker. We used to kill the goose that laid the golden eggs. We now fatten him a bit, educate him a bit, give him a bit of a chance; and we find the result quite satisfactory to us, because he works better and can be trusted with more complicated machinery; so that we are able not only to pay for all his little indulgences out of the extra product, but to find something left for ourselves out of it afterwards. We admit that we were shortsighted in objecting to these indulgences when they were first proposed; but we have found out our mistake and have no intention of going back on them. Only, let it be understood that we can go no further. Some of us, like our friend Livesey,[5] are willing to introduce profit sharing, provided the worker will produce his share in addition to our own and something for us into the bargain; but a step beyond this will drive us out of the country. Many of us do not approve of profit sharing on any conditions, as it leads working men to form an undesirable habit of looking at profits as if profits were their business instead of wages. However, leave that aside for the present. The thing to grasp is that if you take away the incentive of gain, the work will not be done. That may be sordid, but it is human nature."

But here the employer, by implication, does Socialism too much honor. There is really no reason to suppose that under Socialism men will be less sordid in this sense than they are at present. Only, let us be quite clear as to how sordid they are at present. Sordid enough certainly, not to do a job for five pounds if they can get six, but also generous enough to do the same job for four if they cannot get five. Milton took £5 for Paradise Lost because he could not get any more. I should ask £5,000 for the same quantity of pen-and-ink work because I need not take any less. The employer today is emphatically a man who, like Milton and myself, has to take what he can get. Whether as lessee to a landlord, debtor to a capitalist, employee to a big company or trust, employer to a powerful Trade Union, or slave to an inexorable Factory Inspector, he very soon finds out that it is no use to declare that he must have this or that, or he will not play. He *must* play, or go under. If the conditions are made more onerous for him, he must play harder, or reorganize the game. If he has to surrender more of the product, he must increase the product (or adulterate it) by new methods. Ever since Factory Legislation began to be really effective sixty years ago he has protested that another turn of the social screw on him would drive his trade into bankruptcy and his country into ruin; but the screw has been turned again and again; and the result is that his trade flourishes more than ever. It is the farmer's trade, which was left untouched, that is ruined, and has to beg off half its rates.

The process, however, has its limits in the case of certain individuals, if not of the nation at large. There is a point at which the pressure of State regulation from above, and of the acquisitiveness of organized labor from below, will squeeze an employer out of business through the doors of the Bankruptcy Court. Many a mediocrity and many a sweater has gone that way already; and others have gone it who were neither mediocrities nor sweaters, but simply lacked the particular sort of charlatanism which attracts capital and the confidence of bank managers, or the narrowly greedy competitive ruffianism or the wide and powerful grip of the realities of our system which makes a man say "Thou shalt starve ere I starve" and go through with it. But the supply of employing power has never yet failed, although it is usual to say that the stress both of competition and State regulation has incresed enormously. Of that I am not sure. State regulation makes business much easier for capable men by relieving them from the worst sorts of competition. Legitimate competition has been made much more agreeable by compacts which limit it in its most harassing forms. The supply of literate employees to whom parts of the work can be delegated has been increased by popular education. At all events the number of business men who knock off work from Friday to Tuesday is visibly greater than it was: indeed, the week-end itself is quite a recent institution. The man who can only learn a routine and stick to it for eight hours a day may be having a worse time than he used to; but the man who can use his brains for two hours a day has probably a better time than he ever had before in business. I therefore do not admit that Socialism has yet reached the point at which there is a danger of a strike of employers against State regulation, rising wages, and shortening working days. But I am quite prepared to consider the theoretically possible limit next week.

V WILL THE LABORERS EMIGRATE? Suppose, then, that our employers declare that State regulation and labor aggression have gone too far to leave the private employer any interest in his business. Suppose they say that since we will neither let them conduct their enterprises in their own way nor for their own benefit, instead of for that of their workmen and of the nation at large, we may do it for ourselves, and be hanged to us.

This raises a very serious question for the employers. How are they to live? Sulking satisfies the soul up to a certain point; but it does not fill the stomach. Will they demand employment as employees, refusing to give orders and insisting on being themselves ordered and thought for? That is a cock that will not fight against

Socialism. We are too familiar with the Utopian nonsense of our own cranks to be taken in by it from the opposite side. Too often have we urged people to do just this thing—urged women to become well paid and well treated parlor-maids instead of sweated shop assistants, snubbed governesses, dehumanized schoolmistresses, or, worst of all, idle poor relations—urged men to make their sons mechanics instead of clerks, or to give up the struggle for independence in businesses where the employer, when the landlord and the money-lender and the rate-collector are paid, has less left for himself than he has had to pay as wages to all but his poorest employees. They will suffer anything rather than step down. In the army the lieutenant who has nothing but his pay is much worse off than the quartermaster; and for this reason the quartermaster often refuses a commission; but the lieutenant never wants to become a quartermaster. Today men who have hitherto been employers on their own account are frequently driven to become the employees of the trusts whose competition has ruined them, but never voluntarily, never without a struggle, never until not only are the terms far better than they could offer themselves as their own employers, but until they can, in fact, no longer offer themselves any terms at all.

It is not altogether a question of snobbery: it is a question of aptitude. Everybody knows that you cannot make every private a captain. But they are apt to think that you can make every captain a private. No doubt you can; but if he is a born captain you will make him so unhappy that he will be glad to do captain's work for private's pay (or less, if better may not be, and he can live on it) sooner than waste his life by leaving the best he can do undone. If you refuse to pay the man at all—nay, if you even forbid him with threats of punishment—he will hardly let even that prevent him from doing what is in him, though he will, to be sure, take as much as he can get for doing it when he has made his position good. Mr George Meredith did not begin his career by declaring that unless he were paid as well as a stock-jobber he would go on the Stock Exchange instead of writing novels. He wrote novels for less than nothing until people began to read them. And it is quite a mistake to suppose that this sort of beginning is confined to literary and artistic geniuses. The born employer who graduates from the stool of the office boy almost always has to begin his career as employer by exchanging a safe salary and a comparatively easy time for a period of struggle in which he has to work strenuously and pay everybody without any certainty of an adequate return and with a terrifying chance of entire failure. No doubt, when once he has made his ground good, he, like Mr Meredith, will take the fullest advantage of his market; but that does not alter the fact that what is called brain work will always be offered by the man who can do it at the same price or less *(faute de mieux)*, than routine work, and that the very best of it is done today, and always has been done, for nothing but the satisfaction of doing it.

The real danger is on the other side of the hedge: the street side of it. And now the moment has come to turn the tables on the Unsocialists. They talk of driving Capital out of the country. What about driving Labor out of the country? From the revocation of the Edict of Nantes to the depopulation of Ireland and the colossal emigrations which have created the United States of America, the Dominion of Canada, and the Australian Commonwealth, and forced the partition of Asia and Africa upon the European Powers, modern history is full of examples of the urgent need for making your country tolerable to your workers if you wish them to stay in it. Civilization can always keep its geniuses, and even draw them irresistibly from the backwoods to its capitals. Milton did not emigrate, nor Bunyan, nor Pepys. Cromwell turned back at the last moment, and would never have started had he known his own strength at that time. But Tom, Dick, and Harry did emigrate; and they raised from among them the most capable commercial employers and inventors in the world. When the French Revolution broke out, the nobles did not emigrate voluntarily: to get rid of them, it was necessary to convince them that their heads would be cut off if they stayed. And what, pray, became of the one important branch of public service which had depended on them for all its superior officers—the military service? Did the army fall to pieces like an arch with the keystone knocked out? Not a bit of it. The most capable officer in the army, Lieutenant Buonaparte, did not emigrate. He took his chance with the Revolution. And he found generals enough in the stable-yards of France to replace the emigrants, field-marshals and all, to considerable advantage. He was often at a loss for men: indeed, his downfall was due mostly to the fact that he treated the French laborers as mere cannon fodder. But of officers, "bravest of the brave" and so forth, there was never any lack, though there was hardly a gentleman among them. They turned to and became kings on occasion: one of these improvised monarchies survives to this day in Sweden, and is much more successful and illustrious than our own highly connected dynasties have always been. This does not mean that every ostler is a potential general or monarch. What it does mean is that the master spirits do not emigrate and are not afraid of revolutions. Had George Washington been born in London he would have died there. It was John, the nonentity, who emigrated, and thereby lost us George, and, incidentally, lost us the United States. It is your ordinary man whom you lose if you ill-treat him.

Even were the loss of one employer worse than the loss of a thousand laborers, you would still have to face the fact that laborers emigrate in scores of thousands whilst their employers virtually do not emigrate at all, unless they are forced to follow the laborers by lack of custom. The reasons are obvious. A blacksmith can make his living in any country in the world. He knows the language of all the hammers, and can stand the climate of all the forges. But the ironmaster can neither read, write, nor cipher in a foreign land. His power of judging a customer's social position and probable solvency from his appearance is upset: the whole environment in which he has become an expert is snatched away from him: he has to begin life again as a stranger among hostile competitors. He is thus almost as much tied to the soil as his fixed capital, whilst his laborers can find masters everywhere and freehold land in a good many places. Happy would it be for him if he could run away from Unsocialism. For Socialism threatens him with the question: "Are you really a born captain of industry, or have you merely, by going to the office every day and doing 'what was done last time,' picked up a routine the underlying motives and social meaning of which you understand about as much as the boy who switches on the light for your desk understands electricity. For that routine is of so little use to us, that we shall be better with a young man who has nothing to unlearn than with you."

Everybody who knows anything of business at first hand knows that the vast majority of our employers are routineers, who could no more contribute an intelligent statement of their industiral function to this paper than a bee could write the works of Lord Avebury.[6] Routineers can always be replaced, and replaced with profit, by educated functionaries. Consequently when the employers threaten us with emigration, our only regret as to the majority of them is that it is too good to be true.

But how about the possible emigration of the man who does not pretend to organize industry, but who simply spends money in the country, and thereby gives employment to hosts of retainers and whole groups of trades?

There is only one way of obtaining my answer: buy next week's New Age.

VI THE PARASITIC PROLETARIAT.   We have now got back at last to the social function for the sake of which we tolerate the idle man of property. He gives employment.

Everybody recoils from this proposition with a sense of fundamental fallacy somewhere. The fallacy is not very recondite: it lies in confusing two quite different things: employing a man and supporting him. A lunatic employs his keeper: he does not support him. A father supports his daughter: he does not employ her. The idle man of property is like the lunatic: he employs a great many keepers; but he does not support them. He does not even support himself, though he employs himself as best he can, in shooting, hunting, racing, motoring, or as an amateur in the arts and sciences. Both he and all his keepers have to be supported by the labor of those who make the food they consume, the clothes they wear, the houses they live in, etc., etc.

Thus we find that what the idle man of property does is to plunge into mortal sin against society. He not only withdraws himself from the productive forces of the nation and quarters himself on them as a parasite: he withdraws also a body of propertyless men and places them in the same position, except that they have to earn this anti-social privilege by ministering to his wants and whims. He thus creates and corrupts a class of workers—many of them very highly trained and skilled, and correspondingly paid— whose subsistence is bound up with his income. They are parasites on a parasite; and they defend the institution of private property with a ferocity which startles their principal, who is often in a speculative way quite revolutionary in his views. They knock the Class War theory into a cocked hat by forming a powerful conservative proletariat whose one economic interest it is that the rich should have as much money to spend as possible; and it is they who encourage and often compel the property owners to defend themselves against the onward march of Socialism. Thus we have the phenomenon that seems at first sight so amazing in London:

namely, that in the constituencies where the shopkeepers pay the most monstrous rents, and the extravagance and insolence of the idle rich are in fullest view, no Socialist—nay, no Progressive—has a chance of being elected to the municipality or to Parliament. The reason is that these shopkeepers live by fleecing the rich as the rich live by fleecing the poor. The millionaire who has preyed upon Bury and Bootle until no workman there has more than his week's subsistence in hand, and many of them have not even that, is himself preyed upon in Bond Street, Pall Mall, and Long Acre.

Some day a poet will arise to do justice to the amazing system of hypnotic brigandage by which the rich are compelled to burden their lives with all sorts of horrible discomforts and superfluities so that their plunder may be shared with the tradesman and the flunkey. A lady has a pretty dress, made of expensive materials, comfortable, and as good as new. She is forced to take it off and buy a new one of uglier and less convenient shape by a tradesman whom she despises as abysmally beneath her in taste, manners, and social worth. A gentleman who has paid £1,200 for an automobile with a satisfactory low tension magneto and efficient chain drive, is compelled to discard it and pay £1,500 for a new car with a leaky high tension magneto and a wasteful and dangerous live axle, by a salesman whom he thoroughly mistrusts and whom he knows to be as ignorant of mechanics as he is himself. This lady and gentleman, as man and wife, have endless services foisted on them which they do not want; and the moment they accept them, a caste system of more than Indian strictness is developed in their houses, and compels them to employ a separate servant for every separate service. The motor car has hardly made its way into the stable when it is discovered that the chauffeur cannot possibly clean the car; so another man must be retained for that job. Scullery-maids, tweenies, housemaids, parlor-maids, footmen, knifeboys, revolving round cook and butler, lady's maid and valet and nominally ruled by the housekeeper, all cling to some shred of privilege in the form of something they must not be expected to do. A lady with no children and a tiny house in Mayfair with accommodation for six people, tells you that she cannot do with less than nine servants, who sleep under the stairs or anywhere they can. The very buttons and hooks and eyes on her dress are purposely placed so that she cannot fasten them herself. She must have a maid to do it. She knows, of course, that other people are as comfortable as she with two or three servants; but she cannot escape from her nine all the same. They have been made absolutely necessary to her by some power that is stronger than she. She is dragged to the opera, through she may hate music: she is driven to Goodwood, though she may loathe racing: she has to spend weary weeks on a Scotch moor keeping a sort of private shooting hotel for men whom she does not care for, and for whom her husband, who perhaps hates shooting, does not care either. There is no tyranny on earth to be compared with it. It is so complete that a woman who knows just as well as her husband that our English public schools are largely in the condition of the cities of the plain, finds herself as powerless to refuse to send her sons there as the woman whose house is rated at less than £40 a year is to refuse to send her children to the public elementary schools. The parasitic proletariat says in effect: "It is a matter of life and death to us that you should do these things; and since it is we who organize your life for you—you being too idle (and consequently too weak-minded) to organize it for yourself— you shall do them whether you like it or not."

But there is something more and something worse in the matter than this. The parasitic proletariat not only forces the routine of fashion on the propertied classes: it forces the parasitic system on the entire community. These are the plutocratic retainers whom Socialism must convert, coerce, or kill, just as Capitalism had to convert, coerce, or kill the retainers of the feudal barons in so far as they did not very obligingly kill oneanother. The real property owners of this country—the people who are directly parasitic on our industry—are so few and negligible that there are already avowed Socialists enough in the country to guillotine them in a week, if that summary method were still in fashion. Many of them, having no illusions as to the alleged comfort and freedom which the present system is supposed to secure them, and being heartily tired of having everything they do or wear or inhabit dictated to them, and of being imposed upon, cheated, and clumsily flattered at every new chain heaped on them, would not risk a scratch in defence of their slavery. But their parasites, the West-End trades-man, the West-End professional man, the schoolmaster, the Ritz hotelkeeper, the horse dealer and trainer, the impresario with his guinea stalls, and the ordinary theatrical manager with his half-guinea ones, the huntsman, the jockey, the gamekeeper, the gar-dener, the coachman, and the huge mass of minor shopkeepers and employees who depend on these, or who, as their children, have been brought up with a little crust of conservative prejudices which they call their politics and morals and religion: all these give to Parliamentary and social Conservatism its real fighting force; and the more "class conscious" we make them, the more they will understand that their incomes, whilst the present system lasts, are bound up with those of the proprietors whom Socialism would expropriate. And as many of them are better fed, better mannered, better educated, more confident and successful than the productive poletariat, the class war is not going to be a walk over for the Socialists. When Shelley converted the timid revolutionaries of his time by saying "Ye are many: they are few"—when Marx, later on, called on the proletarians of all lands to unite, they were reckoning without Bond Street. I know better. As what is called an art critic, I have made my living in Bond Street by doing the hypnotizing part of the business in the Press: persuading the millionaires that they must buy works of art if they want to pass as people of culture, running up the prices of prima donnas by penning exciting descriptions of their singing, and so on and so forth. And I warn the Socialists that those who live by despoiling the spoilers will not only fight in defence of spoliation more fiercely than the spoilers in chief, but will force these to fight even if they wish to surrender. There is a big and strong sort of seagull called the skua, which never fishes in the sea when it can help it. The skua waits until a common seagull catches and swallows a fish, when it forces the poor gull to disgorge its prey and leave it to the skua. The parasitic proletariat treats the owners of property as the skua treats the gull. It is the skuas, my friends, that we shall have to fight or convert. And the difficulty is that just as the skua prefers a regurgitated fish to one fresh from the sea, a British shopkeeper prefers a lord to a common producer as a customer. William Morris, whose style of dressing made stupid people guess him to be a ship's purser, used to chuckle at the remarkable change in the warmth of his welcome in certain West-End shops when it dawned on the shopkeeper that he was a person of consequence who wanted five hundred pounds' worth of something precious. Dickens long ago gave us the barber who refused to shave a coal-heaver. The original of Dickens's Inspector Bucket was furious because he was sent to arrest a common pickpocket instead of being reserved for murderers and gentlemanly forgers.[7] Until you realize the happiness of licking a duke's boots and the shame of "attending to" a poor person, you can have no conception of the enormous force of snobbery that fortifies property and privilege. The rich, then, do something more than employ the poor. They reflect their glory on them. It is not the duke who enjoys his rank: on the contrary, he is the sole person who does not enjoy it. It is his tailor who enjoys it, his outfitter, his bootmaker, his carriage builder, his doctor, his solicitor, his vicar, his valet, down to the very crossing sweeper who gets a penny from him. Even the executioner who hangs or guillotines him enjoys his importance, and feels that he is demeaning himself when he has to hang a mere commercial traveller the following week.

I have still, therefore, to consider what Socialism will do to the parasitic proletariat.

VII The Economics of Globe-Trotting. From the point of view of the parasitic proletariat the emigration of our proprietary classes would be an unmixed misfortune. Not only would their prey escape them; but their desperation would be aggravated by the knowledge that foreign parasites were profiting by the loss. Under the present system, they have already more than enough of this kind of irritation. For example, an immense capital is sunk in the construction of a trap for pleasure seekers on the South coast of England, called Brighton. Another trap of the same kind is constructed on the south coast of Europe, called Nice, with a subsidiary trap called Monte Carlo. The result is that the richer pleasure seekers break through the Brighton trap and push on to Nice. Parasitic Brighton is naturally furious. Its capital is depreciated or annihilated: every year it has to cater for a poorer class: already it can hardly hold its head higher than Margate, where the air is better. There is no consolation for the Brighton hotelkeeper in Tariff Reform: what he wants is that the out-going tourist be forcibly stopped at our ports and compelled to enjoy himself on his own shores. But here he comes into conflict with that powerful section of the parasitic proletariat which makes motor cars and sleeping cars, and has its hotels for birds of passage on the great routes that lead to Nice. Thus, whilst the parasitic proletariat of Brighton strives to keep the rich at home, another equally powerful section is trying to drive the rich abroad; and as the rich, always seeking exclusiveness—that is, always running away from the poor (small blame to them), and then finding that they want to run away from themselves—tend strongly to do the most expensive thing, and to avoid boredom by globe-trotting, they go abroad more and more, and are plundered by foreigners instead of by their own countrymen. Note how little is said about the enormous export of income that takes place in this way. It is no doubt to some extent compensated by the money spent in England by Americans on their way to the Continent; but it is none the less a dead loss to this country, involving the production and export of commodities which are consumed abroad by foreigners who send us absolutely nothing in return except their own relatively few and frugal travellers.

All along the great railway routes, you hear the echoes of the complaint of the deserted Brighton hotelkeeper. When I first visited Pisa, it was a place at which a stoppage on the journey to Rome was so convenient that even people who had seen the leaning tower and the Campo Santo half a dozen times were to be found passing the night at the Pisan hotels. When I was last there the best hotel was half empty, and the proprietor gave me a piece of his mind, which I shall not readily forget, on the subject of the fast through trains, with refreshment cars and sleeping car, in which travellers pass from Calais or Ostend to Rome without breaking the journey. It is the same everywhere. Each successful trap to catch our rich ruins some other trap, just as Kensington and Hampstead ruined Soho and Bloomsbury.

It will be replied at once that Bloomsbury and Soho are not ruined. True; and for the matter of that, neither is Brighton, and neither will England be when Socialism has ruined every idler in it. But the parasitic industries of the neighborhood have been ruined. The sort of people who used to live in Golden Square and Soho Square hardly know at present where these spots are: new industries and new classes of workers have replaced the old business and retinue of fashion; and this process did not accomplish itself without ruining a good many individuals. The price we pay for our Unsocialism is that progress acts destructively. An improvement does not relieve the people who worked the old method: it ruins them. The railway ruined the stage-coach: the motor car is ruining the railway: the flying machine will no doubt ruin the motor car. It is part of the defence of Unsocialism that its continual threat of poverty gives men an incentive to snatch livelihoods from oneanother; so that, as the invention of new processes is the only honest means of doing this, Unsocialism stimulates invention. That being so, Unsocialism must not bring forward the ruin of any particular class of capitalists as an objection to Socialism. What is sauce for the goose is sauce for the gander. The motor cab capitalist is ruining the old-fashioned cabman without remorse; and when his turn comes to be ruined by the aeroplane; he need not hope that we will remain on the ground for his sake. And similarly, if the Unsocialists, who ruin whole classes and neighborhoods by the introduction of new methods and new machines, imagine that the Socialists will stop because certain classes fear to find their occupation (or no occupation) gone, and certain forms of fixed capital scrapped, they show very little knowledge of human nature. Their own defence in such cases is that though individuals are ruined the country as a whole is benefited. The Socialists have the same plea to offer. Suppose Socialism does ruin the region just north of Piccadilly exactly as plutocracy ruined the once fashionable region north of the Strand and Fleet Street! What of that? Are not these regions more productive than ever? Was not their ruin an economy from the national point of view—even from the metropolitan point of view?

Besides, the ruin was not necessary in the nature of things. It was necessary only in the nature of competitive capitalism. Mere displacement of an industry, or improvement in its methods, has no terrors for the workers in a socialized industry. In the army, when the Snider rifle scrapped the Enfield, when the Martini, scrapped the Snider, when the Lee-Medford scrapped the Martini, no soldier or officer was ruined. Woolwich arsenal was none the worse when the Woolwich Infant was discarded. A private telephone company may ruin a private telegraph company, a private wireless telegraph company may ruin a private cable company; and these disasters may spread through the cash nexus and ruin insurance companies and banks in widespread calamity; but nobody in the postal service is a penny the worse for all this; and nobody out of it would be if the whole business—telephones, cables, wireless and all—were in the same public hands instead of in a half a dozen private competing ones. On the contrary, everybody would be the better; for the time saved and the labor spared by the new methods would be shared by everybody instead of, as at present, going to create a new set of idlers.

Today, one sometimes wonders whether the inventor of the power loom ever hesitated when he thought (if he ever did think) of the thousands of handloom weavers whom he was condemning to starvation; whether the linotype might not make its way faster if it were not so much more humane to wait until all the old compositors are dead; whether the man who first foresaw what an enormous boon the combination of Atlantic steamships and British North and South Western Railways would be, also foresaw the slow starvation of dozens of little coast towns with their tiny harbors, their petty fleets of trading schooners, their populations of skippers and marine store dealers. Aberystwyth, for instance, is today a fairly prosperous watering place and a university town; but there were long years during which it was only a decaying port not knowing what was happening to it except that work was mysteriously going and poverty mysteriously coming. On this side of Unsocialism its friends do not dwell. They tell us always of the fortunes drawn in their sordid lottery, not of the fortunes lost in it. They tell us of how So-and-so helped himself to riches, not of how he helped Thingumbob to bankruptcy. They urge the nation not to keep all its eggs in one basket lest the first fall should smash them. They forget that a policy of separate baskets does not involve a policy of separate owners, and that a still surer plan is to make your basket too big to be dropped and to have too many eggs in it for any shock to smash.

They forget also that one of the greatest economic advantages of living in society is that men can pool their risks and avoid ruinous losses by that form of Socialism which we call insurance. No doubt there are objections to insurance. It gives people an inducement to burn their houses and commit suicide and murder. But as a matter of practical experience it is not found that these inducements prevail except with people already in desperate circumstances. The man who burns his insured premises is either a criminal or is at his wits' end for money. The people who murder their children for the insurance money—a thing quite extensively done, apparently, by the British parent—are so abominably poor that their children die in heaps anyhow. They could not insure at all but for the fact that so many of them have to let their policies lapse from inability to pay the premiums punctually, such lapses being what the companies really gamble in. In reasonably comfortable circumstances the only desire the normal man has concerning insurance is that the event against which he has insured may be put off as long as possible, or, better still, never occur. On the whole, that form of society which provides most completely for insurance of all practicable kinds has an enormous advantage over forms which not only involve bankruptcy at every forward step in industrial methods, but actually depend on these risks for their motive power. Socialism scores heavily against Unsocialism on this point. And when the Unsocialists plead that Socialism may ruin them, we can only reply that it is like their impudence to imply that their own system gives them half as much security.

We see now that such ruin to individuals as may be produced by the transition from Unsocialism to Socialism is not worse, to say the least, than would be produced by the decay of neighborhoods and the introduction of new methods under the existing system. And there would be immense compensations. In my next article I shall give some idea of how they will occur.

VIII   SOCIALISM AND THE SHOPKEEPER.   When Socialism ruins a neighborhood by destroying the industry of catering for the parasitic classes, it does not impair the purchasing power of the community as a whole: it only redistributes it. In fact, it increases it; for if the parasites are starved into becoming producers, as Socialism fully intends they shall be, they become genuine purchasers instead of—not to put too fine a point on it— thieves. The shopkeeper finds that the same operation that has deprived him of his few monstrously rich customers supplies him with a great many reasonably well-off ones, who not only buy more of what they consumed before, but a great many things which they formerly regarded as luxuries beyond their means.

Conceive the Bond Street stationer gazing in white-faced despair at the departure of his last millionaire customer from Park Lane. Enter a tripper from Yorkshire. He orders 750 visiting cards. He insists on their being gilt-edged: domn th' expense! Five hundred are to be like this:—

MR. DEPUTY CHECKWEIGHER JOHNSON.
North Riding Provincial Administration.

16, BOTTY BANK ST. WEST,   THE FIRS,
CLIFTON ON CLEVELAND.   WOODBRIDGE.

Two hundred and fifty are for Mrs Deputy Checkweigher Johnson, with the additional information that she is at home on third Fridays. He also requires a supply of the very best hand-made notepaper, on which the address of The Firs is supplemented by directions in the corner that telegrams should be addressed to Ginger Johnson, Cleveland, and that the railway station (2½ miles) is Woodbridge Junction. The amazed stationer smells the checkweigher's money; says piously "non olet"; and trusts to be favored with the renewal of Mr D. C. J.'s esteemed order. Mr D. C. J., after picking up some further trifles in purses, albums, and leather covers for his Whitaker, postal guide, and A. B. C., goes to the ruined outfitter next door, and revives him by ordering not only half a dozen shirts, but by discovering with delight the existence of the pyjama, and fitting himself out for the night with reckless splendor.

When Mr D. C. J. next goes to Bond Street to renew his wardrobe, he will be a much more refined person. The pyjamas will have done their work. He will have worn them for many months, and lived up to them. Then his wife will come; and if the shopkeeper has been pining for the insolence of his old customers, it is quite likely that she may fill up that void in his aching heart so liberally that he may discover—what so few men nowadays seem able to discover—that it is possible to have too much of a bad thing as well as too much of a good thing, in which case he will be able to assert his dignity without ruining himself. Good manners are a product of equality. Even at present the Bond Street rule of obsequiousness for the shopkeeper and insolence for the customer—which is none the less a rule because it is suspended and replaced by honorable reciprocity of consideration when the parties are not snobs—is not universal. There are thousands of shops in which the shopkeeper and his customer are on the same level socially, the test being that the shopkeeper's son is an eligible suitor for the hand of the customer's daughter. In such cases there are no bad manners. The time will come when every lady who enters a Bond Street shop will do so at the risk of the gentleman behind the counter, when she says "I want a stick of golden sealing wax," replying "Take everything in the shop, including myself." Then there will be a very marked amelioration in the tone of these establishments. Bond Street will become as enchanting as a bazaar in the Arabian Nights: the enormous possibilities of romance in a world where love leaps at first sight across the counter will be realized. Shopping will become romantic and adventurous. Nothing in the possibilities of Socialism takes our breaths away at present so much as the enormous number of people our marriageable lasses and lads will have to choose from, and the huge mass of public opinion which every individual will have to reckon with in his conduct, both for support and opposition. It is highly significant that already, as a consequence of the merging of our gentry in our plutocracy, with its free intermarriage of rank and money, we have begun to talk of sets instead of classes. There will be no end of sets under Socialism; but they will be intermarriageable; they will be large; and the wise man will belong to several of them. Men will belong to the musical set, or the motoring set, or to both; and so will their tailors; with the result that a man will not cease to be a gentleman when he is dealing with a tailor, nor the tailor cease to be a man when he is dealing with a gentleman.

One advantage about the clientèle represented by Mr D. C. J. is that it is numerous. The old saying that the displeasure of a lord is a sentence of death has still its terror for the man who depends on a select fashionable connection. How true the stories are one hears about the way in which fashionable dressmakers are blackmailed into submitting to bad debts by their fear of offending smart ladies, I cannot say; but anyone who reads the cases which occasionally come into court must feel pretty sure that fashionable shopkeepers are much more dependent on the individual customer than, say Mr Gamage, of Holborn.[8] Withdraw your account from a select West End shop, and you will soon receive respectful letters expressing the concern of the shopkeeper and his anxiety to get you back again. The extreme economic instance is the painter whose pictures are bought by only one patron. Such a painter is evidently in a condition of abject dependence on his patron. At the opposite extreme is the cabman, who is so independent of the good opinion of any single customer that it is necessary to protect the cab-hirer by a special code. If any shopkeeper were to attempt to cheat his customers in giving change by the trick of putting down part of the proper sum on the chance of the customer picking it up and going away without waiting for the rest, as systematically as some railway booking-clerks do, he would soon lose all his business.

The moral of all this is that it is better to depend on a thousand casual customers, each of whom is no more to the shopkeeper than a unit in the statistical average, than on ten clients, each keeping a large account. It is better for the public, too, as the popularity of the Stores and Whiteley's shews.[9] Some time ago a canvasser called on me to secure my custom for a new Press Cutting Agency. His argument was that as a new concern was not overcrowded with subscribers I should be sure of more individual attention. Six months later he returned and canvassed me for one of the older institutions, having changed his shop in the meantime. This time he argued that the large firm was on such a scale that nothing escaped them: they could afford to take in every paper in the world, etc. Which ever way *my* advantage lay, there was no doubt at all that the agency with the large connection was the better off. This would be so even if its takings were no greater. A dealer who supplies five hundred customers with three pairs of trousers per year has a safer and steadier income, and much more personal independence, than the dealer who supplies seventyfive customers with twenty pairs per year. The displeasure, insolvency, or death of a single customer is more than six times as serious a loss to the latter than to the former.

Socialism will, however, ruin one sort of shopkeeper very effectually. He who caters for the wretchedly poor will lose his customers for ever. The dealer in farthings-worths of tea, in second-hand clothes, in tenth-hand furniture and bedding, in meat that is really offal, will find his occupation gone. Lockhart will have to set up Holborn Restaurants, Aerated Bread shops, perhaps even Carlton tables d'hôte or perish. The merchants of Rag Fair, who sell you a pair of boots for a penny and an overcoat for fourpence, will lose all their customers, whilst Peal and Poole will have a new world opened before their counters.[10] And here let us pause and meditate on the folly of mankind. Those whose business it is to cater for people who can afford to pay a good price for a good article resolutely oppose a change which would enable everybody to pay a good price for a good article. Those whose business it is to cater for people who demand trash and filth because they cannot afford anything better, raise no outcry against the change, though it would not only empty their shops, but demolish them through the local sanitary authority as nuisances. They would be thrown, with the Park Lane millionaires, on the merciful consideration of a new world, which, let us hope, would be too well off to be unkind to them. Possibly some employment might be found for them in the Treasury Department; for they are mostly born financiers.

Please observe, however, that this enormous expansion of the custom of the better sort of shopkeeper will depend altogether on a positive vigorous Socialism. If you drive his customers to Nice and Algiers, to Biarritz, Paris, and Vienna, and allow them to take their purchasing power with them, which is exactly what the present system is doing, then you simply bleed Bond Street to death. It is no part of the purpose of these articles to reassure Bond Street. I repeat, you can, and do, drive income out of the country by your present system. It creates poverty; poverty creates ugliness and dirt; the English climate makes these more cruel and disagreeable than they are on the shores of the Mediterranean; the railway restaurant car makes travelling easier than it used to be; and the motor car is making it positively delightful. The rich go away more and more; but neither rents nor rates allow for that. Socialism would apply the rents to defray the rates; would spend the balance (as much again) on making the town attractive; would replace the expropriated customer by ten impropriated ones; would nourish trade with unheard of accesses of purchasing power. Unsocialism means the status quo, with just enough *panem et circenses* to put up the rates, and accelerate the movement of the rich towards countries where there is no east wind and no income tax.

Next week we can sum up all these apparent digressions and see how much is left of "Driving Capital Out of the Country" as an anti-Socialist scare.

IX LEFT FOR DEAD. I hope I have now convinced the anti-Socialist alarmists that the question of driving capital out of the country is one which they had better let alone. If there is one matter which a wise opponent of Socialism would carefully keep out of the public mind, it is the unpatriotic internationalism of Capital. Fortunately, there are no wise anti-Socialists. The same stupidity which blinds them to the utter impossibility of dealing with our huge modern communities as simple aggregations of private lives and private properties leads them, like some ironic Fate, to challenge Socialism on the points on which its answer is unanswerable and its counter-attack irresistible.

The weakest point in our Capitalist system is its failure to secure the application of our national capital, as fast as it is accumulated, to the provision of our national needs in the order of their urgency. Thus we want more schoolmasters; and we get more jockeys. We want more recreation grounds for children; and we get more race-courses and motordromes. We want more healthy mothers; and we get more diseased prostitutes. We want more well-planned, wholesome streets; and we get more slums. We want more good houses for the people; and we get more week-end hotels for the plutocracy. We want more bakers, more tailors, more masons, more carpenters; we get more coachmen and footmen and gamekeepers. We want producers, in short; and we get parasites. Finally, wanting all these things, we often get nothing, because the capital is invested abroad instead of at home.

Not only do we get less than we want; we get more than we want. We want one pair of boots; and a hundred competing bootmakers make it for us, and throw ninetynine superfluous pairs into the market; so that the working bootmakers are presently out of work and must starve until the overproduction is absorbed by the wearing out of the boots in use. Competition not only fails to adjust supply to demand automatically: it actually makes a principle of overproduction.

Let me repeat that foolish as this way of applying our capital is, our system does not even secure that it shall at least be applied to our own country. Just take the list of enterprises whose shares are quoted on the Stock Exchange. Count the relative numbers of the home and foreign securities. Note the prices to convince yourself that the foreign ones are just as popular as the home ones. Then talk of the patriotism of private capital without laughing if you can. Again I say, if there is a subject on the face of the earth which the opponents of Socialism would have avoided if they had understood their own case or ours, it is this of capital going abroad. But they have forced it on us; and I hope they are satisfied with the result. I now challenge them to name a single proposal made by English Socialists that would not have the effect of investing English capital in England. Dare they challenge me to name any of their little enterprises—their South African Mines, their South American railways and telephones, their Egyptian and Russian and Turkish and Japanese loans—on the same terms? The impudence of such a challenge would roar and stare at even the stupidest man in the street. And yet it is not more impudent than the pretence that Socialism is driving capital out of the country, and that capitalism is keeping it at home. The two pretences are, in fact, one and the same, and those who are so ignorant or unobservant as to be taken in by it should be at once disfranchised as political imbeciles.

Unfortunately, they are much more likely to be returned to Parliament by other imbeciles in the vain hope that they will save the country from Socialism. People seem incapable of grasping the simplest and most obvious economic propositions when their imaginations are excited by the waving of the red flag. Since I began these articles a paper which has the audacity to call itself The Economist has attempted to criticize me in an article which would hardly pass muster in a parish magazine. I had dealt with the possibility of taxing imported dividends. But this possibility was too large for The Economist. It proceeded to show that if you tax all imported dividends, then, as some imported dividends will be taxed and some not, that will be equivalent to a bounty on the ones which escape taxation. I could have done better than that in my cradle. And yet I once respected The Economist, and have still quite an affection for it—now a purely sentimental one.

It is truly amazing how people lose their heads in opposing Socialism. It presents difficulties enough in all conscience. When I think how recent some of our solutions are, and for how many years we preached our gospel before we saw our way clearly on some of the most pressing practical problems, and how anybody during that time might have posed us by pressing for the solutions we had not yet arrived at, I feel like the Duke of Wellington when he said "The finger of Providence was upon me" to explain how he had escaped without a scratch after spending the day at the front under the terrific fire of Waterloo. With the weak spots in our defences under their eyes, and the weapons under their hands, our opponents do nothing but throw lighted magazines into their own powder magazines when they are not making trenches for us to occupy. They draw up frantic appeals to the ratepayers to refrain from relieving the rates by taxing unearned incomes; and the best reason they can find for that act of self-sacrifice on the ratepayers' part is that the Inland Revenue is a department of Atheism and Free Love. And then they leave the appeal at my house. They are never so proud of themselves as when, to make their appeal against driving capital out of the country more impressive, they secure for their committees and lists of vice-presidents and the like the names of the chairmen or directors of all the most prominent companies for developing mankind everywhere from China to Peru, except in England, the home of Trade Unionism and the Labor Party and the Fabian Society and so forth. It is too silly; they be-little our triumph by their obvious mental inferiority to us. I declare publicly that I am ashamed of my opponents. Since Bradlaugh and Herbert Spencer died, they have not put up a man against us that we could annihilate without turning the sympathy of the pitying spectators against us by our obvious superiority in knowledge, in character, and in brains. And they dare not now appeal to the memory of Bradlaugh and Herbert Spencer, because the mere mention of those names disposes of their attempt to associate Freethinking with Socialism instead of with the opposition to it. From Diderot and Voltaire, Bentham, and Mill, to Mr John Morley, Individualism has not one undamned champion.

I must put down my pen; the slaughter of the helpless is tedious work. Take your capital abroad, Gentlemen, until Socialism stops you; for nothing else can. Nay, take yourselves abroad: we can do without you. If any man chooses to live in France rather than in England, he becomes, in effect, a Frenchman; and the prosperity of Frenchmen in France is clearly not incompatible with the prosperity of Englishmen in England. But it is only fair to warn you that if the sole object of the change of residence is to avoid Socialism, it will not succeed, as Socialism is now co-extensive with developed modern Capitalism. To run from Mr Keir Hardie into the arms of Jaurès[11] is to jump out of the frying-pan into the fire. Still, there is the consolation, dear to your souls, of compulsory military service, of which some of you have a high opinion, in the country of your adoption.

And here let me draw your attention to an interesting point. All over Europe the institution of compulsory military service has given foreigners a strong incentive to leave their country and settle in England or America. More of them have actually done so than Socialism will ever frighten away from any country. But compulsory military service has not been abandoned on this account, though compulsory military service under existing conditions is a very gross invasion of the rights of the individual, because it is accompanied by a superstition and wholly unnecessary suspension of ordinary civil rights. Now, Socialism means finally compulsory civil service, without any deprivation of ordinary rights—nay, with every prospect of a considerable accession of personal property and extension of personal freedom. Is it to be feared that human nature, which has stood compulsory military service, will run away from this? And upon that note of interrogation I close this series of articles.

A previously unpublished report of a lecture delivered before the Liverpool Fabian Society on Wednesday, 28 October 1908.

Socialist Politics

It has really become necessary of late years to begin to explain, rather carefully, what Socialism means, because the thing has spread so much that there are a large number of people taking it up because it has become fashionable, and they have not the slightest idea what Socialism means.

There are a great number of words which get into popular use in a strange way. Not long ago I was lunching at the Savoy Hotel—not because I usually dine there, but I was a guest. At the next table there were sitting a young lady and gentleman, and I heard the gentleman say, "I dont like Vanilla Ices." She said in reply, "Oh, you are a Pessimist!" I have not the slightest doubt that if that young gentleman had proceeded to slip some of the knives and spoons into his pocket, she would have said, "Oh, you are a Socialist."

You notice this interfering Government (a Liberal Government—the very opposite to a Socialist Government) is denounced by the Conservative papers as Socialistic. They do this with the extraordinary idea in their minds that they are discrediting the Liberal Government, while any intelligent man can see that the one claim the Government has over the hearts of the people is just the socialistic tendencies of which they are suspected (and unjustly suspected, I think). I myself have found it to be a great advantage, going through my life, that people who wish to injure me have denounced me as a Socialist; it has immediately raised my reputation enormously. Socialism is really so very popular. If you go to any ordinary man and try to get him, when talking of Liberalism, or Conservatism, or anything else, to tell you on what system the wealth of the country should be distributed, you will find that he will usually come out with some kind of amateur socialist scheme; but if you tell him that is Socialism, he will probably quarrel with you.

Take the Fabian Society. It is generally understood to represent a very moderate and constitutional kind of Socialism. That is true; we are moderate. I assure you that all we want to do is entirely, and totally, and completely, to demolish, and abolish, and put an end to private property in every possible shape and form in this country, and if possible also in the whole world.

You may ask me why we are dissatisfied with private property. The reason is very obvious: Look at the mess it has made of things! Here we are, a great rich country, with great natural resources in the way of coal and iron and so on; we are, in fact, the richest country in the world. There is absolutely no reason why any man in this country should be in the slightest anxiety in regard to money, or in regard to ending his days in a comfortable fashion— absolutely none. It is within our means to bring about a state of things in which the poorest man in this country shall be as secure from starvation, as secure from disgrace and poverty in his old age, as secure from the dread of not seeing his children provided for, as the Prince of Wales is at the present time. Of course you applaud that; you recognize it as being true; but probably you are not going to do anything about it.

Sometimes you see people get out of temper about it. For instance the other day in London, Will Thorne, M.P.[1] got so angry at seeing starving men before him, that he told them to break into the bakers' shop and take the bread. I have no fault to find with the sequel to that. Mr. Thorne is brought before the magistrate and told that what he had said was extremely dangerous. He was bound over to behave himself in future—and now everybody is satisfied. But surely Mr Thorne's position is still unsettled. Could not Mr Thorne turn round and say: "You have told me what NOT to say to these men, but you have not told me what I AM to say"? Apparently nobody has raised the question as to what Mr Thorne ought to have said. The only thing apparently he could have said was: "Ladies and Gentlemen, owing to the peculiar structure of our present system, you will have to starve; there is no remedy for it." Do you think such remarks would have put that crowd into a good temper? I should think they would have been the most dangerous words a man could say, but apparently that is what we want Mr Thorne and Victor Grayson[2] to do. I am almost tempted to say, "I hope some day they will."

The fact of the matter is that it is not merely the question of a crowd of unemployed men; it is not merely a question of these men you see in the streets; it is a question of everyone of us. How many men are there here tonight who are certain that they will not die in the workhouse? I dont believe there is a single man here who has not that possibility before him. I look round at you, and I see it in your faces—faces marked by pecuniary anxiety, faces shewing a nervous apprehension. It is completely unnecessary, this starvation in the midst of plenty. That is the reason the Fabian Society wants to abolish private property. That is the mess private property has made of the job.

Let us go into this question of the abolition of private property. Allow me to talk about my favorite subject, myself: I have property of all sorts; private property and public property. Now, I am a landlord; (I am also a Capitalist by the way; you will not find many Socialists who are not). My land is my private property; that is to say, I can do as I like with my land without any reference to the public interest or the welfare of the people who live on it. If there is a man on that land who goes to a place of worship of which I do not approve, I can turn him out. I can put that land to any use; I can sweep all the people off and turn it into a place for sheep or deer or horses, or I can put birds on to it for the purpose of shooting them. I can treat the land as my private property, and no person has a right to come and interfere. I am the private proprietor of my land. I can do what I like with it; and I *do.*

I am also the proprietor of my umbrella; but here I meet with annoying restrictions. There are a number of people in this country whom I would like to hit with it, and it seems to me that just as I can use my land, I should be able to use my umbrella. But if I am brought before the magistrate and I point out that the umbrella is my private property to do as I like with, the magistrate convinces me that although the umbrella is my private property, I hold it subject to public opinion as to its use. The law draws a sharp distinction between the use of an umbrella, and the landlord's power. Socialists want to curb the power of the landlord just as the owner of the umbrella is restrained.

During the last hundred years there has been a steady conversion going on, and, even as a landlord, I have been more than ever interfered with. Now, I happen to be a landlord in Ireland, and there I have more of a run for my money, for I have always stood the chance of being shot at. But I have always taken up the position of Lord Clanricarde, who sent a message over to his tenants to the effect that if they imagined they were going to intimidate him by shooting his agent, they were mistaken.[3]

However, I think there are many men, factory owners, in Liverpool and Manchester who have inherited their factories from their fathers and grandfathers, and if those grandfathers could only come back and find what their factories had been turned into by the Factory Acts, they would be surprised. The difference is enormous compared with the position a hundred years ago. Then, a man could make a factory what he liked, and they used to like to make it a hell on earth. It is said that nine generations of men were used up in one generation. A man then could do what he liked when he got his people inside the factory. Nowadays he has to keep his factory open to the factory inspector, who keeps things up to the mark, and if the men who work in the factories would use their political power intelligently, and with a direct sense of their own power, their position would be better still.

In all directions there has been a steady encroachment upon the absolute rights of private property; a conversion of these rights into property held only on the condition of public rights being considered. Formerly, if two men were producing a certain article, according to the law of competition if one wanted to master the other he was able to adulterate; but nowadays we say: "You must not compete in that way; you must find some other way." Another way is for one man to find cheaper labor, and make the men work longer hours and so increase production; we have begun to make up our minds to say that we will stop THAT kind of competition; we are not quite certain yet, but we have begun. We do stop the worst extremes in that direction.

So you see that all through the community there is a steady growth of public conscience, and men are beginning to see that instead of being a lot of units, we are living in a community, where we ought all to be able to live a fuller life, and live it up to an ethical standard. We are now saying, instead of "First reform ourselves in order to reform others," that we must first reform others and the effect will be to reform ourselves. We also begin to see that a man cannot reform himself outside of the general mass. People come to me and say: "You're a Socialist with a lot of money; why dont you give it away?" But Socialism does not mean giving away your property; it means trying to get a little more of the results of your labor. You see, it would be no use for me to divest myself of the shares I hold. There are such a lot of gentlemen warning you about capital going out of the country, and these gentlemen are actually those who are Chairmen of Companies for the express purpose of sending English capital to every blessed spot of the universal globe except England. I challenge any man here to name a single proposal Socialists have made that would send capital out of the country; they have all been proposals that would keep investments of capital in England for the benefit of the English people. The deceit of our capitalists to turn round and accuse us of this conduct is enough to take my breath away. A stockbroker sends me a list of investments, and three parts of them appear to be investments in foreign countries.

Now, let us get back to my Private Property. Here comes a very odd thing about me; curiously enough, when it comes to my particular kind of work, the community gets a strong fit of socialism, and treats me in a socialist way. I am not only a landlord and a capitalist, but a worker also—and as a worker I really do produce the things I sell. I do not go down to the Club and leave my managers to do the work. I cannot do that. I write plays and books, and if the theatre managers and the public want plays from me, they wont take one written by a man I employ. I cannot even trust the punctuation to a boy at twelve shillings per week. If ever there was an article that did incorporate the sweat of a man's brain, it is the manuscript of one of my plays. Now, why do you treat me so differently from the other people who have water, gas, or cotton shares and businesses of one kind or another? As they have built up their businesses, so I have built up mine. You allow them to keep their property for ever and ever, and hand it on to their sons and grandsons and great-grandsons, who have done nothing for the money it brings in. Why dont you do so with me? No, you get common sense, and you turn round to me and say: "If your son wants money, he had better work for it; if he wants to live on the profits of plays, he had better write plays." At the end of fortytwo years, the plays and books I write become the nation's property, and anybody can use them. You did the same thing to Shakespear; you did not even give him fortytwo years; and yet there are people like Sir Christopher Furness[4] who tell you that if you dont pay people who have enormous brains—people like Sir Christopher Furness and Shakespear—if you dont give them enough money, say enough to buy 30,000 acres, and to give them two or three big ship-building yards, they wont work; their brains will cease their enormous productivity. Well, all I can say is, that a great deal of the hardest work I have done with my brain, I got nothing at all for. Shakespear wrote his plays without having any property in them; he had to sit on them very tight indeed. There you have a curious fact: You take me, a person you all admit to be the most estimable, the most magnificent on the face of the earth—the Author, the Poet—you cut all my work at the end of fortytwo years and my sons cannot enjoy the fruits of my labor. Yet any man who, in the course of a mere money-grubbing existence, scrapes together an amount of property, you allow him to have his property for ever and ever, and perhaps make him a Peer. After all, I put it to you, is it fair to me? Why not have a Duke of Shaw? I suppose the reason you dont do that, is that you find you get the plays without the extravagance. Why dont you try the experiment the other way round? Why dont you cut short the profits of the other gentlemen?

Then, there are a great many people in the world more useful than writers (though you must not say I said this); look at your inventors. I have gone through factories and examined the machines (by the way, I feel sure I could have invented the most of them in five minutes), and there is a certain amount of machinery in the world which is very ingenious; and yet you only allow a man fourteen years' property in his invention, and charge him an ever-increasing fee with each succeeding year, and yet a man who gets hold of that invention and exploits it, you allow him to have the property he heaps up, for ever and ever; while the inventor very often starves. I have known a good many inventors; most of them invented something nobody wanted, but the men who do invent something you want very often have to borrow money to take out their patent, or have to sell or mortgage a part of their share, and by the time the thing is on the market, it has gone out of their hands, and they do not even have an interest in it for the fourteen years.

Thus you see, in two of the most notable departments of human intelligence—industrial invention, and literature and art—you have found you can get the best class of work by giving rights of property which are strictly limited in the case of the literary man to fortytwo years and in the case of the inventor to fourteen years. Why dont you go a little further, and, when you find a number of persons who are afraid of being cut off short, and when they are kicking up a row in the newspapers, talking about the sacred rights of private property, and how the country would tumble to pieces if you interefered with them—why dont you point out that it has been done already, and it has not brought about that result. It does not discourage literary or industrial invention. I wish it did! You cannot stop men from inventing.

Now let us go from one class of society to another, and see who stands to gain by Socialism and who stands to lose. Of course, if you take the working classes in the mass, they have long discovered that they stood to gain. They gain by making the state interfere with industry, so that more and more they are able to work, not on terms dictated by the employers, but on terms which are regulated by the State. You all know the history of the working-class movement of the last century. You know that they first tried to oppose private property by forming trade unions. Then they found trade unions could do little until they got political power behind these unions— that is to say, until they got factory regulations. As you know, the working classes have not only agitated for the regulation of their labor, but have put pressure upon municipal bodies to get standard wages; but you neglect these regulations of labor, and the standard wages are not always paid. You have regulation wages in Liverpool, and they are not paid ("Shame"). It is all very well to say "Shame," but whose shame is it? It is the shame of the working classes, and they should try to get persons on the Municipal Council who will call the attention of the Corporation to those regulations, and get them carried out. It has been done in London and in Sheffield, and it could be done here. If the gentlemen on the Council are determined it shall not be done, it will not be done; and if you want it done you had better replace those men. The working classes are already pressing the Government. They have already got little old age pensions, very little, but it is a beginning. It does seem a hard thing a Government like this should have been unable to go further then five shillings a week at say ninety, I forget what the age was, I have a bad head for figures but I know it was an advanced age. The reason they said it was impossible to go further was, that it would cost fourteen millions of money, or perhaps, as somebody said, twenty millions. They could not lay their hands on twenty millions. Are you aware that every year in this country you are paying 630 millions of money to people who dont earn it? What is the use of saying "Shame"? It is not shameful; it is ridiculous. It is not as if there was any secret about it; they tell you themselves they get it; you get the figures from the income tax returns. It seems to me they get rather more than they say they get. Here you are every year throwing away this money to the tune of 630 millions. Well, *you* dont see where a great deal of it goes to; I do. I idle about a good deal when ever I get the chance. I have gone, for instance, [on] a trip round the Mediterranean, and have seen along those beautiful coasts, one town after another where there were no vulgar industries, such as you have in Liverpool. Everything was charming; there you see beautiful Opera Houses, Casinos, delightful Villas, and the whole thing is going on lubricated by an enormous mass of gold which is tumbled about in heaps—YOUR gold! There are different seasons at these places. First the Italian season, when prices are low. Then the German season, when prices are moderate. Then the English season, the prices are high; they take it out of the English people. There you see this waste—this enormous, outrageous waste—going on; and as you see it you know: HERE is your 630 millions; here is all the money that is being driven out of the country by our existing system; and then you think of the slums of Manchester and Glasgow (of course I know there are none in Liverpool); then you think of the anxious lives of the poor; and yet the labor of these people is producing the mass of money which is spent in this wasteful and extravagant manner. One has a sort of impulse that if you had command of the British fleet you would like to shell those towns. Then you come to your senses and say, "No, these are nice places; let us take the fleet back and shell the slums at home." Once when I spoke to a mob in London, they wanted to burn Marlborough House, but I told them it was a nice house and advised them to go and burn their own insanitary places in the East End. They would not; they did not feel quite sure about it. I never was a success as a mob agitator for that very reason. It is not necessary to go to the Mediterranean to find this waste. You find it at your own pleasure resorts; you find it in Brighton and Eastbourne and other places; and, curiously enough, you find the people of Brighton are becoming Socialists; they only want the rich to be rich enough to stay at Brighton, and not rich enough to get across the Channel.

Now, you are fighting against this waste a little, and one of the ways you are fighting is that the working classes are steadily pressing for a number of things to be provided for them. Not only old age pensions, but also houses to be built by the authorities; and they are getting them; and, mind you, the provision of houses as now carried on is a sort of fraud on the ratepayers, because the ratepayer is persuaded they pay for themselves, but it is not true. The working man is getting his houses put up at the expense of the ratepayers. Then again, he is clamoring for more education for his children. At the present time it has become an act of folly for any man of moderate means to send his son to a private school, because it is sure to be worse than a public school. The working man's son is getting his elementary and his secondary education out of the public money, and that secondary education provides a ladder to the university, so it is quite possible with the aid of scholarships to get a university education at the public expense. But the working man wants more. He is constantly being egged on by Socialists to ask for more, and we are not going to stop egging him on.

There is no difference between the Liberals and Conservatives on the question of old age pensions. The Conservatives say, if you would only let them in, and allow them to have a tariff, they would give you bigger old age pensions. So the thing goes on.

But, I ask you now, where does the middle class come in, in all this? The middle class has to pay for it; for, politically, it is the most helplessly foolish and absurd class that ever existed on the face of the earth. Just consider the situation: The working classes are represented in Parliament. They have an independent Chairman and whip of their own. They call it "The Labor Party." On the other hand, you have our great capitalists and landlords represented in Parliament, but our middle classes are not represented at all. They may have a few representatives in the Irish Party (everybody is poor in Ireland, but everybody in Ireland belongs to the middle classes), but their business is looking after the Irish Question, and

not the English; so you may say the middle classes are not represented at all in Parliament; and they are *proud* of the fact. They vote
for the rich people, because they believe they themselves belong to
the upper classes. I remember being disgusted on one occasion,
when reference was made to me as belonging to a middle-class
family. It is true my father was not so well off as he might have
been, but still—he was a SHAW! It was the mere accident of his
being a younger son that he was not able to keep up the position he
had been used to. But he had a second cousin a baronet, and I used
to consider myself somebody in the world—until I made the discovery that nearly every other man had a father who was second
cousin to a baronet.

You have to remember the arrangement of English society. In
Germany, if you are of noble descent, your descendants are noble
to the end of time, and there is a distinct line drawn between you
and other classes. But in England, according to the laws of primogeniture, it is only the eldest son who is considered the gentleman.
Let us suppose you are a Duke. You will probably have £50,000 a
year. That is not a very great amount; an American millionaire
would consider it merely a fair income. (You must have been
touched when you heard of that millionaire who said, "Gentlemen,
it is all very well for men like us, but the men you have to consider
are the poor devils who have only £10,000 a year".) To them, Dukes
are no longer rich men; yet you will find Dukes here and there with
£50,000 a year to keep their houses going, and, having that income,
they have a good many children. Suppose a Duke has six children.
(He might have more, but put it at six.) Every one of these children
is brought up in a house carried on at the rate of £50,000 a year,
and they dont know how to live any other way. And yet it is only the
eldest son who inherits the Duke's £50,000 a year; and the others
have to put up with very little. The daughters are already married
to American millionaires, and under such circumstances may make
allowances to their younger brothers. But take the younger son:
perhaps he will be a Lord through courtesy for life; but the effect
of that is, he is expected to have more money than he has, and you
put this man into society, and the only rate of living he knows is the
rate of £50,000 a year. He is bound to live beyond his income, and
he gets more and more into debt, and when he hands the thing on
to his son, he is embarrassed. If your father lives at the rate of
£1,200 a year and leaves you £600 a year, he leaves you in the same

fix; and you know the dreadful thing that happens in a generation or two: some member of that family has to make up his mind to WORK for a living, and perhaps goes in for a profession; a clergyman, or a doctor, or something low like that, and he, in turn, tries to give his sons a good education. But he cannot give it to all. The next thing is, the son is not successful perhaps, and is bankrupt. Then comes the time when the son has to become a clerk. Then perhaps one says his son had better be a skilled tradesman, and another son has to become a laborer. So, remember, the laborer you talk to, who is one of the working classes, can look back to his great-great-grandfather, who was a Duke. Well, what does he do? One of his sons gets so sick of poverty that he goes in for and gets a scholarship, and perhaps another son makes another flight and gets a business together. If clever, perhaps he is able to add to his money what he borrows from other people. Perhaps he marries somebody with a little money, and he makes a bit at business, and the end of it is, we get back to the Duke again.

All through English society you have this going-up and coming-down, and so you have the difficulty of giving this country a class consciousness; they are all conscious of belonging to the upper classes, which they consider in the nature of a halo of smug respectability and reflected glory.

The political bearing of all this is obvious; it explains the reason why the middle classes think they are voting for their own class when they vote for the rich and upper classes. They really think a man with £300 a year can be represented by a man with £30,000 a year. It is convenient for the upper classes.

It has been said of the Tories that they were willing to do anything for the poor except get off their backs; and it is true. It is the Liberal who says, "If you do anything for the working classes you will pauperize them." They have an idea that by giving the workers private charity it is not pauperizing. The Tories recognize that in order to keep and maintain their position they must keep the working classes in a good humor; so they give them housing, education and the rest, but they do not give these at their own expense. Nothing is ever done by the House of Commons at the expense of the House of Commons, so long as it can be put on the shoulders of someone else. Why should they? So the workers have to pay. The rich say, "We are willing to give you anything, but we cannot pay the bill ourselves. Therefore, we had better make the ratepayer pay"; that is to say, the great mass of the middle classes; and, if you please, the ratepayer is beginning to grumble. What does he want? He keeps dreaming that the rates can be reduced, and votes for the candidate who talks of his anxiety to put down the rates; and though the voter hears this over and over again, and the rates have not gone down, he clings to this idea, that the rates can be abolished. I almost wish you, in Liverpool, would try this middle-class idea, and return a Council who would do away with the rates, and I would like to see what sort of a town it would be to live in, with no police service, or health authorities, and nothing at all done in the town unless somebody could make a profit by doing it. I wonder if the ratepayers ever think what the effect would be if their idea was carried out. If I was a representative on this body, I would have the rates increased considerably. I would have public expenditure increased, because there is plenty of money to be got without coming on the middle classes if they would only open their eyes and see where to go for it.

Consider how the financial affairs of this country are carried on and think of what goes on in the House of Commons. You have the Chancellor of the Exchequer, who comes forth and says, "I want so much money to conduct the business of this country; where am I to get it? I want £120,000,000." If there is a little war on, it might be more. He says, "What have I got to start with? There is the interest on the Suez Canal shares; that is a little. Then there are the stamp duties; that is a little more. Then if I sweat the Post Office: if I screw down the wages of the men and women in the Post Office: if I charge the public more for their services: there will be more profit, and all that will help. Then what else is there? Let me see: Suppose for instance I were to charge more for the working man's smokes, a shilling for three-halfpence worth of tobacco; I might get some more money that way. Then of course, there are the drinking habits of the people; if they would drink hard, I might get something more." At last he gets down to within a margin of what he wants, and he goes down to the House of Commons and tells them all the efforts he has made to get money, and says, "Gentlemen, having got everything I possibly could out of the workers, I am sorry to say I will have to get the rest by the Income Tax; the Income Tax is going to be a shilling in the pound." Then the country is up at once; the middle classes are indignant; there is a tremendous row. Well, do you think a shilling in the pound is a

high income tax? Dont you think it would be a good thing to discriminate about your income tax? You dont levy the income tax
square on everybody. If a man has £160 a year, you dont take any
tax from him. Then there are a series of abatements up to £700 a
year. Then you let the full force come upon those with over the
£700. After a long agitation by the Socialists, this year the momentous step has been taken of making a distinction between "earned"
and "unearned" incomes. You must know, if you know anything
about the Liverpool Fabian Society, that ever since it was started, it
was urging upon you the fact that some incomes were earned, and
some were not. At last, the cat is out of the bag, and the House of
Commons has made the distinction; they say a difference must be
made. (I am sorry to say they make me pay a shilling in the pound,
because unfortunately they made it out that I made more than
£2,000, and they have come to the conclusion that if I earn more
than £2,000, I did not earn it quite fairly.) Dont you think you
should make the earned income tax sixpence in the pound, and the
unearned one-and-sixpence in the pound? (Great Cheering). Since
you receive that in such a hearty manner, why not go further, and
tax the earned incomes a penny in the pound, and the unearned at
five shillings in the pound. My friend Sidney Webb had the com-
pliment paid to him of having something he said posted on the
walls all over London; he suggested that the ground-rents in London should be taxed twenty shillings in the pound; but Mr Webb is
an extreme man. I am not; I would be content with nineteen and
six in the pound. And remember, all this is possible if the people
would only send different representatives to the House of Commons. You could re-distribute the income of the Country. All this
money wasted on the Mediterranean could be stopped and got at
by means of the income tax. If the Corporation of Liverpool ever
want to get anything from the large number of rich men who at
present seem to own the City, let me give you a hint how to get it:
Buy their concerns from them, and let them know beforehand you
want them, that will send the price up. Then you will give them the
maximum percentage for compulsory purchase. Say you give
twenty per cent extra—dont be stingy. And then afterwards, get a
bit of your own back by putting a Municipal income tax on the
money you have paid them. It is done, I assure you, at the present
time, elsewhere. One of the most essential duties of a Government
is to take lots of money. They take this money and distribute it

through the Local Government Board; and that might be done on a much larger scale if you would only intelligently use your political power. You might turn Liverpool into a much more beautiful and healthy City, and do it without costing the ratepayers one farthing. You might do it without taking out of the pocket of anyone who is doing service for the community by working for his living.

There is just another little question before I come to the end of my lecture. You must remember that if you make up your mind to intercept this drain upon the industry of the Country—these large masses of surplus wealth drained off into the pockets of the upper classes—you must find means of employing the money. You cannot put it into the till of the Chancellor of the Exchequer, and expect him to sit down and do nothing with it. You must remember that in the service of the rich a number of people are employed. There are the men who are their servants, and the various other people who are depending on the incomes of the idle rich. That is one of the reasons so many people help and vote for the idle rich. Their attitude is an intelligent one, for they say, "When the Duke robs the community, I will go and rob the Duke," only, they generally do something for their money: they do a certain kind of work. So, if you begin to take the money, you must begin to fertilize the industry of the country with it, and with that money which has employed people in the hands of the rich, you must find employment for the people, but in a more useful manner. This money must be used by the community as industrial capital.

Take, for instance, the case of Liverpool: Why on earth do you allow Liverpool to be built by private people? Surely the building of Liverpool concerns the people of Liverpool? But when you impose Building Acts, you say to private builders, "You can build the town, but you must build it in a particular sort of way; you must not build a house in the middle of Lime Street." If I was a builder, I would say, "Let me build the town as I please, or else, build it yourself." The whole town ought to be built by those responsible for its regulations, and yet you are not allowed to build your own town. The only houses that the public authorities are allowed to build are the working-class houses; that is to say, the one class of property that does not pay and cannot pay. The private contractor may build any kind of structure he likes, from a cathedral to a hencoop, but until he can make a handsome profit he refuses to build. If you went to a private builder and told him he would not be allowed to build big buildings, what would happen to the builder? He would be bankrupt. Our municipal housing schemes dont pay; the city of Liverpool will never be able to make money building houses for the working classes alone.

Remember, the profits made by public bodies are real profits; they are not so much percent paid to idlers at the expense of the workers; the profits got by the local authorities *are* profits; then there are the great invisible profits, the increase in happiness and health; these are not shewn in the books of your town. The commercial man comes along and says he wants your books audited, and I blush (at least, I am trying to) when I hear of business men of Liverpool or Manchester or other big towns, and see how they are taken in by that silly nonsense about Municipal Debt, and that kind of thing. Municipal Debt is Municipal Capital. When they collect money to use in their businesses it does certainly go into their balance sheet as Liabilities, but the commercial men call it "capital" and when it is doubled they boast about it. Yet if the Municipalities double *their* "capital," these men say, "Oh! you are plunging into Municipal Debt deeper than ever." Did anyone ever hear such nonsense from people who ought to know better? Why, it would not impose on a cat! You see it has not imposed on an innocent literary man like myself!

Here you have the bits of a program, and now you can take them home and piece the bits together. I think you will begin to see that Socialism is a business scheme, based on facts and figures.

I want you to understand thoroughly that I have not come to Liverpool to establish Socialism in Liverpool. If you ask me to, I wont! It is YOUR business, not mine. What is more feeble than to think that the whole people of this country expect that half a dozen people like Thorne, Quelch, Grayson, Hyndman, and myself, are going to walk into England and establish a new political and industrial system, in spite of the people themselves, and tyrannize over them.[5] It is very complimentary to us. It is extremely flattering to me. I am a very extraordinary man myself, and can do extraordinary things, but there is a limit to my appetite for doing other people's business. You may depend on it, if you dont choose to establish Socialism, Socialism wont be established. And remember, Socialism is a very elastic thing; it is a thing which comes on gradually, and you can stop it whenever you like. Whenever a little bit of Socialism is adopted, people cease to call it Socialism. After you

have followed our advice, you talk as if we were advocates of Free
Love, and Atheism and other things. I dont know the meaning of
"Free Love," except that I know there is a certain thing to be got in
the streets of Liverpool and other great cities, and I wish the gentlemen who so frantically denounce "Free Love" would be a little
more concerned to bring about a state of things in which no woman
would be driven to such a sort of business by mere want. (Loud
applause.) I am glad I trapped you into that applause, for it is not a
mere question of a woman selling her womanhood; it is a question
of men every day selling their manhood; it is that which makes the
present system intolerable. If we all felt we worked for the country
at large, and not for private employers for private ends, with our
lives twisted for the benefit of some private man, there are many of
us who would make a sacrifice willingly for the community. We do
get a great deal of work done without paying an extravagant price
for it. In the Army and Navy you get good work done for a salary
which is small. There you have, of course, the particular dignity
which is attached to the profession; they are in the service of their
country. When our capitalists say, "We organize industry, and we
must get everything that is produced; everything that is added to
the wealth of the country should come into our pockets." Surely, if
we are to have any respect for them, it should be that what they add
to the wealth of the community should come to the community.
What would you think of General Roberts,[6] if, after having won a
battle he claimed to have the country for himself, and said, unless
you give this country to the man who saved it on your field of
battle, he would not fight any more!

When Sir Christopher Furness talked to his men the other day,
and claimed that the men who organized industry would never get
the work done unless you gave them all that their brains produced,
I say he really spoke just as meanly and unpatriotically and with just
as great a want of sense as General Roberts would if, after saving
this country in battle, he claimed this country as his own.

I dont want these gentlemen to be poor; I abhor poverty, and
hate the working classes because they are poor. I myself have not
only an objection to giving money, but I hate people to ask for it. I
dont want to be poorer, but I want the other people to be richer. As
a matter of fact, I am a man of extremely moderate requirements;
if you give me £2,500 a year, it will be quite good enough for me. It
would be quite possible to give everybody in this country a standard

of comfort and security equal to that represented by £2,500 a year if we had the thing properly organized.

Well: in the course of an hour and twenty minutes I have tried to remind you of things you have not thought of. If you want to find out more, you can find out from the Fabian Society. It is a simple Society, and we sympathize with poverty because we ourselves are not poor. We are like the captain of the sinking ship who got into the boat first and said "Now I can give my orders calmly; if I had stayed on the bridge, I could not have kept my head." We have been able to look at the general position of politics, and, by going about talking as I have been talking tonight, we think we shall stimulate the working classes to go on, and make the middle class understand, if they continue as they do at present to help the upper classes, they will be absolutely crushed, as ratepayers, between the propertied classes and the working classes. There is no possibility of them saving themselves by making a combination with the upper classes; the upper classes will still keep on trying to throw the whole expense on the ratepayers. The only chance of the middle class is to form a combination with the working classes, and throw the expense necessary to transform our country from the wretched place it is into a handsome and happy country, upon the enormous fund of unearned income which is at present being wasted.

The thing must proceed gradually; you must put up your shilling in the pound income tax and get it up bit by bit, and take more and more men from the middle and working classes and put them into public employment until finally you have covered the whole field.

It is only a little question of taxation. You need not do anything except by constitutional means. By taxation you avoid compensation; it is pure confiscation, quite legal and usual. There is no need for anything except your power through the ballot box. You will see it is a good system, and if you like it, you can go in for more of it.

And now, if you want to know more, you had better ask me questions.

The Unmentionable Case for Women's Suffrage

One of the most blackguardly debates that ever took place in the House of Lords was that in which the women who had sat on the old London Vestries were disqualified from sitting on the new Borough Councils. The argument which prevailed was that the Borough Councils would include aldermen, and that a woman could not possibly be an alder*man*. This joke pleased the Peers immensely. It stimulated that vein of facetiousness in which the health of the bridesmaids is proposed at old-fashioned weddings; and women vanished from the London municipalities for some years.

I believe that this unseemly piece of mischief and bad manners could have been prevented if it had been possible to give publicity to the most pressing reasons for the presence of women on public bodies. I made an effort to save the situation by writing a letter to The Times; but The Times blushed and threw my letter into the wastepaper basket, after, I presume, carefully tearing it up lest it should shock the dustman. For it was unfortunately necessary for me, in the course of that letter, to throw over the customary polite assumption that women are angels.

English decency is a rather dirty thing. It is responsible for more indecency than anything else in the world. It is a string of taboos. You must not mention this: you must not appear conscious of that:

you must not meddle with the other—at least, not in public. And
the consequence is that everything that must not be mentioned in
public is mentioned in private as a naughty joke. One day, at a
meeting of the Health Committee of the Borough Council of which
I was a member, a doctor rose to bring a case before the Committee. It was the case of a woman. The gravity of the case depended
on the fact that the woman was pregnant. No sooner had the doctor
mentioned this than the whole Committee burst into a roar of
laughter, as if the speaker had made a scandalous but irresistible
joke. And please bear in mind that we were not schoolboys. We
were grave, mostly elderly men, fathers of families. It was no use
being indignant or looking shocked: the only effect of that would
have been an impression of ill-natured Puritanism. There is only
one absolutely certain and final preventive for such indecency, and
that is the presence of women. If there were not other argument
for giving women the vote, I would support it myself on no other
ground than that men will not behave themselves when women are
not present.

I recall another scene in the same Committee before the House
of Lords had driven the women off it. This scene illustrated quite a
different point: namely, that the average man is a silly sentimental
gossip where women are concerned, and will not keep women up to
the mark unless women are present to keep *him* up to the mark.
The question arose as to whether a young woman should be prose-
cuted. She had caught scarlet fever whilst at work in London, and
had immediately flown to her family at Esher by omnibus and rail.
This was as serious an offence against the Public Health Acts as she
could have committed; but the men on the Committee were unequal to the occasion. "What would any poor girl have done?" said
the leader of the party in power; and I found myself unable to
disagree with him. The law is one of those entirely reasonable ones
which are nevertheless inhuman, because our social arrangements
do not present a reasonable alternative to the thing which it forbids. Unless innocent people attacked with infectious disease
drown themselves in baths of carbolic acid, they can hardly avoid
exposing somebody to infection on their way to bed; and as a poor
and ignorant girl knows of no refuge but her parents' house, to
punish her for taking the only means of getting there that she
knows of and can afford is beyond my sense of public duty. But had
the offender been a young man, I might have taken a sterner view.

As it was, a vestrywoman arose and "went for" us. "Mr Chairman," she said: "I protest against this mawkish pity." We quailed. She proceeded to ask us whether, if our children or our wives or our nurserymaids had been in that bus, we should have found the young woman's thoughtlessness quite so touching. In the end she compelled us to arrange that when the offender was well she should be officially visited and threatened and reproved, so as to make her thoroughly conscious of the enormity of her conduct. I beg to say that I am still on the side of the unfortunate girl, deeming it altogether the fault of the community that she knew of no refuge or help save in her parents' house; but the incident illustrates the fact that the influence of women on public bodies is antisentimental, and much needed to correct the tendency of men to exceed in the opposite direction.

The unmentionable question of sanitary accommodation occupied a good deal of the time of the Borough Council. I invite the male reader to give his mind to this with some care. The sumptuous public lavatories which now provide the poor man with the only palatial luxuries he ever uses meet two requirements, one of which, being frequent and simple, costs him nothing; whilst the other, involving the use of a separate private apartment, costs him a penny. If this charge of a penny were extended to the gratuitous accommodation, which is used perhaps a thousand times for every once of the other, there would be an explosion of public indignation which would bring to its knees at once any municipal authority which dared to impose it. Women had two grievances in the matter under my Borough Council. The first and worst was, that in most places no sanitary accommodation was provided for them at all. But this, at least, was known and understood. The second, which no man ever thought of until it was pointed out to him, was that even where accommodation was provided, it consisted wholly of the separate apartment at a charge of one penny: an absolutely prohibitive charge for a poor woman, and a very serious expense up to that income, well advanced in three figures, at which housekeeping allowances are so generous that pennies cease to have any importance. The moment it became known that I was one of those ungentlemanly and unromantic men who reject the angelic theory of womanhood, I received piteous anonymous letters from women begging me to get that penny charge at least reduced to a halfpenny. These letters, and the reports and complaints as to the condition of all the little byways and nooks in the borough which afforded any sort of momentary privacy, revealed a world of unmentionable suffering and subterfuge.

Then began a grotesque struggle for more accommodation. It raged for years round a site in High Street, Camden Town. The opposition, though resolute and desperate, was not direct. It is true that one councillor, on other questions an enlightened man, of gentle manners and humane public spirit, passionately protested against "this abomination," as, in an excess of horror, he described the projected lavatory. Another councillor objected on the ground that the water supply would be used by flowergirls to wash the violets which he occasionally purchased for his buttonhole. Another, when told that women demanded the accommodation, urged that persons who so far "forgot their sex" should not have anything provided for them at all! But it was easy to kill these objections by ridicule, as the Council was only too ready to laugh on the slightest provocation when so highly humorous a subject was under discussion. The really effective opposition took the form of alleging engineering and traffic difficulties, which were carefully manufactured for the occasion. The pains taken at this game, and the money spent on it were amazing. To this day I do not understand how it can have been worth my opponents' while to dodge the project as they did. The climax was reached when, to test the excuse that the lavatory would form a dangerous obstruction to traffic, a wooden obstruction of the exact dimensions of the proposed lavatory was placed on the site. That brought out all the power of the vestryman over the petty commerce and petty traffic of his district. In one day every omnibus on the Camden Town route, every tradesman's cart owned within a radius of two miles, and most of the rest of the passing vehicles, including private carriages driven to the spot on purpose, crashed into that obstruction with just violence enough to produce an accident without damage. The drivers who began the game were either tipped or under direct orders; but the joke soon caught on, and was kept up for fun by all and sundry. In the end the thing was so grossly overdone, and the conspirators were so indiscreetly proud of their cleverness in having "worked it," that it produced no effect except the inevitable comic one. None the less, the lavatory was not made; and we were presently arguing about another site and the alleged impossibility of making anything underground in London without wrecking the water-pipes and drowning the metropolis in a general inundation. My career as a councillor came to end before anything was done. And this was the period during which women were excluded.

Another difficulty of the same nature was exposed when, before the exclusion of the women, they had succeeded in making the vestry appoint a woman as inspector of factories and workshops. The first result of this was that a factory belonging to one of the best-known firms in England had to build more than a dozen closets to bring the sanitary accommodation for the women they employed up to the bare requirements of the Acts. The state of things before this may be imagined. The exclusion of women from the Borough Council left the inspectress in a difficult position. The barrier of the unmentionable arose between her and the members of the Health Committee. It was all the higher because the inspectress was generally an educated woman of university rank, not at all conversant with the sort of local tradesman who regards the subject of sanitary accommodation as one to which no lady should allude in the presence of a gentleman. The vestrywomen had always known what the inspectress was doing; but I, during my six years as a councillor, would never have discovered the fact of her existence but for the monthly salary list and the occasional necessity of re-placing her when she left us. It was made clear to me that the truth about the female industrial worker will never be found out by male inspectors or by male councillors.

The unmentionable aspect of the Housing question is very un-mentionable indeed. The primitive form of housing for the human family is the cabin consisting of the single room, still to be found in all its mudfloored simplicity in Ireland. There is one bed for the whole family: the parents sleeping in the middle, the boys on the father's side, and the girls on the mother's. At the other end of the scale of civilization every individual has a separate bedroom. The concession of this privilege to the children is a matter of course when there is money enough to make it economically possible; and where it is not, there is at least one room for the boys and another for the girls, except when the poverty is so extreme that no segre-gation at all is feasible. Thus, for everybody but the husband and wife, the absence of a separate room is admittedly one of the priva-tions of poverty. But in their case the superstition of the nuptial chamber introduces an element which defies reason and decency. Even in circles where the husband's "dressing-room" is a matter of course, and is always provided with a bed, it is still necessary for married couples who maintain separate bedrooms to make that fact known before they accept invitations to stay at other people's houses; and instances are not unknown in which aristocratic hostesses with plenty of rooms to dispose of have been so scandalized by what they regarded as a violation of the sanctity of marriage, that they have indignantly refused the desired accommodation with an intimation that the persons asking for it ought to be ashamed of themselves.

Behind this unwholesome prejudice many odd little weaknesses are hidden. I once knew a very clever lady who had a great dread of widowhood, and a resolute objection to the provision of a separate room for her husband. She was not jealous; and she was not prejudiced. But she was afraid of ghosts, and would have slept with anybody rather than sleep alone. The habit of sleeping in company can be acquired like any other habit. The crew of a battleship, hung up by the hundred in festoons of hammocks that almost touch oneanother, prefer the accommodation to single rooms on shore.

Nevertheless, the practice is an indefensible one. However indifferent people may be to privacy and ventilation, however jealous they may be of the slightest relaxation of the chain that binds them to oneanother, there are times and circumstances which make the practice of condemning two people to share the same room frightfully cruel. Suppose, for instance, one of the party becomes consumptive, and begins slowly to cough, cough, cough, all the way to the grave. Even in the still quite recent days before infection was feared, married people were driven almost mad by want of sleep from this cause. I knew one man who told me passionately, after his wife's death, that if he had not been a coward he would have killed her to save her from the racking cough that went on all night long, and racked him almost as cruelly as it racked her. It very nearly killed him: she died just in time to give him a chance of recovering from the strain. And, unfortunately, he did not recover. He had taken to drinking to make himself drowsy and indifferent: and he presently drank himself to death. Here the husband was the sufferer; but what about the unfortunate wife who may not have her bed kept sacred even when she is bearing children? One just touches this terrible subject, and flies from it. I do not know what date the latest criticism assigns to the book of Leviticus; but it is melancholy to think how far British domesticity falls short of the decencies of the ancient Jewish code. I wonder how much of the modern antipathy to marriage is due to this cause that no one ever mentions. The time will come when it will be incredible that people should have submitted to such a condition as the British double bed. One can understand their getting used to it; for people can get used to anything, even to the family bed of the cabin or one-roomed tenement; but to make it an institution! to glory in it! to wallow in it! to insult those who object to it! Surely that indicates either an extraordinarily morbid state of mind, or a love of company and intolerance of solitude which cannot be universal. I strongly suspect that, though we never mention it, the cry for the vote is often really a cry for the key of one's bedroom.

This is not a question for women alone. Nothing is more exasperating than the common assumption that all the sensitiveness, the delicacy, the privacy which is outraged by our existing matrimonial habits are on the side of the women. The line of cleavage in such matters does not run between the sexes: it runs between those people whose natural delicacy and individuality is too strong for habit and inculcation, and those who find the custom bearable enough to follow without thinking. The men who are dissatisfied must be reinforced by the women if they are to make any headway in their contention that the housing problem is a problem of providing every individual with a separate, private, inviolable apartment. Indeed there should be two such apartments; for a boudoir is a necessity to the higher life as well as a bedroom; and it is one of the grievances of women at present that, when only one boudoir is available, the man seizes it and calls it his study.

To some extent this demand is being met among well-to-do people by the shrinkage of the family. If people who formerly had eight or ten children now have two or three, and they still inhabit the old family mansion, the appropriation of four rooms by the parents may be possible. But this remedy for domestic overcrowding is set off by another social change. Even when the old large houses are still used, the servants tend to encroach on the accommodation formerly reserved for "the quality." Servants also want separate rooms, and object to be packed by twos and threes in basements or attics only fit for cellars and boxrooms. Mistresses of houses are finding out that it adds enormously to the amenity of home life to raise the standard of gentility in personal habits for their servants.

At the other end of the social hierarchy the horrors of the one-room tenement are being exposed statistically from many new points of view, especially that of national costliness. When Lord Shaftesbury and Tennyson tried to startle the conscience of the nation by letting slip the unmentionable fact that the one-room tenement produced incest, we simply pretended not to hear, knowing that nobody dare pursue the subject. But now that it has been demonstrated that one-room life means huge burdens on the ratepayer, we are beginning to concern ourselves about it. We are finding out that high vitality, with its products of health and decency, pays us; and that overcrowding and promiscuity mean high rates, doctors' bills, and low efficiency of labor. We are face to face with the task of rehousing the population; and the very first question we should consider is whether man and wife are two individuals requiring at least two rooms, or one individual requiring only one bed.

There are, of course, many points of housing which men are sure to muddle hopelessly unless they are helped out by women; but they are not unmentionable, and therefore do not come within the scope of this article. Also, it must be understood that I do not pretend to have exhausted the unmentionable matters. In the borough which I helped to govern for six years there were long sections of main streets in which almost every house was a brothel. I explained that phenomenon in my play entitled Mrs. Warren's Profession; but the brothel proprietors sheltered themselves behind the schedule of taboos which constitute the decency of the King's Reader of Plays; and the play may not be performed in this country; whilst in America it exposed me to a savage press campaign against my character and my play, led by a newspaper which was shortly afterwards heavily fined for deriving a considerable part of its revenue from advertisements of Mrs. Warren's houses. That is what provoked me to say that decency is indecency's conspiracy of silence. Even I have not said a tenth of what ought to be said. The little I have written has not been written without effort; for I am sorry to say that the heroic impudence which is the quality most needed just now to ignore the taboos is beyond my strength. Still I hope I have said enough to show that the exclusion of women from public life is not only an injustice—we have to put up with many injustices—but an abomination.

Shaw's contribution to the first issues of the Daily Citizen, *18 and 19 October 1912.*

What about the Middle Class?
A Lay Sermon

I It was some twelve years after my first appearance on the Labor platform as a Socialist that my attention was turned to the wretched plight of the middle classes. During those twelve years I had delivered innumerable public addresses on Socialism to audiences of working men from the point of view of the working classes, by which I mean the point of view they would take if they understood their own situation, and did not all regard themselves as members of the middle and upper classes compelled for the moment to resort to manual labor to tide over temporary reverses.

It happened then that my success as a writer of plays roused a good deal of curiosity and even some intelligent interest about me in the better-off sections of the community. The Labor and Socialist organizations, which had before then put me up to beg the attention of audiences in market squares, at street corners, on park pitches, and in the cheaper public halls, and had been well content when my eloquence resulted in a collection sufficient to pay the expenses of the meeting, now found that the readiest way to get out of debt and make a little money for future emergencies was to hire the best hall in the town; announce a lecture by Bernard Shaw; and make a substantial charge for admission. The result was, of course, a complete change in the class of my audience. Thus I remember that on my first visit to Walsall I spoke to rows of black-faced men. I knew that they were not Christy Minstrels, because their lips were as black as their faces; but whether they were sweeps, colliers, or workers in some grimy industry unknown to me I could not tell. On my second visit many years later the rows of black men, with the whites of their eyes glittering strangely at me in a badly-lighted room, were replaced by rows of ladies sitting in a flood of electric light in the smartest hats the wealth of Walsall could procure. And here and there, squeezed in between their fineries, were the fathers and sweethearts of these ladies, mostly with an air of having been brought there against their wills to listen to paradoxical tomfooleries from a person with whose views they had no desire to be identified. The black men would have described them as a collection of young toffs and old geezers.

Now, it was clearly no use talking to high-collared toffs and frock-coated geezers as I had talked to the industrial blacks. Their immediate interests were too sharply opposed. They hated oneanother like poison. They would not speak to oneanother; would not eat with oneanother; would not sit in the same part of a theatre; would not intermarry; and would not believe any good of oneanother, though, underneath their clothes, they are exactly the same animal. They were robbing each other without remorse by process of law. The toff was sweating the black: the black was forcing the toff to pension him, educate his children, and do various odd jobs for him out of the rates and taxes.

Nine-tenths of the art of popular oratory lies in sympathizing with the grievances of your hearers. The working man being shut out by charges for admission beyond his means, I said not another word about his woes, but set to work to draw a terrible (and perfectly true) picture of the growth of his power of putting pressure on Parliament to provide more and more of the things he had already begun to help himself to out of the rates and taxes, culminating in the near future in that unexpected but inevitable improvement on the old age pension, the pension for life in the shape of full public provision for the unemployed. I shewed that all these costly reforms would be thrown on the rates, because the middle class was not represented in Parliament, and even if it was would be in a minority, writhing between the upper millstone of the plutocracy and the nether millstone of the Labor Party. I shewed how the oligarchy of big capitalists by which we are really governed had, with the full approval of the Labor Party, thrown the whole burden of national insurance against industrial accidents on the shoulders of the employers; and how, when the greater question of national insurance against illness was tackled, and shelved by the monstrous and shameless injustice of throwing the cost on the employer in direct proportion to his services in organizing the national labor, and mostly in inverse proportion to his income, the working man and his representatives in Parliament thought it an excellent arrangement. And it certainly suited me personally very well, as I said to a builder of my acquaintance who employed some hundreds of men on one-ninth of my income (I employ one secretary). And I freely expressed my very poor opinion of the workers and the employers for not striking against the contributions and forcing the Government to get the money by super-taxing unearned incomes.

I also set to work to make the middle class "class conscious" as the Marxists say. And this was not easy, because the middle-class man thinks he is actually a gentleman, whereas the working man only thinks he would have been a gentleman if his great-grandfather, the Honorable Thomas Noddy, had not lived beyond his younger-son's allowance. Now, it happens that a middle-class man engaged in commerce cannot be a gentleman, as any real gentleman will tell him. The whole point of being a gentleman is that you will not accept payment for your work, and that you insist on the country keeping you in a handsome manner and treating you respectfully in consideration of your doing the best you can for it because you ought. *Noblesse oblige*. A middle-class man is a commercialist who says, like Lord ****** that he does not see why he should do anything unless he is paid to do it, nor why he should add anything to the productive power of labor unless he gets the increase of product as his reward: in other words, unless he feels sure that he is benefiting nobody but himself. That is why real gentlemen call Lord ****** a vulgar tradesman, and want to abolish the House of Lords, now that it has become nothing but the commerical-room in the great hotel at Westminster.

To make a middle-class man class-conscious, you have first to explain to him that as organizer of production to the community he is so vitally necessary and important that no revolution could possibly enable the State to do without him. This pleases and reassures him, though it would please him more if he understood his own business better. Second, that the commercial method of organizing production condemns him to be a cad who does everything for pay and nothing for honor, love, or patriotism. And this he is apt to get huffy about; but he cannot rub it off; and it is the shame of it that will finally convert him to Socialism if anything will.

I cannot stand the man who wants the whole product of his labor, whether he is a doctor or a duke. It is not the fellow's stupidity and ignorance in imagining that anybody, even Robinson Crusoe, could possibly put his hand on anything and say, "This owes its existence to me, and to me alone." We are all too stupid and ignorant to afford to be impatient with oneanother on that score. It is the poverty of soul that wants to grab and consume instead of to give, to create, to leave a surplus. The economic grievance of the worker today is not that he produces more than he consumes; for the man who does not want to do that is a spiritless creature with no proper pride in him. The real horror of the laborers' lot is that this continual gift of theirs to the world, instead of raising it steadily towards its final destination of becoming heaven, is consumed and wasted by wretched idlers and their parasites, so that the surplus becomes a curse instead of a blessing, and rots the society it should ennoble.

Our ridiculous hesitation over the very simple duty of killing these parasites would be respectable if it were due to the fact that they have a right to demand the option of honest work, and that our society is so villainously organized that we are not prepared to offer them that option. But we really have no such intelligent scruples. If we had we should dare not to deal as we do with the unemployed and the tramp. The root reason for our forbearance is that we would all be thieves and wasters ourselves if we could, and therefore, even with the chances against us at millions to one, we keep the door open to theft and dishonor.

II How to give the Englishman a social conscience: that is the difficulty. At present he will do anything for money, provided only everybody else is doing it, or trying to do it, too. He sweats the working man, or allows himself to be sweated by his employer, not for his country's present or future, not for the love of God, nor even for the fun of the thing, but for the benefit of the waster and the self-legalized thief who (very properly) despises him. And this silly thing he does because he hopes to share the plunder himself some day, and regards the waster-thief as a superior creature, just as poor folk two hundred years ago called highwaymen gentlemen of the road and pirates gentlemen of fortune.

This, again, is not to be disposed of by telling the middle-class employer that he is a dupe and a snob, though he usually deserves both assurances. What is behind the sham gentleman of today is the ideal gentleman of all time, who works, not because he is paid, but because he ought and because he likes. And this ideal gentleman gets his income not because he works, but solely because it is desirable and pleasant and good for the world that he should be well off, healthy, and handsome: he and his womankind as well. There is nothing whatever wrong in a man having an "independent" income. Everyone should have such an income. What is ghastly and revolting is that a man should have no income at all unless he can bribe some other man to share with him. The gentleman, with his pension for life and his respected position, is in the right place. The instinct which leads us all to aim at getting up beside him is a perfectly sound one. He alone is honorable who is neither bought nor sold, and need submit to no man's insolence. Neither the labor-monger at twenty shillings a week nor the profit-monger at twenty pounds a day can pretend to be his equal: they can cut off his head, but not his dignity.

But if a gentleman does not work, and accepts the bribe of the laborer or employer, he becomes a thief, a sponge, a parasite, and an enemy to his country. Yet what else can he do under existing conditions? If he refuses to pay wages and accept rent and interest, he starves both himself and the workers and employers. If he does his share of the ordinary work of the world, he takes the bread out of the mouth of the laborer who would otherwise be paid for the job. If we are all to be gentlemen, then, as we cannot all write books or be Cabinet Ministers or officers in the army, or philosophers or discoverers or experimenters of one sort or another, we must also be navvies and carpenters and masons and engine drivers and dustmen and such like jolly things. But our stupid middle-class men do not think them at all jolly. They actually think it better to sit in an office day-in-day-out for thirty years, dictating the same letter in the same commercial jargon to different customers all wanting the same thing, than to make embankments and build houses and drive locomotives. When one of their sons has sense enough to revolt against the unnaturalness and absurdity of this hideous office life, he becomes some sort of artist, only to discover that dislike of commerce, though it is the first social instinct of a born gentleman, does not necessarily imply artistic talent.

To the middle-class man all this seems ridiculous, old-fashioned, and what, if he studies history, he calls feudal. His mind is bound like the feet of a Chinese lady; and he binds the minds of his children with the fanaticism of a Chinese mother. With ruin and destruction and waste all round him, and anxiety and the fear of bankruptcy and poverty always at his elbow, he persists in thinking that the commercial system not only works, but is the only practical system. It is hard to make him understand that it does not work and never has worked, and is, on the whole, the most miserable and short-lived failure of all the failures of history.

Last month I had to spend some time in the French city of Nancy. As it stands, it is very largely the work of the eighteenth-century aristocrat, Stanislas, ex-king of Poland, the sort of man the middle classes guillotined after the Revolution.[1] Nancy is a remarkably handsome town as far as Stanislas is responsible for it, with noble squares, golden gates, triumphal arches, broad spaces of air and visible sky instead of the dirty strips familiar to our city children, splendid public buildings, and statues and fountains that are at least pleasant, refined, and interesting, if they fall short of the deeper art of earlier centuries. Your middle-class man will come straight from some filthy hole created by his class and his system in the Potteries or in Lancashire, and gape at the style and dignity of Nancy without being in the least shaken in his conviction that the redemption of the world was effected when he and his like cut off the heads of Stanislas and his like. And if he reads in the museum, as I did, the municipal edicts of Stanislas, he will probably be too ignorant of the most elementary public business to know that they are almost word for word the sanitary by-laws which reformers are today trying to induce our middle-class local authorities to adopt, and which, even if adopted, could not be carried out because of our commercial system, as Mr Lloyd George will find out when he tries his pet scheme of forcing the landlords to put their houses in order, and finds the streets full of homeless people, turned out, in consequence of his improvements, to make room for "a better class of tenant" than existing commercial humanity. The truth is that if the spirit of Stanislas were as dead as his body, our system could not stand for a day: it would collapse under the oppression of its own stupidity and impracticability in as short a time as it takes to starve men into revolutionary desperation.

But if you could really make an end of Stanislas you would make an end of human society. What keeps the social fabric together at this moment, in spite of the disintegrating forces of Commericalism, is the fact that most things are still done in Stanislas's way, and not in the way of the Manchester school. The vulgar tradesman, when he has ignobly grabbed his millions and bought his seat in the House of Lords, or his knighthood, or his baronetcy, tries to live *en grand seigneur* as well as a man can who has had all the essential principles of feudal nobility carefully rubbed out of him, and all its besetting vices of self-deification and class rancor carefully rubbed into him from his cradle. But, these repentant-brigand millionaires could do nothing to save the situation, if it were not that the great mass of the people are still doing their feudal duty: that is, taking it as a matter of course that they should produce more than they consume, and accepting equal pay with all their fellows in the trade, or charging customary prices for customary articles and services, according to their notion of how a man in their station ought to live, without prating about the infinite diversity of their talents and characters, or clamoring for extra shillings under pretext of realizing that silliest, basest, and fortunately, most utterly impracticable of all Utopias, the Utopia in which each person gets paid in exact proportion to his personal qualities, duly estimated, no doubt, by a department of State phrenologists working in an anthropometric laboratory, and assisted occasionally on ethical points by the bench of bishops.

The really grave question today is whether the Labor movement means anything more than an attempt to put forward middle-class claims on behalf of the working class. If so, it will land the working classes in as horrible a mess as the middle-class hell politely called the United States of America. When the English working man resolves to be a gentleman (which includes the right to carry arms, by the way), he will be on the road to emancipation. But if he has only resolved to be a successful tradesman and have the full product of his labor to himself, he might be described as being on the road to the devil if it were possible to pretend that he is not there or thereabouts already. For what has been happening during my lifetime is the Americanization of the whole world. I have a personal interest in the process, because I know well that when it is complete, the middle-class tradesman will crush people like me just as the middle classes of France and Switzerland would have crushed Rousseau (for telling them the truth) if the French aristocrats and the King of Prussia had not protected him.

But I do not despair. America must and can be born again, and re-christened Whitmansland. My countryman, Goldsmith, informed an incredulous public in the eighteenth century that "honor sinks where commerce long prevails." In the seventeenth century Bunyan uttered the same warning against the growing power of "Mr Badman," *alias* Mr Middle-Class Tradesman. In the nineteenth century, Carlyle, Ruskin, and Morris took up the parable. And Bunyan, Carlyle, Ruskin, and Morris all came out of the trading class: Goldsmith, as the son of an Irish beneficed clergyman, being the only exception. Our titled persons, no longer a nobility, look enviously at the large gains of commerce, and strive to share them and to marry their children to the children of commercial millionaires. Our more prosperous working men hanker thoughtlessly after middle-class respectability, and are as convinced as anyone that Ruskin and Morris were fantastic dreamers. It is in the middle class itself that the revolt against middle-class ideals breaks out: that is why the revolt of Labor has taken place at the call of middle-class revolutionists. Neither peer nor laborer has ever hated the bourgeoisie as Marx hated it, nor despised its ideals as Swift, Ibsen, and Strindberg despised them, nor exposed its essential infidelity and its degradation and subornation of Christianity as Rousseau and Butler did. I defy any navvy, or any duke, to maul the middle class as Dickens mauled it, or as it is mauled today by Wells, Chesterton, Belloc, Pinero, Granville Barker, Galsworthy, Bennett, the young lions of the provincial repertory theatres, or

G. Bernard Shaw

Morning Post, *12 March 1913.*

The Case for Socialism

Socialism, translated into concrete terms, means equal division of the national income among all the inhabitants of the country, and the maintenance of that equal division as the invariable social postulate, the very root of the Constitution. The problem Socialism offers to the politician and the economist is how to make this postulate workable. At present we make it a social postulate that every inhabitant shall wear clothing whether he or she be rich or poor, sober or drunken, idle or industrious, honest or dishonest; consequently if any person has no clothes the State must provide them whether the clothed person can pay for them or not, the reason being that nakedness is an intolerable spectacle. Under Socialism the clothes would have in their pockets the quotient of the national income divided by the population, on the ground that pennilessness is intolerable, and that overwhelming economic, political, and biological evils are produced in society by inequality of income.

The Socialist has thus the advantage over our Parliamentary parties of knowing precisely what he is aiming at. Since Peel introduced our modern income tax in 1842, every Chancellor of the Exchequer has been engaged more or less in redistributing income by means of taxation. Sir William Harcourt's death duties and Mr Lloyd George's supertax have forced us to face the real nature of the process.[1] Mr Lloyd George knew what he was doing, as far as any Cabinet Minister ever knows what he is doing, which is perhaps not saying much. No attempt will be made to repeal the supertax by the next Unionist successor of Mr Lloyd George. The demand for redistribution of income is now an active motive force in the country, especially in the middle class; and it will soon be a fully conscious one. Yet neither Mr Lloyd George nor the Unionists who will have to carry on his work at the next swing of the pendulum have as yet asked themselves where they will stop. They instinctively raise cries: they never know what the cries mean. They support or oppose "the Budget." They propose "Land Reform." They no longer shy at "Minimum Wage." They regard these things as ends in themselves. But they are all means to the end of redistributing income. Sooner or later we shall have the parties bidding against oneanother for votes by promises of Redistribution Bills; and Redistribution will mean, not Redistribution of Seats, but Redistribution of Income.

When the question becomes as definite as that, the parties will have to make up their minds as to the proportion in which income is to be distributed. The man who thinks that the Astronomer Royal should have less than his grocer; that his grocer should have less than the King; that the King should have less than a Beef Baron or a Steel President; that a widow with six children dependent on her labor should have less than her bachelor brother, and so forth, will finally have to say how much less, and why.

The Socialist is the only man who has already made up his mind on these points and concluded, or rather foreseen, that the only permanently possible proportions are equal proportions. Socialism is sometimes described as Collective Ownership and Control of the Means of Production, Distribution, and Exchange. But this is a necessary part of any system of distribution except our system of property and competition, which is not a system at all, but the abandonment of our livelihood to a private scramble in which so many get nothing that it cannot be called distribution at all, and so many get next to nothing that they are not satisfied. When you begin, as you presently must, to interfere with this scramble by establishing a Poor Law, taxing rent and interest, imposing humane conditions on factory owners, fixing wages by law, and supporting the unemployed, the scramble gets out of hand, because certain farms, mines, and industrial concerns are only just worth working when labor is sweated to the last degree of human endurance, and is forced to submit by the alternative of starvation. Such enterprises are said to be "on the margin of cultivation." If we suppress the alternative of starvation and protect the workers in these marginal industries from sweating by Factory Acts and Minimum Wage Acts and the like, they are no longer worth working. They are abandoned; and the protected workers find themselves starving in the streets.

Here politicians will point to actual experience, and say that, as a matter of fact, this does not happen. It does not happen at first. The first effect of palliative legislation, which never ventures very far, is to compel the proprietors to set their wits to work to increase the product by introducing new methods, speeding-up old ones, and putting more brains and capital into the concern generally. It is then found that workers produce more in ten hours than they did in twelve; that railway traffic managers forced by law to work on the block system find out that it is possible to run expresses within two minutes of oneanother instead of ten: in short, that sweating does not pay as well as the philanthropy of Bournville and Port Sunlight.[2] But when the most economical methods have been made general by the pressure of palliative legislation, it will be found that perfect economy has its margin as well as sweating, and sooner or later the point vainly prophesied by Nassau Senior and other old-fashioned economists will be reached, and the palliative legislation will make the marginal concerns unworkable. If such concerns are to stand minimum wage, shortening of hours, and the other improved conditions of labor which are cheerfully borne and sometimes even voluntarily established in the concerns which have plenty of rent, interest, and profits to cut into, all the concerns in the trade must be pooled, so that the big surpluses in the middle of the pool may cover the deficits at the margin. This pooling is Collectivism, and this is how ameliorative and redistributive politics—"Socialistic legislation," as they are called—are driving us to Collectivism.

But pooling is a well-established capitalistic process as well as a proletarian one. The Trust is a pooling of all the concerns in an industry. Pooling is good for the marginal investor, the marginal landlord, and the marginal employer, just as Factory Acts and Minimum Wage Acts are good for the marginal workman. Thus the stars in their courses seem to fight for Collectivism. It has the support and advertisement of The Times as well as of The Labor

Leader, of The Morning Post as well as of The Clarion. The louder the outcry against Socialism, the busier its enemies are in reconstructing the industrial organization to suit its purposes. The most resolute defenders of property in the abstract are energetically throwing their own properties into great common stocks and depending for their livelihood on entries in bank passbooks. The air resounds with cries of "Atheist, Free-Lover, Thief, Scoundrel, Assassin: have it your own way: we are building up the Collectivism you demand whilst you are raving at street corners." Well may the Bishop of Oxford³ say that "no one can persuade him that there is not a Providence at work in the great movement we call Democracy." I quite agree with the Bishop.

But Collectivism is not Socialism. We have pooled the London water companies, the London bridges, and the telephones, just as we shall presently pool the railways; but the income they yield is distributed as unequally and absurdly as ever. I am a railway shareholder, and should be very glad to have the railways nationalized, as it would mean, in effect, Government security for the income I get from the money you, dear reader, pay for your tickets. Complete Collectivism is quite compatible with the maintenance of privileged classes and rich idle classes at the expense of a proletariat in which the hewers of wood and drawers of water would receive barely enough to keep them alive when their work was needed, and be flung into the gutter to starve or into the common workhouse when it was not needed. It is that possibility that lures the Unsocialist into the paths of Collectivism, and finally induces him to urge forward the work of replacing our scramble, in which Socialism is impossible, with a Collectivism in which Socialism is just as possible as Unsocialism, and much more probable.

The struggle will come over the distribution of the product of Collectivism. At present we need not compel anyone to work, because if he does not he will starve unless he is a man of property. But guarantee him an income from the day of his birth to the day of his death, and hold firmly to the resolve that, whatever else you will allow him to be, you will not allow him to be poor, and you will be forced to find some means of making him work on pain of national bankruptcy. You dare not, under such conditions, tolerate a single ablebodied idler, male or female, or encourage a morality which places idle extravagance above industrious energy. The ridiculous German anomaly of allowing a man to shirk civil service on the ground that he has an independent income, whilst the possession of a thousand billions will not exempt him from military service, will explode itself: the Germans will shoot a man for idling as they now shoot him for cowardice in the field. And when every man must get his quota and earn it, of what use will it be to be spacious in the possession of dirt or dividends? Pooh Bah[4] will then be in the position of the Irishman who took a sedan chair and found that there was no bottom to it. "But for the honor and glory of the thing I might as well have walked."

When Collectivism has gone far enough to make Socialism possible we shall come to those overwhelming objections to inequality of income, a statement of which would be too long for the few hours which limit a daily newspaper's life. Fortunately equal incomes are too familiar as a fact to be incredible as a theory, except to the handful of people who live on the haphazard gains of property or exceptional talent instead of on the regular wage of average labor, which takes account of status, but not of personality. Our present rule is, and always has been, equal incomes for all in the same rank. Democracy means that rank shall not carry privilege, and that all classes shall become one class politically. And "politically" will mean industrially under Collectivism. When there is one class it will seem quite natural that there should be one income. Even I, who, on the basis of personal ability, should, I suppose, have about fifty thousand times the income of an average member of the House of Lords (as conceived by the Radical Press) do not object. And if I am satisfied, who has any right to complain?

Verbatim report of an address delivered before the Political and Economic Circle of the National Liberal Club on Thursday, 1 May 1913. Published in the New York Metropolitan, *December 1913, in pamphlet form (Part 85 of the* Transactions of the National Liberal Club: Political and Economic Circle) *on 9 January 1914, and in* The Socialism of Bernard Shaw, *edited by James Fuchs (1926).*

The Case for Equality

When I speak of The Case for Equality I mean human equality; and that, of course, can only mean one thing: it means equality of income. It means that if one person is to have half-a-crown, the other is to have two and sixpence. It means that precisely. You, Mr Chairman, have spoken of equality of opportunity. The difficulty about that is that it is entirely and completely and eternally impossible. How are you going to give everybody in this room equal opportunities with me of writing plays? The thing is, I say, a ghastly mockery. In one sense it might be said: "Well, any of us are welcome to try our hands at play-writing." I might say that and smile. But I am quite safe in saying that to the majority of you it is just exactly like saying to a beggar: "Well, my friend, Mr Barnato made a large fortune: you have the same opportunities as Mr Barnato; go and make that fortune," at which Mr Barnato would smile; but it is of no use at all to the beggar.[1] The fact is that you cannot equalize anything about human beings except their incomes. If in dealing with the subject you would only begin by facing that fact, it would save you a very great deal of trouble in the form of useless speculation. I have chosen this subject for tonight because it is an extremely practical and important political subject. You have been for a long time using the power of Parliament to redistribute income in this country more or less. The very moment the Income Tax was introduced by Sir Robert Peel, somewhere in the 'forties—1842, I think—from that moment you were beginning to effect a redistribution of income. If you just glance over the subsequent succession of Chancellors of the Exchequer, you will find them all redistributing income unconsciously, until you come to Sir William Harcourt with his death duties, Mr Asquith with his discrimination between earned and unearned income, and Mr Lloyd George with his Supertax, all doing it consciously.[2] The object of super-taxation, and the object of the threatened land taxation, is to effect a further redistribution of income in this country. There is another point which has not been quite so closely observed as that. The working classes have been using their power, at first indirectly, and of late years directly through the Labor Party in Parliament, to effect a redistribution. This used to be a redistribution in kind. Instead of getting money, the working classes got municipal dwellings; they got education; they got sanitation; they got the clearing away of slum areas; and this mass of municipal work was largely paid for by rating richer people than themselves, and by grants-in-aid, which came from the Income Tax, from which the working classes were exempt themselves. Thus they were deliberately transferring wealth from one class to another by Parliamentary power. They were redistributing part of the national income, and diverting it in their own direction. This went on for many years; but a few years ago they took an entirely new departure. Instead of saying, "We will get more schools out of you; we will get more houses out of you; we will get more plumber's work out of you," they suddenly took the step which was sooner or later inevitable, and said: "We will have some money out of you. We will have some money straight out of your pockets into our pockets to do what we like with." There was an apparent precedent for this in Poor Law outdoor relief, or the giving of public money to poor persons on the ground that they are poor. But when you passed Old Age Pensions, then, for the first time, you had money paid down without regard to the differences between one person and another. It was not given exclusively to the people who were poor, except that there was a certain limit of income, which was really rather a concession to the snobbery of the people who did not like to take it than a real essential difference of principle. The fact remains that a few years ago the Chancellor of the Exchequer began to put his hand into the national pocket, and to give every person aged seventy of the working class, without reference to his ability or sex, if he claimed it and had not a certain income at the time he claimed it, the sum of 5s. a week. The recipients of that 5s. a week included among them every possible variety of character. They all have exactly the sum of 5s. a week, no more and no less. Here is a process which has begun, and a process which we all know is going to go on. We know that that 5s. a week will not remain at 5s. a week. We know that it will be presently 10s. a week (Dissent.) I should have thought that every-body here present would know that in New Zealand at the present time it is 10s. a week; and that the Labor Party knows it; and that it is 10s. a week at an earlier age than the age of seventy. If any man present is simple enough to believe that it is going to stay at 5s. a week, I ask him to retire to the smoking-room downstairs, because he is congenitally (I must say it, though I say it without malice) incapable of understanding any address that I possibly can give. I take it now you are all convinced that it will not stay at 5s. a week; and I hope there will be no hesitation about this also: that the Supertax is not going to remain at what it is at present. I think you must all admit, though some of you may deplore it, that the Super-tax is going to go up, which means a further redistribution of income in this country.

Having put the matter on a thoroughly practical basis, I now want to ask you whether you have made up your mind what is going to be the final result of this process; because if you are not like the mere opportunists who are outside the Political and Economic Circle and in the smoking-room downstairs—if you re-ally are serious in your pretensions as members of this Circle, you must either have made up your minds already on that point, or you must be in the process of making up your minds; you must be asking yourselves what is the final level to be? I am here tonight to say that I have quite made up my mind as to the only possible solution of the question. I am going to shew you that my solution, which is the solution of an equal distribution, is one which has overwhelming practical arguments in its favor.

Perhaps the strongest argument to people who are not very fond of abstract thought, is that equality of income is the only plan that has ever been successful, the only plan that has ever been possible. It is the plan that has always prevailed; and it is prevalent at the present time to a greater extent than any other rule of distribution. The moment you begin to try and think of any other, you are met with such difficulties and such absurdities that, however reluctant you may be to come to the solution of equality, you are finally driven to it by the elimination of every other solution, except, of course, the solution of the mere brute scramble that we have at the present time. If you take our Civil Service and our Military Service, you find that equal pay is the rule. If you take our trades, you will find that equal pay is the rule. Wherever you turn you find in every class of society a certain conception of what constitutes a becoming livelihood in that class of society; and everybody in it aims at and claims an income representing that standard. Nobody seriously asks to have more than the other persons of his class. Every soldier of the same rank gets practically the same pay; every policeman of the same rank gets the same pay; every colonel gets the same pay; every general gets the same pay; and every judge gets £5,000 a year. You do not find Mr Justice Darling getting up and saying: "I really think that because I have put a little humor into the proceedings, I ought to have an extra allowance."[3] Nor do you find that the judges who put a little extra stupidity and cruelty into the proceedings, ever suggest that their salaries should be reduced on that ground; nor do the people who admire and uphold their cruelty and stupidity propose that they should get any more.

Now supposing you do not agree, supposing you think there should be some other standard applied to men, I ask you not to waste time arguing about it in the abstract, but bring it down to a concrete case at once. Let me take a very obvious case. I am an exceedingly clever man. There can be absolutely no question at all in my case that in some ways I am above the average of mankind in talent. You laugh; but I presume you are not laughing at the fact, but only because I do not bore you with the usual modest cough, and pretend to consider myself stupid. Very well. Take myself as an absolute, unquestionable case. Now pick out somebody not quite so clever. How much am I to have, and how much is he to have? I notice a blank expression on your countenances. You are utterly unable to answer the question. In order to do so, you would have to compare us in some quantitative way. You would have to treat human capacity as a measurable thing; but you know perfectly well it is not a measurable thing. Taking some person whom we will call x, an average man, you may think I am fifty times as clever as x; and you may think that I, perhaps, ought to have fifty times as big an income. But if anybody asks you: "Where did you get that numerator of fifty from, and what does your denominator represent?" you will be compelled to give it up. You cannot settle it. The thing is impossible. You cannot do it. Every attempt you make in that way reduces itself to absurdity in your hands; and that silly dream of the nineteenth century which began with: "The career open to the talents,"[4] the idea that every man could get his value; all that is the vainest Utopian dream; and the most ridiculous, the most impracticable idea that ever came into the heads of men. The reason it has been talked about so much, is that the people who were talking about it had no serious intention of ever bringing it into practice and never pleaded it in practice except as an excuse for giving somebody less than themselves. It would have been far more sensible to go at the question in the old mystic, religious way; when you would have immediately seen that all human souls are of infinite value, and all infinities equal.

It is now plain that if you are going to have any inequalities of income, they must be arbitrary inequalities. You must say flatly that certain persons are to have more than others, giving no reason for it. I am quite sure again, from the expression of your faces, that you have not any reasons. Well, I will give you one. As you know, obedience and subordination are necessary in society. You cannot have a civilized society unless tolerably large bodies of men are willing to obey other men, even by executing orders that they do not themselves understand. That is the real foundation of our traditional feudal inequality. In order to make a common man obey some other man, you had to take some means of making that other man an uncommon man; and the simplest way was to set him apart from common men by giving him more money, by putting him in a different sort of dress, by making him live in a different sort of house, by setting up a convention that under no circumstances could his son marry the daughter of the common man, or the common man's son marry his daughter. In short, you resorted to idolatry to secure subordination in society; for the man so set apart became literally an idol. I do not deny that idolatry served its turn; but I suggest to you that modern democracy and modern conditions are exploding it. The very idols themselves have made the fatal mistake of allowing the invention of photography and the half-tone process to destroy the glamor on which the whole social structure is based. So long as you have a peer or millionaire who is known only by name and by reputation, people may believe him to be a great man, quite unlike themselves; but the moment you put his portrait into the papers, it is all up: the shew is given away. The time has gone by for the old privacy, the old mystery, the old seclusion; that is how our idols are beginning to get found out in all directions. The whole movement of Liberalism in the history of the world—I do not mean the Liberalism of Parliament, or the Liberalism even of this Club, which, as you know, has very little to do with Liberalism at all—the history of Liberalism in the world, when you understand it thoroughly, has been the history of Iconoclasm. In America they will not allow their ambassadors to put on the uniform that European ambassadors wear; and they will not allow their judges to assume the ridiculous costume our judges put on to persuade people that a judge is not a man, but Justice incarnate; and they do not allow their President to put a crown on his head, in order to produce illusions as to its interior. I think you will admit that nowadays, in spite of the costumes of our judges, and in spite of our crowns, there is very little of such illusion left. As a matter of fact, the popularity of our last two monarchs has been due, I think you will agree with me, not at all to a belief in them as extraordinary and supernatural persons, but to the precisely contrary belief in them as rather good fellows, much like ourselves. I am glad you agree with me; because that disposes of the last and only argument in favor of inequality of income: absolutely the last and only one.

Now I come to the objections to inequality, which have been too little considered in this country. I am going to shew you that there is an overwhelming political objection to it. I will then shew you that there is a still more overwhelming economic objection to it; and I will finish by shewing you that there is a biological objection to it which, in my opinion, outweighs all the others. Let us begin with the political objection. As long as you have inequality of income, you may have Franchise Acts, and you may have votes for men, and votes for women, and you may have votes for babies if you like, but there will be no such thing as real democracy in this country. There will be class government of the very worst description. There will be class government based on plutocracy, as there is at the present time; and there will be no possible real representation of the people in Parliament. It does not matter how high the characters of the members may stand. I will take two gentlemen who are at the head of Parliamentary life at the present time. Take Mr Asquith on the one hand, and Mr Balfour on the other. How can Mr Balfour or Mr Asquith represent men with £300 a year; much less men with £50 or £60 a year? How can they pursue in Parliament the interests of men with only a very small fragment of their income? I say, furthermore, that even if they wanted to do it, they would not be let do it. I say they are subject to public opinion. I say that public opinion is manufactured at the present time by newspapers; and I say that the newspapers are absolutely in the hands of the plutocracy. The extent to which they are in the hands of the plutocracy I could illustrate in fifty ways; but you cannot be so destitute of intelligence—I have no right to assume that you are lacking in intelligence at all—as not to feel this every day of your life. If you do not feel it, there is nothing that I could say which would convince you of it; but the extent to which our newspapers are under the personal control of the plutocracy, I may illustrate by a harmless little incident.

A little while ago I had the pleasure of holding a public debate in Queen's Hall with Mr Hilaire Belloc. It was reported at some length in all the newspapers of London. It was considered an event of sufficient public importance to occupy from one to three columns—the three columns were in a highly conservative paper in London. All over the country the newspapers had reports. But there were two papers that made absolutely no mention of the debate. One of them was The Times and the other was The Daily Mail. It has remained a profound mystery why those papers took absolutely no notice of a debate of which they were informed; and at which they were represented by their reporters. The only conjecture that was made on the subject was based on the fact that one of the speakers, by an unfortunate slip, mentioned Lord Northcliffe not as Lord Northcliffe but as Mr Harmsworth.[5] Now, gentlemen, I am not so absurd as to suppose that Lord Northcliffe went down to the offices of those two papers of his, and said: "This blasphemer has called me 'Mr Harmsworth,' as if I were not Lord Northcliffe; never mention him in my papers again." I do not believe anything of the kind; but I am perfectly prepared to believe that the gentlemen in his employment may have been so under the influence of Lord Northcliffe's position, and may have been themselves so unjustly mistrustful of Lord Northcliffe's breadth of mind, that they may have thought it safer on the whole not to mention the debate, in which they would have had to report that deplorable slip; and so got out of the difficulty by not mentioning it at all. Any of you who are in public life must know that the moment you take part in any anti-plutocractic movement you are boycotted by the newspapers. Nothing is reported and worked up in the newspapers except the interests of the plutocracy. Those papers form public opinion. Public opinion cannot be formed in any other way. The consequence is that you have no genuinely popular government in this country. I will give you just one other instance which comes back to my memory: it is also a personal one. I once went to a meeting on the temperance question. That meeting was addressed by me; and it was addressed by a bishop. Under ordinary circumstances, when a meeting is addressed by me and addressed by a bishop, the bishop is very fully reported; and I am somewhat briefly reported. On this occasion, it happened that I said something (being a life-long teetotaller, and the meeting talking a great deal of nonsense about publicans) in defense of the publican. The bishop did not speak in defense of the publican. He spoke in the conventional manner against the liquor trade. The consequence was that in The Times next day my speech was reported at full length; and the only thing that was mentioned about the bishop was that "the Bishop of Kensington then addressed the meeting." When Bishop Gore, who was then Bishop of Birmingham, delivered a most eloquent protest in London against the assumption that political science, any more than religion, was on the side of industrial sweating, he fared worse than the Bishop of Kensington; for he was not mentioned at all except by one morning paper, which shortly afterwards changed its editor.

Gentlemen, leaving the question of the Press, you know that every one of you wants to get into Parliament. I have never yet met a member of the National Liberal Club who did not intend to get into Parliament at some time, except those who, like our Chairman, are there already. Well, most of you will get no further than taking part in other men's election meetings. You will hardly ever have an opportunity of speaking on behalf of a man who really represents your opinions. Nine times out of ten, for the sake of what you call the Liberal Party, you will be speaking on behalf of a rich man. You will be answering for his magnificent Liberal principles; you will be explaining his views on the Welsh Church, and on Home Rule, and on Free Trade. And the gentleman on whose behalf you are speaking, and who will be returned if your oratory is successful, will be sitting there on the platform wondering what on earth you are talking about, but perfectly prepared to foot the bill, to pay the expenses, to bribe the constituency on the chance of getting into Parliament. Doubtless, when he gets into Parliament, he will go into whatever lobby the Liberal whip tells him is the proper lobby to go into. That is what you get in the shape of democracy; and that is all you ever will get as long as you have inequality of income.

Now I come to the economic objection; and you will all now please put on your best expressions, being all of you political economists. Now, Gentlemen, I am really a political economist. I have studied the thing. I understand Ricardo's law of rent and Jevons's law of value. I can also tell you what in its essence sound economy means for any nation. It means, Gentlemen, just what sound economy means for any individual; and that is that whatever powers the individual has of purchasing or producing, shall be exercised in the order of his most vital needs. Let me illustrate. Suppose you find a man starving in the streets. You are sympathetic: you give that man sixpence. Suppose that man, instead of buying some bread and eating it, buys a bottle of scent to perfume his handkerchief with, and then dies of starvation, but with the satisfaction of having his handkerchief perfumed! You will admit that that man is an unsound economist, will you not? You will even declare that he is a lunatic? Well, allow me to tell you, Gentlemen, that is exactly what this country is doing at the present time. It is spending very large sums on perfuming its handkerchief while it is starving, and while it is rotting. How are you going to remedy that? As long as you have inequality of income, that mad state of things is compulsory. If one man has not enough money to feed his children properly, and another man has so much that after feeding and clothing and lodging himself and his family as luxuriously as possible he has still a large surplus fund, you will find that the richer man will take his surplus purchasing power into the market, and by that purchasing power set the labor of the country, which ought to be devoted to producing more food for people who have not enough food, to the production of 80 horsepower motor cars, and yachts and jewels, and boxes at the opera, and to the construction of such towns as Nice and Monte Carlo. The thing is inevitable. Production is determined by purchasing power and always will be. If you were to attempt to do away with money and with purchasing power, then you would have, in order to satisfy your nation, to ascertain what every man particularly wants and likes;

and, as that would be impossible, you would have to give every man exactly the same thing, with the consequence that the man who wanted a racehorse as a luxury would get a gramophone, and the man who wanted a gramophone would get a racehorse. In order to enable men to determine production according to their own tastes, you must give a man his income in the shape of purchasing power. By that purchasing power he determines production; and if you allow the purchasing power of one class to fall below the level of the vital necessities of subsistence, and at the same time allow the purchasing power of another class to rise considerably above it into the region of luxuries, then you find inevitably that those people with that superfluity determine production to the output of luxuries, while at the same time the necessities that are wanted at the other end cannot be sold, and are therefore not produced. I have put it as shortly as possible; but that is the economic argument in favor of equality of income. All the arguments which have been brought forward against it, and all the more personal considerations in favor of inequality, seem to me, as an economist, to be practically swept away by the overwhelming weight of that economic objection.

I now come to the biological reasons for equality. I do not know, Gentlemen, what may be the outcome of your experience in progressive political work, but I must confess to you here that I, having devoted more than thirty years, the most active part of my life, to political questions in their most serious aspect—not to the ridiculous game, not half as interesting as golf, which you call party politics and with which you debauch your intellects and waste your time, but to the genuine problems of the condition of the country and the condition of the people: in short, to the life of the country—I must confess to you that all my experience and all my thought on the subject have left me with very grave doubts as to whether mankind, as it exists at present, is capable of solving the political and economic problems which are presented to the human race by its own multitudinous numbers. If you take a few persons like ourselves, and put them into a new colony, in a climate which is not too rough, to make little pioneer villages like the pioneer villages in the days before Capitalism overwhelmed America, in that village you may get a reasonable and decent kind of life, a rough life, but a natural life; not in any very high sense a civilized life, and certainly not a cultured life; but a tolerably human kind of life. But the moment you attempt to go beyond the village stage, the moment you attempt to create the complicated political, social, and industrial organization required by our great modern empires and cities, the human constituents of these communities are hopelessly beaten by the problems created by that organization, and by their own numbers. Our House of Commons, to do it justice, does not even pretend to know what it is legislating about. Read its speeches on the subject, and you will find that it practically gives up the problem. It goes on in a hand-to-mouth fashion trying to remedy grievances, making five or six new messes every time it clears up an old one. You see measure after measure brought out, accompanied by extensions of the franchise; but all the time we are going more deeply into the mire, and increasing the evils I have been fighting all my life. Although people are constantly assuming that these evils are being got rid of, I assure you that they are not being got rid of at all; and the reason of that, it seems to me, is that we are not capable of getting rid of them. We are a stupid people; and we are a bad-looking people. We are ugly; we have narrow minds; and we have bad manners. A great deal of that is due to the effect of being brought up in a society of inequality. I know perfectly well what happened to myself. I can remember one of my earliest experiences in life was my father finding me playing with a certain little boy in the street, and telling me I was not to play with that little boy, giving me to understand that he was a very inferior and objectionable kind of little boy. I had not found him so. I asked my father "Why?" He said: "His father keeps a shop." I said to my father: "Well, but you keep a mill." Therefore my father pointed out to me that he sold things wholesale, and that this little boy's father sold things retail; and that, consequently, there was between me and that boy a gulf which could never be respectably bridged; and that it was part of my duty and part of my honor to regard that boy as an inferior, which I did ever after, in so far as I could safely do so, having regard to the fact that the boy was a more vigorous and larger boy than myself. I was also taught, being an Irish Protestant boy, what Protestant children are habitually taught in Ireland: that the great bulk of my fellow countrymen, being Roman Catholics, were condemned to eternal damnation. Perhaps you can see that this was blasphemy; but in my opinion the doctrine that the wholesaler should excommunicate the retailer was a much more dangerous blasphemy. At all events, when you are brought up, as you inevitably are in a society like ours, with that sort of blasphemy being continually dinned into your ears; when you are taught to be unsocial at every point, and brought up to be unsocial, then any little chance that your natural endowments at your birth may have left you of being able to grapple with the enormous problems of our modern civilization—problems that demand from you the largest scope of mind, the most unhesitating magnanimity, the most sacred recognition of your spiritual and human equality with every person in the nation—is utterly destroyed. That is why I doubt whether these problems can be solved by us, brought up in that way. To solve them, you need a new sort of human being.

And now we have come to what we call Eugenics. Ever since the time of Plato—and I dare say the subject was practically as old in Plato's time as it is now—sensible men have always said: "Why cannot we breed men with the same care that we breed horses?" (Hear, hear.) Several gentlemen say "Hear, hear." Have they ever tried it? You must always test yourselves, when you have these ideas, by asking yourselves how would you begin. Suppose we could go as a deputation to Parliament, and were allowed to address Parliament at the bar of the House, and impressed them with the importance of this problem to such an extent that they passed an Act and sent it through the Lords, and got the Royal Assent, indemnifying us and giving us power practically, we here, to make an attempt at breeding; to pick out a mother and father and try to produce a better sort of human being; we should not know where to begin. You see it is all very well when you come to breed a horse, because when you want to breed a horse you know the sort of horse you want. If you want a racehorse, all you care about is that the horse should be a very fast horse. If you want a draught horse, you know that all you want is a powerful horse. You do not bother about the horse's soul; you do not bother very much about its temper; you do not care whether it is a good horse in the pulpit sense of the word. You want a horse that will go round a racecourse in a shorter time than any other horse. Or you want a horse that will carry a hundredweight more than any other horse you can get hold of. It is quite simple, because you know the sort of horse you want. But do you know the sort of man you want? You do not. You have not the slightest idea. You do not even know how to begin. You say: "Well, after all, we do not want an epileptic. We do not want an alcoholic." (It is a barbarous word, but drunken people are now called alcoholics.) But for all you know to the contrary, the superman may be a self-controlled epileptic fed exclusively on proof spirit, and consuming perhaps ten gallons a day. You laugh; but the thing is entirely possible. You do not know what a healthy man is. All your doctors are not able to tell you. All they can tell you is that if you bring them a healthy man, they will very soon have him in bed. Still less do you know, Gentlemen, what is a good man. Take a vote as to whether I am a good man or not. Some people will tell you that my goodness is almost beyond that of any other living person. They will even tell you that I am the only hope of religion in this country. You will not have to go very far to find persons who are of exactly the contrary opinion. I tell you that you really do not know. I think the very first thing you have to do is to face the fact that you do not know, and that in the nature of things you never can know. Your capacity does not run to it. You have no clue, as far as your own judgment is concerned; and, therefore, you are thrown back on the clue that Nature gives you.

Let me propose to you an experiment which I am always proposing to large audiences in this country. I ask you tomorrow in the afternoon, if it is a fine afternoon, to walk down Park Lane or Bond or Oxford Street, or any well-frequented thoroughfare, and to look carefully at all the women you see coming along and to take a note of how many of those women you would care to be married to. If we are to judge by the utterances of some of our Moral Reform Societies, the members, when they walk down Oxford Street, are so wildly and irresistibly attracted by every woman they meet, old or young, that nothing but the severest and most stringent laws restrain them from instant rapine. I cannot imagine how any man gets himself into such a deplorable condition of mind as to believe that this is true of himself, much less of any other sane human being. There may be some men of low type, who are nearly indiscriminate in their appetites; but I am perfectly certain, with regard to the great majority of men, that they may very often walk down Oxford Street without meeting one single woman to whom they could tolerate the idea of being married; and they will in any case be fortunate (because I like the sensation when it comes to me) if, on the most crowded day and in the finest weather, they meet two women for whom they feel that curious physiological attraction which we all recognize as the sex attraction. That attraction means something. If that attraction meant something destructive and ruinous to the human race, the human race would have been wiped out of existence long ago. It is what you call the Voice of Nature. You fall in love as the saying is. You see a woman whom you have never spoken to, about whom you know absolutely nothing at all; you do not know her character, and you do not know her aims; but you look at her and fall in love with her. If you were a free person in a free society, you would feel very strongly in love with her; but nowadays you seldom feel more than that timid little—what shall I call it?—sort of sinking feeling, which is about as much as, in our present society, is left of any of our natural emotions. But you do feel some attraction. My contention is that this attraction is the only clue you have to the breeding of the human race, and I do not believe you will ever have any improvement in the human race until you greatly widen the area of possible sexual selection; until you make it as wide as the numbers of the community make it. Just consider what occurs at the present time. I walk down Oxford Street, let me say, as a young man. I see a woman who takes my fancy. I fall in love with her. It would seem very sensible, in an intelligent community, that I should take off my hat and say to this lady: "Will you excuse me; but you attract me very strongly, and if you are not already engaged, would you mind taking my name and address and considering whether you would care to marry me?" Now I have no such chance at present. Probably when I meet that woman, she is either a charwoman and I cannot marry her, or else she is a duchess and she will not marry me. I have purposely taken the charwoman and the duchess; but we cut matters much finer than that. We cut our little class distinctions, all founded upon inequality of income, so narrow and so small that I have time and again spoken to English audiences of all classes throughout the Kingdom, and I have said to every man and woman in the audience: "You know perfectly well that when it came to your turn to be married, you had not, as a young man or a young woman, the choice practically of all the unmarried young people of your own age in our forty million population to choose from. You had at the outside a choice of two or three; and you did not like any of them very particularly as compared to the one you might have chosen, if you had had a larger choice." That is a fact which you gentlemen with your knowledge of life cannot deny. The result is that you have, instead of a natural evolutionary sexual selection, a class selection which is really a money selection. Is it to be wondered at that you have an inferior and miserable breed under such circumstances? I believe that this goes home more to the people than any other argument I can bring forward. I have impressed audiences with that argument who were entirely unable to grasp the economic argument in the way you are able to grasp it, and who were indifferent to the political arguments. I say, therefore, that if all the other arguments did not exist, the fact that equality of income would have the effect of making the entire community intermarriageable from one end to the other, and would practically give a young man and young woman his or her own choice right through the population—I say that that argument only, with the results which would be likely to accrue in the improvement of the race, would carry the day.

I am sorry there are no ladies present here. There ought to have been, to have full justice done to the last argument. But the final argument which prevails with me is that it is half-past nine. I hope I have given you enough to talk about for some little time. I hope you understand that equality means equality of income. In justification of equality of income, I have given you a political argument, I have given you an economic argument, I have given you a biological argument; and now make what you can of it.

[At this point, four members of the National Liberal Club—John A. Hobson, Roger C. Richards, Arnold Lupton, and Richard Whiteing—responded to Shaw's remarks. Hobson contended that, although a minimum standard of food and clothing for all individuals was an estimable goal, equality of income would not bring mankind to that standard. Human beings, he argued, are not equally capable of making good use of income just as they are not equally capable of assimilating the same size portions of food nor equally capable of dressing well. Different capacities, in brief, necessitate different levels of income, an opinion, Hobson said, which was shared by many intelligent men in the Independent Labor Party. Richards took exception to Shaw's criticism of the "human material" in the House of Commons, reminding the audience of Gladstone's words, "We must work with the instruments we have got." He also quarreled with two other points made by Shaw: first, that it would be wise to equalize purchasing power since purchasing power determines production, and second, that sexual attraction is a safe guide to improving the species. Richards answered the first by asserting that "it is perfectly possible that when a man is spending his wealth on motor cars, he is indirectly increasing the purchasing power of those people who are making the motor car" and the second by pointing out that, while it is generally agreed that consumptives are among the most sexually attractive people, their offspring can hardly be considered an improvement of the species. Lupton reminded the audience that the strong state was made possible by inequalities of income. By skillfully employing their money, the rich, Lupton maintained, were responsible for the increase in scientific knowledge; and the technological advances resulting from scientific experiments, in turn, were responsible for the success of a nation such as Britain. Whiteing rejected Shaw's biological argument for equality. He said that it was impossible to determine with any certainty the product which might result from a given sexual union. Using Pen Browning, the son of Robert and Elizabeth Barrett Browning, as an example, Whiteing maintained that geniuses do not necessarily produce a genius.[6] Regarding the distribution of income, Whiteing insisted that the best course of action was to follow Proudhon's formula: "From every one according to his powers, to every one according to his needs." This formula, he argued, was better than the mean notion of not working except for financial reward suggested by Arnold Bennett in *The Truth about an Author.*]

Mr Bernard Shaw: Mr Chairman and Gentlemen: One of the interesting points in the debate to me is this: that I am supposed to be addressing a Liberal assembly, and yet the first gentleman, my friend Mr Hobson, who stands up, apparently with a sort of vague idea that he ought to oppose me, takes the most extreme anti-Liberal position that it is possible for any human being to take. What Mr Hobson advocates is distribution to people of what? Let me say *x* quantity of commodities which are good and proper for them. Who is to decide what is good and proper for them? Mr Hobson tells us, by way of illustration, that some people do not know how to wear clothes properly. In whose opinion? Mr Hobson's, clearly. But Mr Hobson's taste cannot bind nations. It shews how entirely Liberalism must have departed from the atmosphere of this Club, that a man should have been able to fall back here on this old, vague notion that you can settle everything by getting some person or other to decide what is good and what is proper. Let me take another expression used by Mr Hobson. He said in effect: "Are people equal in making good use of their income? They are not, and therefore what you have to do is to give more to the people who make a good use of their income than to the people who make a bad use of it." He, apparently, has not considered who is to decide the remarkable and important point: What is a good use of one's income? If there is anything in Liberalism at all, it is the repudiation of the pretension of certain persons to determine for other persons whether they are acting properly or becomingly, or not. My reply on the whole to Mr Hobson is, that he is in the wrong Club, or he would be if this were a Liberal Club. I leave you to consider that dilemma.

There was another very important thing said by Mr Hobson; and it was a true thing, although he did not put it quite in what I call an accurate way. He said that the Labor men themselves—he has been talking to a member of the Independent Labor Party, he tells us—are revolting against this simple doctrine of equality. They are not revolting against it, because it has never been preached to them. It is not part of their doctrine. But it is quite true that Labor is now getting more and more political power; and the important fact you have to face is that the Labor men are not gentlemen; that is to say, that they have been trained up for generations in the idea and habit of each man selling himself for as much as he can get. The consequence is they are thoroughly against this idea of equal distribution. Every man of them thinks that he should have more than somebody else. Every mechanic may think that he should have the trade union rate with the other mechanics. Every fitter may think so. But suggest that the laborer should have it, and hear what he says! These are the men into whose hands, by exploiting them, by selling them in the market, you have hammered from their very birth this abominable idea that men should be bought and sold according to what can be got out of them. These are the men who are gradually waking up to the fact that political power is within their reach as soon as they make up their minds to give up idolizing the upper classes and to make use of their power. That is not a cheerful prospect to me. I am trying, as far as I possibly can, to introduce the sounder and juster ideal of economic equality, and to shew the utter and final impossibility of going on with the plan of every man trying to get as much as he can, and a little more than other people. Does Mr Hobson look upon that plan with any real complacency after devoting his life to studying the evils that have been created by that system? I cannot understand it, especially in a man of Mr Hobson's really public-spirited character.

Now I come to Mr Richards. Mr Richards began by saying I have no constructive scheme. How does he know? I came here to put before you the Case for Equality; and I put the case for equality. If you will assure me that if I give you a constructive scheme you will accept my principles and adopt it, I will give you a constructive scheme. What is the use of talking about a constructive scheme of things people do not want to do? I presume, this being a political-economic circle, you are concerned with principles on which you can act. As a matter of fact, as soon as you have got the will, you will find out the way. There is no difficulty about a constructive scheme of equal incomes; because, as I have pointed out to you, equal incomes are the rule throughout the world, class for class. A thing you have found practicable within every class does not become impracticable when you spread it from one class to the other, especially as at the present time it overlaps many classes.

Mr Richards seems puzzled because I criticized Parliament and then said we could not, under existing circumstances, get anything better. But where is the contradiction? I said that, under existing circumstances—that is to say, the circumstances of inequality—you had a Parliament which could not possibly represent the people of the country; but I also let it be very clearly inferred, if I did not say so in so many words, that if you established equality, you would get a better Parliament. It is quite true that, under existing circumstances, you will not get anything better. That means that under existing circumstances you will not get anything else but existing circumstances. That is a very profound observation; but it does not carry you any further.

Then Mr Richards said, very naturally, that he is quite sure that Mr Balfour understands the feelings and desires of a man with £300 a year. I do not doubt it; but I want my representative in Parliament not only to understand my feelings and desires, but to understand my working difficulties, which is a very different thing. The very knowledge which Mr Balfour may have of our common feelings and desires, applied as it is in his case to an income of, say, £30,000 a year, may lead him very much more astray as to life on £300 a year than if he had no such knowledge; because, in that case, he might go and ask the man with £300 a year what he wants, which he never does do at the present time. As to that little point raised by Mr Richards about the motor car, I will say nothing about it. I do not think it would be kind. Mr Richards says, very truly, that his father was more sensible than my father; and now look at the result! To come back to important matters, see how Mr Richards and Mr Hobson, both believing themselves to be Liberals, are practically favoring principles which mean the utter destruction of all

Liberalism in this country. Nobody in the Tyrol, said Mr Richards, is allowed to marry without a certificate of fitness for marriage. Here is a Liberal who believes that there is a person in this world qualified to give a certificate of fitness for marriage! I have no doubt there are men so utterly ignorant of science; there are men so infatuated with the sort of thing that we call scientific training; there are men so absurdly conceited that they do conceive themselves to be fitted to say to their fellow-men: "You are fit for marriage," or "You are not fit for marriage"; but is it safe to put any power, even to the extent of casting a vote, into the hands of men who believe in these supernatural powers? As a matter of fact, all you can get, in the Tyrol or elsewhere, is the appointment of certain officials who will undertake to examine a person, and to say: "This man has a certain kind of disease; and he ought not to marry within a certain period, nor perhaps at all." This idea of a certificate of fitness for marriage, this notion implied by Mr Richards, that you can settle the biological difficulty by allowing certain persons—selected God knows how—to decide whether their fellow citizens are fit for marriage, is one of the things that make me absolutely despair of Liberalism in this country. I am going to tell Mr Richards one thing. He said: "Is the sex attraction a safe guide? And do not certain diseases make people attractive?" Attractive to whom? I remember a friend of mine, who was very strong on heredity, used to be indignant with people who were consumptive and married oneanother; and he used to try to dissuade them. I used to say, "What are you trying to do? When you find a consumptive person, are you going to marry him to another consumptive person, or are you going to marry him to a healthy person, and corrupt a healthy person by so doing?" Some years afterwards I said to him: "You do not bother about these things as you used?" He replied, "No, I do not. I found, as a matter of fact, you need not bother about it, because these people who have struma are very attractive to oneanother. They marry oneanother and have sixteen children, who all die before they are six years of age, which is an admirable result from the general point of view." I do not put that down as a scientific proposition; but I say that when you begin to meddle in a small way with Nature, you soon find that Nature can do much better than you.

I now come to Mr Lupton; and I have no particular quarrel with him; but he said one thing which I must criticize. He said: "Where

would science be without surplus income?" Well, I do not know
anything that has corrupted science more than surplus income. I
do not suppose any generation of men that the world has seen ever
hoped for so much from science as the generation I belong to.
When I was a young man there seemed to be a glorious period
coming. It was the period of Tyndall and Huxley and Darwin and
Helmholtz; and we were getting rid of that horrible, corrupt sort of
thing which supposed itself to be religion in those days, a thing
which can hardly be conceived by enlightened people now. We
thought there was going to be a golden age of science; and now
what have we got? Mr Lupton knows better than most of us what
science has become now, under the corrupting influence of men of
enormous incomes and very bad habits as regards eating and drinking, who live—if you can call it living—in a continual state of terror
about their diseases, and to whom science means the payment of
enormous sums to gentlemen whose science consists in cutting out
your appendix. That is the effect of surplus riches on the progress
of science. The scientific method of using your brains conscien-
tiously and honorably within the limits placed by the deeper interests
of humanity is not worth £300 a year now to anybody. All the
honors and emoluments go to people who promise to secure long
life and health to rich people by all sorts of abominable inoculations
and conjurations. Then take the surplus money which has not been
applied even to spurious science, and look at the enormous waste of
it upon luxury and destruction of all kinds. All that surplus income,
in an intelligent community, might have been made available for
the purposes of science, and for the purposes of art, and for the
purposes of literature. But you throw this surplus wealth into the
hands of idlers, who give nothing for it, and are corrupted by it; so
that the money is wasted and turned to harm and destruction—all
that money which was potentially available for science—and yet you
say that surplus income encourages science! It is inconceivable to
me that anybody can believe such a thing. As a matter of fact,
science manages to steal a little of it. It occasionally gets a statue
when it is dead, or has been persecuted out of existence.

Now I come to the speech of Mr Whiteing, at the end of which he
drifted into entire agreement with me; but when he sat down he
forgot to acknowledge that, after working his way through a long
speech, he had arrived at my particular solution. He said, however,
that I despaired of my own solution, because I said that there was

very little to be done in the matter. I did not say that. On the
contrary, I said that there was a great deal to be done in the matter
of biological selection. I said that if you equalize income (and that is
doing a great deal) you will practically render the whole community
intermarriageable; and I said, and I believe, that that would make
enormous changes. I do not understand why Mr Whiteing tells me
that, under those circumstances, I despair of my own solution.

Mr Richard Whiteing: We all intermarry.

Mr Bernard Shaw: Excuse me: we do not intermarry. I challenge
Mr Whiteing, with his income and his position as a man of letters,
to go into the aristocracy and see whom he can marry. I ask him to
go among the common people, and see how many of those people
he would be willing to marry, if he got the chance. I say Mr Whiteing by himself is an instance of a man who, with his qualities and his
talents, ought practically to have had a chance of proposing to any
woman in England; but how many have you had a chance of, Mr
Whiteing?

Then Mr Whiteing said: "What is to prevent a man from running
away with somebody else's wife?" I have never known anything that
has prevented a man from doing so, or could prevent him, when he
had made up his mind to do it, except the lady's refusal. If any
gentleman wants to run away with my wife, and he has determined
to do it, and she has determined to do it, I simply do not know how
to prevent it. I think at the back of that question of Mr Whiteing's
there was that very curious association of ideas which so repeatedly
trips me up. People imagine that when I say a thing, I not only
mean what I say (they very seldom give me credit for that), but they
imagine I must mean a great deal more. When I suggested that the
community should become intermarriageable all through, I did not
suggest any sort of alteration in your existing marriage laws. I did
not suggest for a moment that when a man went and proposed to a
lady, or the lady came and proposed to a gentleman, it might not be
a perfectly valid reply for the lady to say: "I am very sorry, but I am
already married"; in which circumstances, I presume, the gentleman would take off his hat and say: "I am very sorry. I can only
apologize, and go away to die of a broken heart, or to see whether I
cannot find some other lady equally attractive to me." What I said
was quite independent of whatever marriage regulation you may
happen to make. All I say is that I want the available choice extended within your marriage regulations, whatever they may be.

I think Mr Whiteing was a little hard on Pen Browning. He painted one or two quite reasonable pictures; better than I could paint, at any rate. But granting that he was no genius, this idea that if you marry a person of genius to another person of genius, the result will be somebody of genius, is a very crude sort of eugenics. You must allow the human stock to lie fallow for a while; and it was too much to expect the child of Elizabeth Barrett Browning and Robert Browning to begin immediately to go ahead at the rate that the father and mother did. I should expect several generations to elapse before you could get another such splendid growth as that. Another thing is, I am not at all certain that the attraction between Robert Browning and Elizabeth Barrett Browning was, in the first instance, a genuine physiological attraction. Mind you, those two people could write and talk the birds off the bushes when they wished to do so. If any woman wrote to me sonnets such as Elizabeth wrote to Robert, I am very much afraid she would have got round me, whether she attracted me physically or not. Mr Whiteing came really at the end to the right point. He said that Arnold Bennett, for saying certain things, was writing like a bound-er; and in a way he was. As I said myself—and Mr Whiteing really meant the same thing—the ideal that we need to bring before the people of this nation, and every other nation, is the gentleman's ideal. What is the ideal of the gentleman? The gentleman makes a certain claim on his country to begin with. He makes a claim for a handsome and dignified existence and subsistence; and he makes that as a primary thing, not to be dependent on his work in any way; not to be doled out according to the thing he has done or according to the talents that he has displayed. He says, in effect: "I want to be a cultured human being; I want to live in the fullest sense; I require a generous subsistence for that; and I expect my country to organize itself in such a way as to secure me that."

Also the real gentleman says—and here is where the real gentle-man parts company with the sham gentleman, of whom we have so many: "In return for that I am willing to give my country the best service of which I am capable, absolutely the best. My ideal shall be also that, no matter how much I have demanded from my country, or how much my country has given me, I hope and I shall strive to give to my country in return more than it has given to me; so that when I die my country shall be the richer for my life." When you have a man of that type, you never find that he asks for more than any other man. Such a man never says: "I want a handsome and dignified existence; but a less handsome and dignified existence is good enough for other people." He never says it, or thinks it. It is part of his conception of a handsome and dignified existence that it should be an existence shared with other men enjoying the same grace and dignity. If any man wants a better life, he should not seek for that life for himself alone, but should attain it by the raising of the general level of life. The real constructive scheme you want is the practical inculcation into everybody that what the country needs, and should seek through its social education, its social sense and religious feeling, is to create gentlemen; and, when you create them, all other things shall be added unto you.

Uncorrected verbatim report of the National Guilds League lecture delivered at Kingsway Hall, London, on Thursday, 29 January 1920. Published as a supplement to The Christian Commonwealth *on 6 February 1920.*

Socialism
and the Labor Party

I do not think I shall talk to this audience about Socialism and the Labor Party, because probably you have had quite as much of both subjects lately as you can stand. On the whole, having talked a great deal in my time about future possibilities, I think, by way of putting a little novelty into my lecture, it might be well to deal with the existing state of society; because in my experience almost all the opposition which reformers meet with arises not really from any particular objection which people have to the reformer's plan but to their extraordinary ignorance of the existing state of things in which they themselves live, which they very often firmly believe does realize the plan of the reformer as far as it is humanly possible for it to be realized. There are plenty of people, ordinary citizens, who vote Municipal Reform and vote Unionist and all that, and if you asked these people what their ideal of society was they would give you on the whole a Socialist ideal of society, and they would account for all the discrepancies between that ideal and the existing state of things by the fact that they have noticed that some people drink occasionally too much, and so forth. Now the really basic fact in our modern society in this country, practically all over Europe, and whenever civilization extends, is that it is organized solely for the support of a particular caste who are occupied in pursuit of a very old profession. It is a robber caste. Now robbers are people whom we all ought to treat with very great respect, because we may learn very important lessons from them. There is nobody who is compelled to be so completely practical and hard-headed as a robber. What you call an honest man, who practically feels himself safe, surrounded by an organization which prevents his being severely molested in any way so long as he allows himself be be robbed—such a person can theorize to an almost unlimited extent. He can join various political parties, he can spend his life in disputing with other honest men as to the best way of bringing about the millennium—and there is no doubt that disputing about the best way to bring about the millennium is certainly the best way to prevent the millennium ever being brought about. But you do not find that any kind of robber has any time for that sort of thing. If a couple of burglars start out to get at a particular safe, and there are men who are doing that at this particular moment—I do not mean that I have any private and particular knowledge of any such case, but it is a statistical fact that there are men at this present moment who are setting out to break open a particular safe which they believe to contain valuable goods—you may be perfectly certain they are not going to stop on the way to dispute as to whether the safe should be opened in a Liberal manner or a Conservative manner; they have no time for that sort of nonsense. They, however, know perfectly well that the policeman is their enemy. They do not indulge in speculations as to his being a man and brother. No nonsense whatever of that kind. They know he is a man who will prevent them from opening the safe if he can, and submit them to a very severe penalty if they get into his hands. Therefore, their measures are taken without any sort of nonsense. You do not for instance find them raising questions as to the principles of tolerance as applied to policemen. They do not say, After all you should tolerate the policeman up to a certain point. You should allow him to do just as he likes provided he doesnt entrench on the liberties of any other policeman. They go for the safe and they know a policeman will go for them to prevent them; and they take measures accordingly. They also do not discuss questions of democracy. Any two burglars know they are an energetic minority. The idea of democracy is entirely abhorrent. They know that owners of safes are in a majority and they know their profession and existence depend on the energetic minority getting to the safe in defiance of the wishes of the apparently apathetic majority. All this they are taught by experience, and, accordingly, this which is true of a couple of burglars is equally true of any governing class which is founded on the principle of taking and taking by violence what you can get at the expense of the people who produce it. You do not produce wealth by your exertions, but wait until other people have produced it, and forcibly possess yourself of that wealth, and you do so by the method of fighting and you do it by physical violence. You get educated if you are organized as a State by the practical nature of your work, and you become for your own purposes a very efficient class. When the thing becomes politically organized, therefore, you find that military force, *i.e.,* violence, is organized on a large scale, but also the practical exigencies of the case convince the robber class, if I may call them that, always that they must go to the root of the thing, and they must educate public opinion, create public opinion in favor of robbery. Therefore, they always take care to set up a church, and although the principles, the professed articles of religion, of that church may be what they like, the robber class always takes care that the actual persons who administer and preach in that church shall be attached to their own class, either as actual members of it or adherents.

Furthermore, they get hold through that church of the schools; they get hold of the children at a very early age and teach them that practically their first duty to God is to allow themselves to be robbed in that station of life to which it has pleased God to call them. The whole thing is organized and carefully carried out with the method of violence from the beginning to the end, from the fact that the child is beaten in school if it demurs to the propositions put to it there, up to the fact that if adult persons rebel, they also are coerced by it. And the result is, as I say, that a robber state is a very practical and efficient State. Such a State, of course, has to be very largely recruited. Usually the robber class tries to set up round itself a convention which will exclude. It refuses to intermarry with other classes of society, but there comes a time when the phenomenon that is known as Capitalism comes into the world. It is discovered that robbing in the crude way of putting on a suit of armor and getting a number of people at your back, who are not provided with either lodging or sanitation, and you cram them into a castle and let them sleep about anywhere they like, you go out with those people at your back—but merely to rob with lance in rest and sword, although very exciting and a good training and all the rest of it, is an extremely poor business compared with the organization of wealth in the way that is known to us under the Capitalist system. Accordingly, your robber class in its first stage when it consists of robber barons, and the gentlemen whose castles you may still see along the Rhine and a few a little nearer home—there are even some quite new houses of that particular description—but the old-fashioned robber-baron doing that sort of thing has very largely passed away, and what remains of him—and this is very important—is a tremendous public opinion that it is every man's duty to fight for his country, meaning for the robber class for which his country exists. But at any rate the point is that that particular phase did not pass away until there was firmly established in the world the idea that the first point of honor for every man was that he was to be ready to fight. Of course, there were stages in which readiness to fight meant readiness to rob, but when it was discovered that by means of the Capitalist system it was not necessary to rob directly with your own hands, that you could get vulgar persons to do it, the point is that the old public opinion remained, that the honorable thing to do was to fight, and that although a man might escape all obligations of honest work, although he might live selfishly on the labor of other people in an entirely shameless fashion, and even claim honor for doing it, and educate children to honor him for doing it, nevertheless, the point of honor did remain that he was bound on occasion to risk his life and bound to fight. Very well, now when your Capitalist system which I need not describe at any great length to you, you are quite familiar with it as a working fact, when your robber class began to be rather less active, not absolutely to rob its own living by the strong hand, but only confined its military activities, in command of large armies, to overcoming other people's land and fight any other robber classes which formed themselves in other countries, the production of wealth became a matter of the organization of labor, and that was done by comparatively vulgar persons belonging to what is called the middle class. The middle class began to have a very high opinion of itself somewhere about the 17th century. There is a book which occupies in relation to the middle classes the same position that Karl Marx's Kapital does to the modern Socialist proletariat; that book is called Robinson Crusoe. I dare say that many of you have read Robinson Crusoe with the sense of reading a romance about a man who was wrecked and lived on a desert island, and you probably read it very young. But if you will reflect you will recall that almost on every second page of that book there was a certain amount of moralizing about the advantages of the middle station of life. It really was the preaching of the advantages and benefits and happinesses of the middle station of life which nerved Defoe to make the effort of writing Robinson Crusoe.

The middle class undertook the business of robbing the working classes for the benefit of the robber class, but naturally as that was rather a difficult business it expected to get something for itself, but the middle-class man, standing as he did between the working classes on the one hand, and perhaps I had better begin to call them the proprietary classes, because robber class is not a respectable or polite thing to say at the present time, but at any rate you know the middle-class man took the land which was the property of the proprietary class and he took the money which owing to their possession of the land they had been able to save; because if you give people land they become very rich; that is to say they have more money than they want to spend. The moment a man has more money than he wants to spend he saves, but he does not do it beforehand unless he is very foolish; because a man who saves when he has not spent as much as he needs is starving himself and his family. He is a foolish person and in fact a criminal person and ought to be punished for it. But if you give a man £50, £100 or £1,000 a day—and that is the sort of income people have nowadays—you can see that then money saves itself, and these people who had land and capital—the only profession they had was fighting. They still had the point of honor; if there was a war they were bound to go and fight and they did. But they had plenty of other things to do—they had hunting, shooting, dancing and occupations of that kind. Even one or two per cent of them took to art and literature. But you see land was no use to them because they did not want to dig. Capital, saved up money, was no use to them because they did not understand business. Accordingly, the middle-class man came in and said "Give me your land and your capital; I will pay so much for it," and then with that land and capital he organized labor, having a knowledge of business, and gave the laborer just enough to keep him alive on not too luxurious a scale, and having set the laborer to work, having produced certain goods or rendered certain services for which the public paid him very well, he had a lump of money in his hand, so he paid the landlord his rent, paid the capitalist his capital, the laborer his wages and kept the rest to himself, and called it his profit. But you will understand that all the time he was the organizer of the robbery which the robber class originally did for themselves with a few retainers, and as he became the effective working person concerned he naturally became very powerful and indispensable.

What course did he politically take? Instead of taking up with modern Socialist ideas he being always by the nature of his position against the working classes, knowing that the more he gave to the working classes the less there would be left for himself, and knowing the working classes in their unreasonable way always wanted to get as much as possible, and leave as little as possible for himself, he got into the tradition that he was against the working classes, and also being able to read and write, which in those days the working classes were not, he regarded himself as being naturally on the side of the robber class. He very naturally, in fact, wanted finally to become a retired robber himself, to do what the robber class had done, that is retire from the active business of robbery, handing it over to somebody else. Therefore, his object was to accumulate profits until he became rich enough to belong to the robber class. But the robber class did not like that; they wanted to retain their exclusiveness. They said, You are a vulgar tradesman. If all these fellows who have factories and shops, and talk to vulgar people like workmen and grab money, if these men are to come amongst us with their comparatively rough manners—the sort of manners a Manchester man has, for example—we cannot retain the beauty, dignity, and exclusiveness of our life. Then the middle-class man said, I am determined you shall: I am going to break down your privileges; I am determined to bring about a state of things in this country in which any man who can rob can get into the robber class.

Now what is the name of that creed? What is the name of that determination? The name of it, gentlemen, is Liberalism, and its colors are still nailed to the mast by my friend Mr Asquith. I say quite unreservedly that I do admire Mr Asquith for going to Paisley the other day. If he had been like some other statesmen, who think of nothing but pleasing their audiences and getting votes, I can imagine Mr Asquith beginning by saying the world was advancing, ideas were changing, and Liberalism had learned a great deal from Labor. Not a bit of it. He nailed his colors to the mast and practically began his campaign by saying, "Gentlemen, I have learned nothing and I have forgotten nothing."

And that is as far as we have got at present. We have got the old exclusive robber class back in its old form. It was broken down finally by the French Revolution and the Reform Bill of 1832 in this country. Now the Liberals may claim that they have achieved what I said they were out to achieve. Here am I; I have a very high opinion of my own social position, but I have not got a title. I think the nearest relationship I can claim to a title is a third cousin, but, nevertheless, I have only to put money in my pocket and I can go anywhere. You see the intermarriage of the upper classes; they positively seek intermarriage with vulgar Americans who have made money in trade. In point of fact that is what is keeping our old nobility to a very great extent alive—a mixture of blood and money. Your countries are governed in that way. You have now got, not the old limited aristocracy of the robber class, but that large, that democratic sort of robbery we may call plutocracy. A career is open to the talented, and society is open to the rich. The particular talent to which a career is open is that of getting as much money as you can out of other people's pockets and putting it into your own.

I myself, and, I believe, the organization for which I am speaking and most Socialist societies and a good many eccentric philanthropists here and there, want to turn their backs on this particular principle. They want to stop robbing. They want to go in for general co-operation for the good of the community, in short for Socialism. Is there any likelihood, any sign of the formation of a Party in this country which will absolutely throw over the idea of robbery and go in for co-operative and common production for the benefit of the whole country? which will take as its motto that it wants the greatest distribution of life and life more abundantly in the old form, which will do away absolutely with idleness, and not only with idleness but with nonproductiveness, and which will set up a new ideal of a gentleman, the old ideal being a man who had no visible means of subsistence; which will set up this ideal for a gentleman, that in the first place he shall pay his way from the beginning to the end of his life; he shall not leave the world any poorer than he found it; and going on from that to such eminence and virtue as may set a man above his fellows, that shall be measured to the extent by which every man leaves the community in his debt; that the world is the richer for his having lived: for everything that he has consumed in the course of his life he has produced an equivalent for it, and not only that, but has produced more than that equivalent, he has produced what the Marxist would call a surplus value, and that surplus value has gone to enrich the whole of the community.

The question I want to deal with tonight is the question of whether there are any signs of such a party existing. I must frankly say I do not see that there is any party which is able really to say that it is animated right throughout by that particular spirit. There is a party which talks about the class war and which conceives that there must come in society what has been called a definite confrontation of classes, the proprietary class on the one hand and the proletariat on the other. Unfortunately there is no such confrontation possible in existing society, because the utmost you can get people to go at the present time is they will admit rather reluctantly that, on the whole, it is a disgrace for a man to be idle. That is not of the slightest use. You must look further into the matter and get people to see that it is not a question of whether a man is idle or not, it is a question of whether he is producing anything or not, because once you get your robber basis which exists in society at the present time what is the inevitable result of that? The object of the governing and robber class is to become as comfortable and live as luxuriously itself as possible. Therefore the way it will manage the wealth of the community which it gets into its hands is to set apart the smallest possible portion of the wealth to keep the great mass of the working people alive, the people who are actually producing the necessaries of life for oneanother.

Let me illustrate: if you are what you may call a lady or gentleman—I do not suppose if you were you would be in the Kingsway Hall tonight—but suppose you are a young lady and gentleman and you get married. If you were really a lady and gentleman and you set up housekeeping together you could not get on with less than nine servants, not with any degree of decency. I daresay many of you comparatively vulgar ladies and gentlemen here—we only call ourselves ladies and gentlemen because we are called so at election times—get on with no servants at all. Or there may be people who get on with one servant, what you here call a "general" servant and what is called in Ireland, with a great deal more point, a "thorough" servant. Some of you may be able to get

on very comfortably with two but, you see, if you stick at two servants you can get along, but the moment you go beyond that—you
may perhaps, if there are children to be looked after, go as far as
three—but the moment you go on to four you require servants to
wait on those servants, and that is finally how you get the nine
servants. You find you make a sudden jump, a fresh lot of servants
are required to attend on oneanother. And in the same way it is all
very well for a governing class to set apart a proletariat to produce
for them, but these proletarians, if they are attending directly to
the wants of the upper classes, must have another proletariat to
attend to them, to produce food for them, and accordingly you get
a sort of lower layer of people who are producing food, lodging,
and clothing for poor people, but you get all the nicest looking and
best mannered of them gathered up and taken into the industry of
directly ministering to the convenience and the comfort of the
robber class. Not only is that the case with regard to personal servants, people in the house, such as parlor maids, footmen, and all
those people, but there are professional men, and the ablest professional men naturally like to have rich people to attend. In the first
place, they can get very much larger sums for unnecessary surgical
operations, and if it comes to poor people they have got to operate
on poor people for nothing in hospitals; they do it willingly because
in that way they learn how to operate on the rich people, but the
rich people pay very highly. Again, if you are a lawyer, you like to
have the estates of rich people to look after. If you keep a shop,
there may be shopkeepers in this room, and you all know the darling object of your life is to have a high class of custom, that is to say,
you like to have a shop in Bond Street. I was looking in a shop in
Bond Street the other day at a metal vase, and a friend said to me:
"That is a pretty little thing"; it was a William and Mary piece of
metal work. We went into the shop and my friend said, as one does
in these curio places: "If that is going for the sum I do not mind
giving £20." They said: "The price is £2,500." That in a country
which is in debt after a war. There are people who are giving sums
like that. But you see there comes gradually a large mass of people
who are by no means idle people who are very hard-working
people, but they are in the social sense not in the slightest degree
productive people. If you take the surgeon who saves the life of an
idle millionaire, he has inflicted a very great injury on society. If he
were a genuine patriot he would kill the millionaire in order that

there might be one idler the less to feed, and to do our surgeons justice, I must say they generally do kill them.

But what I am trying to call your attention to, and I do not think I need elaborate the fact much more, is that you get finally a real, genuine, useful, and productive proletariat which is producing food, clothing, and everything else that is needed by the workers of the world, and, on the other hand, an enormous parasitic proletariat, as the robber at the top of society is a parasite on the whole of the country. This parasitic proletariat is parasitic on the parasites:—

Big fleas have little fleas
Upon their backs to bite them,
Little fleas have lesser fleas
And so ad infinitum.[1]

It absolutely knocks on the head the idea that you can get a definite confrontation of classes, a clearly-cut class war by the plan of getting into any particular party all the workers by hand and brain. You cannot get that union and you will see if you try to get a political union you have only to contrast broadly the North of England and the South. Very roughly speaking, in the North of England, the manufacturing and productive districts, you find the genuine proletariat; in the South you find the game-keeping class, the enormous masses of servants, tradesmen, who wait on the rich; yacht builders, sailors, hotelkeepers; and these people are the parasitic proletariat, and when an attack is made on the incomes and privileges of the robber class you find the parasitic proletariat rally immediately to the defence of the people they serve.

At the present time the current of politics is being a little disturbed. Before the war, for example, all the suburbs round London were places where the Unionist class lived; that is to say, where the parasitic worker lived; there you found not only had you no chance of getting a Labor member in at an election but no chance of getting in a Liberal. The Conservative always got in by an overwhelming majority. In the general complaint, disgruntling, and upsetting by the war these ladies and gentlemen are sometimes beginning to give a few Labor votes, but they will soon settle down to their own interests and see very plainly that in so far as great masses of them are living on the incomes of the upper classes they must rally to their side politically and defend them. And remember this applies even in the numerous cases in which the middle-class man is now a proletarian. You know, of course, that proletarianization of the middle class has been proceeding very rapidly; that is to say, a man who fifty or sixty years ago as a matter of course, the middle-class man who started in business for himself or in partnership with another middle-class man, two of them together, having a couple of thousand pounds capital, that man at the present time has no chance of starting in business for himself; he is an employee of a Joint-Stock Company. The Joint-Stock Companies themselves are being rapidly absorbed by large combinations of Joint-Stock Companies. When you go into a little tobacconist shop or oil shop today you are very unlikely to be going into the shop of an individual shopkeeper; it is practically the premises of a big trust and the man who occupies it is an employee of those firms. And when tired of your marketing in those places you go to the public house for a drink you know, in the majority of cases, the publican is not really an independent publican; he is in what is called a tied house; he is not really free, he is becoming more and more an employee of the brewer or distiller or, if you like, largely an employee of the Public House Trust—which is a very excellent institution in its way—but the point is, whereas formerly he was in business for himself and lived on profits, he is now an employee and is living on a salary and percentages. Nevertheless, do not suppose the inevitable and immediate result of that must be he becomes proletarian in sympathy, that is to say, he will go the political side of the genuine productive proletarian; nothing of the kind: if the business he is in is a business for building yachts or 80 h.p. motor cars, or maginificent country houses, or tremendous hotels, and developing seaside resorts, he will know his interest in life is to try and keep up the profits and monopolies and privileges of that particular kind of business, and he will virtually support the robber class.

Now that is a very depressing prospect. All your notions of getting a magnificent Labor Party perfectly clearly divided, the notion that on the one hand all the people who live by labor will get up and expropriate the expropriators is replaced by the conviction that on the contrary the expropriators, the proletariat will get up and cut oneanother's throats, the robber class providing plenty of newspapers inciting them to do it and financing them when they come in strongly on the side of the parasitic proletariat. Now what is the way out? I am afraid it is going to be a very difficult way out and I think I will now go back to the beginning of my lecture and begin it all over again. You may remember I began with the tremendously practical education of the robber class, the way they had, by the mere exigencies of their wealth, all nonsense about democracy, about toleration knocked out of them; that they believed in an energetic minority. There is a party in Europe making considerable progress which has been educated the same way. It is in a country called Russia. The Russians are a very curious people. You know that they went into the war with great enthusiasm on our side—or I do not know whether it was not that we went on their side, there is a good deal of dispute as to who got in first—but we all agree of course that the Kaiser began the whole thing, and as a result of that I want to call your attention to the fact that we have not progressed so very much since the middle ages. You may remember when that king (was it not King Edward), who laid a long siege to the town of Calais in France, insisted, out of pure rage at their having fought him so long when he expected the surrender of the town, that they should send out six of their merchants with ropes round their necks in order that he might hang them and get some satisfaction. You may remember his wife, Queen Philippa, who was not an English woman by the way—but for the matter of that he would have hanged you if you called him a Frenchman—being in an interesting condition, and very sympathetic at the time went down on her knees and begged him not to hang those people; and being a mediæval barbarian he thought better of his temper and let them off.[2] I want to know what about those German persons whom we are demanding to have delivered to us with ropes round their necks? Is there any woman going down on her knees to ask if they may be let off? We know it is the old story over again. It is very well to talk of trying these people for deeds connected with the war. I have no objection to men who commit atrocities of any kind feeling there is a point at which they will be held responsible, but if that is going to be carried out it wont be exclusively German officers. If we pick out German soldiers and officers or German officers alone then you may go through any ridiculous form you like of pretending to try them; it is the old case of the bourgeoisie of Calais over again; it is pure and simple vengeance and nothing else, and it is vengeance in order to try and get votes. One election has been won by offering to hang the Kaiser, it being a perfectly well understood thing all the time that the Dutch Government would not surrender the Kaiser, and I desire publicly here to thank the Dutch Government for their extraordinary generosity and magnanimity at a time when they might have blackmailed us almost for anything by threatening to give up the Kaiser to us. They asked nothing. I remember some time ago I asked a Dutch gentleman, "Are you going to give up the Kaiser?" His answer to me was "Holland has a history," and that was the only remark he made. We also have our history, the old Calais history. I hope it will not be repeated. One has the satisfaction of being able to say the real truth about it and to find there is an English audience who appreciates it. I would like some of those gentlemen who are trying to get votes to know what an English audience really thinks about it when the case is fairly put before them.

The Russians seem to very thoroughly appreciate the practical lessons of history that we learned from the early experiences of the robber class. The Russian soldier did a very eccentric thing. He went on for a long time fighting; he was made very uncomfortable; then he had a curious idea, he suddenly stopped fighting, went home, and seized the land of the country. That from the point of view of the robber class in other countries was the first great atrocity. It may have been an atrocity but it was a jolly practical atrocity, and when they began to organize, they started on the idea which I suggested, that they were going to organize the industry of the people for the benefit of the people, that they were going to extirpate idlers, and democracy stood in the way. There is only one really interesting statesman in Europe at the present time and his name is Nicholas Lenin. Nicholas Lenin had a tremendous controversy on the subject of democracy with a German Social-Democrat, Karl Kautsky.[3] Kautsky said all the usual things which Socialists have been saying, which I have said all my life, the thing must rest on the will of the people. You have no right to introduce Socialism until you get a vote, until you get majorities throughout all the constituencies in favor of Socialism. I have always said that my reason at bottom has been this, that I knew perfectly well as long as I waited for that I would never be asked to do anything but talk. I have talked all my life and I have managed to get beyond the age of sixty without ever having been called on to do anything really dangerous or important. Accordingly, I intend to go on talking in that way, but Lenin did not see that. Lenin entirely agreed with Mr Winston Churchill on the subject and with the robber class. Lenin said, These things are not done by the great mass of the people making a vote, they are done by an energetic minority which has got a conviction and is determined to go on carrying out that conviction until it is stopped. That is precisely what our upper class did, what they are doing, and have always done. It is the practical thing to do. There is no use in waiting until the mass of the people throughout the country, who know a little about football and very much less about politics, whose business is not politics and you cannot move them in the matter at all, there is no use in waiting to get the majority of votes from them with all the powers of the press and newspapers bemusing and bewildering and bedevilling them with all sorts of nonsense. We Socialists· when we are a little comfortable are perfectly willing to wait, but the people who really want to have something done, like Lenin, do not wait. When Lenin saw a Constituent Assembly muddling about doing nothing he did not wait but went ahead and like our governing classes there was no nonsense about democracy; he organized the thing in such a shape that it would work. He got his combination of Soviets, a certain method of indirect election which was not at all what we call a democratic method of election because it was very indirect, it was doubly and triply indirect, but susceptible of being managed in such a way that Lenin got working with him the sort of men he wanted to agree with him, which is precisely how our governing classes work elections in this country, and there was no nonsense about toleration at all. He believed in Socialism, in organizing the proletariat. Those were his ideas and he put it down as a minimum of social morality: We are not going to have any more idling or unproductiveness; we do not allow liberty of opinion with regard to that; if you have any doubts about that we regard you as a dishonest person and we shoot you. They shot him; he has several bullets in his body; that will shew he was educating them practically. But he realized when it came to the point that as between the people who believe in a great system of what is practically the robbery of the poor, and the people who believe in another system, an intelligent minority, they have simply to fight it out with what forces they have at their command. Of course, the very first thing he had to institute was what Mr Lloyd George has held up in the House of Commons as his blackest atrocity, and it is felt I think by every respectable man to be his blackest atrocity, he introduced compulsory labor. He actually said every man must work or he will starve. He had not much food to give the people who did work, thanks to the fact that we are trying to starve them out; you do not get much to eat in Russia, but at any rate what there was going he gave. Only if people would not work they did not get any tickets, and they got on as best they could, they lived on their own fat. That was the great atrocity. He was after all carrying out compulsory labor for the benefit of the system of society. He was carrying out the ideas of the upper classes in this country who are also in favor of compulsory labor. Only they find the threat of starvation is sufficient to do the compulsion in this country, except on themselves. Lenin was logical: he brought in a method of compulsory labor from which nobody could get utterly exempt. We have a system of compulsory labor in this country which applies to everybody except people with a considerable amount of property. They can escape from it because they cannot be starved out.

Under Lenin's system you do get starved out. Lenin did something else which is perhaps the most remarkable thing. Supposing the Bolshevik Red Army captures you; what is it that happens to you? You are told beforehand if you are a European you are fighting Bolsheviks because you know they are monsters and committing atrocities. You are told if the Bolsheviks capture you, they will put you slowly to death over a period of twentyone days by cutting off the tips of your fingers and nose and ears, and by horrible scientific tortures slowly kill you, therefore you fight pretty hard— if you believe it. Supposing you are taken personally, in spite of your heroic struggles—if you are an Englishman you naturally do struggle, if not to the death, still very close to it. But supposing you are overwhelmed by numbers, say one Englishman by 200 Bolsheviks, what happens to you? You are brought into a military depot and the first thing that happens to you is they give you a meal, and when you are in a tolerably good humor a man comes in with a lot of literature; he says, "Are you an Englishman?" You say, "I am an Englishman"—proudly. He immediately produces a bundle of Bolshevik literature in English, and you are set to read that literature. You are not given anything else to do. Of course, if they would let you do anything else, being an Englishman you would do it rather than read—play football, for instance—but they throw you back on your own mental and intellectual resources to such an extent that you begin to read their literature. Then you find out the truth about what they are actually doing. They send you about three times a week to the theatre and let you go about pretty freely and see what is going on. They give you these things to read just like the upper classes in our Church schools; they stick their ideas into your mind.

I am emphasizing this thing they have taken from our governing classes. They recognize the fact that you must get at people's minds. What they are doing to the mind of the adult person they are doing to the children of Russia. The children of Russia are now taught to believe from the very beginning that it is dishonest in the last degree for a person not to be a productive worker and not to pay his way in society. I must not carry the parallel any further. I think this is a very good loose end to leave off. I think it is a good place to stop and begin thinking about it. As I say I do not see in the Labor Party as it at present exists the Party which will act solidly and practically and thoroughly and radically and unitedly like the Party represented by Mr Winston Churchill, which I have impolitely called the robber class, and like the Bolsheviks. I see in the Labor Party the most extraordinary heterogeneous mass of people, full of opinions of different kinds. I see there are Methodists and atheists; jingoes and conscientious objectors; there are Protectionists and Free Traders; I see the most amazing mass of people of all sorts and kinds immensely equipped for any kind of discussion, for the most violent electioneering, and for no action whatever.

We have got to simplify the matter. If we believe in the principles which I have sketched out, being the principles that I myself believe in, this belief in the obligation of every man to leave the world in his debt, or at least to pay his way, then that must be made to be a religion; it has got to be the basis of the whole religion in the country. I am tired of seeing Labor and Socialism rolling the stone up the hill with frightful labor only to have it rolled down again. Here you have seen movement after movement, the movement of the Utilitarians, the movement of the Free Traders under Cobden and Bright; the Christian Socialists under Kingsley; the Marxite Socialists, you have seen the Labor Party by an immense amount of labor, by talking on platforms, as I am doing now, get one generation of men educated into ideas about Free Trade or Socialism or what you like. What does that matter to the upper classes? Those men die out and meanwhile the children are coming into the schools where they are taught from the very beginning the creed of the robber class. When I began work as a Socialist I remember seeing a paragraph in the paper about America. They said, "Arizona is aflame with Christian Socialism." They talked of the Knights of Labor. We were led to believe all America was ringing with Socialism. Thirty or forty years have passed since that time and now men are being put in prison for periods of twenty years in America for being co-operators, Radicals, and things of that kind. The stone is always rolling back. It is because we do not go to work in the practical way of Mr Winston Churchill and Nicholas Lenin. I take off my hat to both gentlemen. It appears to me until we get to work in their ways it will be all talk, talk, talk, and nothing coming of it.

An article published in The Labour Monthly, *October 1921.*

The Dictatorship
of the Proletariat

The proletariat is the vast body of persons who have no other means of living except their labor.

A dictatorship is the office of an individual whom the people, made desperate by the absence of government, and unable to govern themselves, have invited or allowed to dictate a political constitution for their country, and control its administration, and who has the necessary will and conscience to use that power from his own point of view, to the complete disfranchisement of every hostile point of view. At present the term is extended from an individual to an oligarchy formed of an energetic minority of political doctrinaires. Where the doctrine is that point of view must be that of the proletariat, and that the proprietariat (the people who live by owning instead of by working) must be disfranchised, expropriated, and in fact exterminated (by conversion or slaughter), then we call such an oligarchy, or allow it to call itself, the Dictatorship of the Proletariat.

As the proletariat is necessarily always in an overwhelming majority in modern industrial States, and cannot be finally and physically coerced except by itself, nothing can stand long between it and such a dictatorship but its own refusal to support it. The proletariat is not oppressed because its oppressors despise it and mistrust it, but because it despises and mistrusts itself. The proletariat is not robbed by persons whom it regards as thieves, but by persons whom it respects and privileges as specially honorable, and whom it would itself rob with the entire approval of its conscience if their positions were reversed. When it falls on itself and slaughters itself in heaps, tearing down its own cities, wrecking its own churches, blowing its own children to fragments, or leaving them to starve in millions, it does so, not because diplomatists and generals have any power in themselves to force it to commit such atrocities, but because it thinks it is behaving heroically and patriotically instead of suicidally. It obeys its rulers, and compels malcontents to submit to them, because its conscience is the same as that of its rulers.

As long as this sympathy exists between the proletariat and its rulers, no extension of the franchise will produce any change, much less that aimed at by the so-called Dictatorship of the Proletariat. On the contrary, adult suffrage will make all change impossible. Revolutionary changes are usually the work of autocrats. Peter the Great, personally a frightful blackguard who would have been tortured to death if he had been a peasant or a laborer, was able to make radical changes in the condition of Russia. Cromwell turned the realm of England into a Republican Commonwealth sword in hand after throwing his parliamentary opponents neck and crop into the street, a method copied by Bismarck two centuries later. Richelieu reduced the powerful and turbulent feudal barons of old France to the condition of mere court flunkies without consulting the proletariat. A modern democratic electorate would have swept all three out of power and replaced them by men who, even if they had wanted to, would not have dared to suggest any vital change in the established social order. Napoleon, because his mandate was revolutionary, was much more afraid of the French people than of the armies of the Old Order. There was a good deal of truth in the contention of the early French Syndicalists that aggrieved sections of the people had more power of obtaining redress under the old autocratic form of government, when they could interfere in politics only as a riotous mob, than under modern democratic parliamentary forms, when they interfere only as voters, mostly on the wrong side.

Accordingly, a real dictatorship of the proletariat cannot be advocated as leading necessarily to better results than the present dictatorship of the Proprietariat. It might easily lead to worse. It would almost certainly do so in certain respects at first. It is advocated because certain changes which Socialists desire to bring about cannot be effected whilst the Proprietors, politically called the Capitalists, are predominant, and could not be maintained unless the Proletariat were permanently predominant. Consequently we have on the one hand the fear that the proletariat in power would play the devil with the whole business of the country and provoke a reaction into oligarchy or Napoleonism, and, on the other, the belief that Capitalism will wreck civilization, as it has often done before, unless it can be forced to give way to Communism.

Fundamentally it is a question of conscience. So long as the average Englishman holds it to be self-evident, not that he has a natural right to life, liberty, and the pursuit of happiness, but that Lord Curzon is a superior being, and Nicolas Lenin a dirty scoundrel and no gentleman—so long as an ordinary British coroner's jury can be depended on to bring in a verdict expressly and gratuitously exonerating the prison authorities from all blame when they admittedly kill a Conscientious Objector by forcing food into his lungs under pretence of feeding him, so long will the political power of the proletariat, whether it come to them as the spoil of a revolution, or be thrown to them by their masters as a move in the parliamentary game, do nothing to change the existing system except by lopping off from it the few safeguards against tyranny won by energetic minorities in the past.

It follows that the task of the advocates of a change-over to Socialism, whether they call themselves Labor leaders, Socialists, Communists, Bolsheviks, or what not, is to create a Socialist conscience. (The task of the Capitalist and Imperialist is much easier: it is simply to trade on a conscience that already exists, and feed it by suitable incitements administered to children in nursery and school lessons, and to adults in newspapers and speeches.) And when this task is accomplished, there is still the very arduous one of devising a new constitution to carry out the new ethic of the new conscience. For there is all the difference in the world between driving an old locomotive (a Government is essentially a locomotive) and inventing and constructing an aeroplane. And there is the same difference between operating the established Capitalist system, and devising, setting up, and administering the political, legal, and industrial machinery proper to Socialism. Unitl this is done, no admission of Labor leaders, Socialists, Communists, or Bolshevists into Parliament or even into the Cabinet can establish Socialism or abolish Capitalism. Mr Henderson and Mr Clynes[1] may be just as anti-Capitalist as Messrs Trotsky and Lenin; but they can no more make our political machine produce Socialism than they can make a sewing machine produce fried eggs. It was not made for that purpose; and those who work it, though they may stand out for better wages and treatment for the workers, and perhaps get them, are still working the Capitalist machine, which will not produce anything else but Capitalism. The notion that we have in the British constitution a wonderful contrivance, infinitely adaptable to every variation in the temper of the British people, is a delusion. You might as well say that the feudal system was an exquisite contrivance adaptable to the subtlest *nuances* of the cotton exchange of Manchester.

What, exactly, does making a new constitution mean? It means altering the conditions on which men are permitted to live in society. When the alteration reverses the relation between the governing class and the governed, it is a revolution. Its advocates must therefore, if they succeed, undertake the government of the country under the new conditions, or make way for men who will and can. The new rulers will then be faced with a responsibility from which all humane men recoil with intense repugnance and dread. Not only must they, like all rulers, order the killing of their fellow creatures on certain provocations; but they must determine afresh what those provocations are to be. Further, they have to see that in every school a morality shall be inculcated which will reconcile the consciences of their executive officers to the carrying out of such grim orders. That is why reformers cling so desperately to gradual modifications of existing systems rather than face revolutionary changes. It is quite easy to sign a death warrant or order the troops to fire on the mob as part of an old-established routine as to which there is no controversy, and for which the doomster has no personal responsibility. But to take a man and kill him for something a man has never been killed for before: nay, for which he has been honored and idolized before, or to fire on a body of men for exercising rights which have for centuries been regarded as the most sacred guarantees of popular liberty: that is a new departure that calls for iron nerve and fanatical conviction. As a matter of fact it cannot become a permanently established and unquestioned part of public order unless and until the conscience of the people has been so changed that the conduct they formerly admired seems criminal, and the rights they formerly exercised seem monstrous. There are several points at which Socialism involves this revolutionary change in our constitution; but I need only deal with the fundamental one which would carry all the rest with it. That one is the ruthless extirpation of parasitic idleness. Compulsory labor, with death as the final penalty (as curtly stipulated by St Paul), is the keystone of Socialism. "If a man will not work, neither shall he eat" is now evasively interpreted as "If a man has no money to buy food with, let him starve." But a Socialist State would make a millionaire work without the slightest regard to his money exactly as our late war tribunals made him fight. To clear our minds on this point, we must get down to the common morality of Socialism, which, like all common moralities, must be founded on a religion: that is, on a common belief binding all men together through their instinctive acceptance of the fundamental dogma that we must at all costs not only keep the world going but increase our power and our knowledge in spite of the demonstration (any Rationalist can make it) that the game, as far as the individual is concerned, is not worth the candle except for its own sake.

What, then, is the common morality of Socialism? Let us begin with the unquestionable facts on which it is based. The moment a child is conceived, it begins to exploit its mother, and indirectly the community which feeds its mother (to exploit people meaning to live parasitically on them). It is absolutely necessary to the existence of the community that this exploitation be not only permitted, but encouraged by making the support of the child as generous as possible. The child is in due time born; after which for several years it has to be fed, clothed, lodged, minded, educated and so forth on credit. Consequently, when the child grows up to productive capacity, it is inevitably in debt for all it has consumed from the moment of its conception; and a Socialist State would present it with the bill accordingly. It would then have not only to support itself by its productive work, but to produce a sinking fund by which its debt would finally be liquidated. But age has its debt as well as youth; and this must be provided for beforehand. The producer must therefore during his working years pay off the debt of his nonage; pay his way as he goes; and provide for his retirement when he is past work, or at whatever earlier age the community may be able to release him.

Now these are not new facts: they are natural necessities, and cannot be changed by Capitalism, Communism, Anarchism or any other ism. What can be changed, and drastically changed, is the common morality of the community concerning them.

The Socialist morality on the subject is quite simple. It regards the man who evades his debt to the community, which is really his debt to Nature, as a sneak thief to be disfranchised, disowned, disbanded, unfrocked, cashiered, struck off the registers, and, since he cannot, as Shakespear suggested in the case of Parolles,[2] be transported to some island where there were women that had suffered as much shame as he, that he might begin an impudent nation (for Socialists do not desire to begin impudent nations, but to end them) subjected to all the penalties of a criminal and all the disabilities of a bankrupt. Every child in a Socialist State would be taught from its earliest understanding to feel a far deeper horror of a social parasite than anyone can now pretend to feel for the outcasts of the Capitalist system. There would be no concealment of the fact that the parasite inflicts on the community exactly the same injury as the burglar and pickpocket, and that only in a community where the laws were made by parasites for parasites would any form of parasitism be privileged.

Our Capitalist morality is flatly contrary. It does not regard the burden of labor as a debt of honor, but as a disgracefully vulgar necessity which everyone is justified in evading if he can, its ideal of the happy and honorable career being a life freed from all obligation and provided gratuitously with every luxury. In its language, success means success in attaining this condition, and failure a life of labor. This grotesque view is made practicable by the fact that labor is so productive that a laborer can not only pay the debt of his childhood, meet the expenses of his prime, and provide for his old age, but also support other persons in complete unproductiveness. If nine men combine to do this, they can support a tenth in outrageous waste and extravagance; and the more poorly the nine live, short of disabling themselves as producers, the richer the tenth man will be. All slave systems are founded on this fact, and have for their object the compulsion of nine-tenths of the population to maintain the "upper ten" by producing as much as possible, and allowing themselves to be despoiled of everything they produce over and above what is needed to support and reproduce themselves on the cheapest scale compatible with their efficiency.

The two moralities have only to be plainly stated to make it clear

that a change from one to the other must be revolutionary. The
Capitalist system admits of so much apparent progress that super-
ficial thinkers easily persuade themselves that it will finally progress
into Socialism; but it can never do so without making a complete
volte face. Slavery is always improving itself as a system. It begins by
working its slaves to premature death. Then it finds out that badly
treated slaves do not, except when they are so plentiful that they
can be replaced very cheaply, produce so much booty for their
masters as well-treated ones. Accordingly, much humanitarian
progress is effected. Later, when modern industrial methods of
exploitation are discovered and developed competitively, it is
found that continuous employment under the same master cannot
be provided for the slave. When this point is reached the master
wants to be free to get rid of the slave when he has no work for him
to do, and to pick him up again when trade revives, besides having
no responsibility for him when he is old and not worth employing.
Immediately a fervent enthusiasm for liberty pervades the
Capitalist State; and after an agitation consecrated by the loftiest
strains of poetry and the most splendid eloquence of rhetoric, the
slave is set free to hire himself out to anyone who wants him; to
starve when nobody wants him; to die in the workhouse; and to be
told it is all his own fault. When it is presently discovered that this
triumph of progress has been, in fact, a retrogression, the Progressive reformers are again set to work to mitigate its worst effects by
Factory Acts, Old Age Pensions, Insurance against Unemployment
("ninepence for fourpence"), Wages Boards, Whitley Councils,[3]
and what not, all producing the impression that "we live in a progressive age." But this progress is only allowed whilst the workers
are gaining in efficiency as slaves, and their masters consequently
gaining in riches as exploiters.

   A further comparison of the two moralities will shew that
whereas the Socialist morality is fit for publication, the Capitalist
morality is so questionable that every possible device has to be
employed to reconcile the workers to it by disguising its real nature.
As a reasoned system it has never been tolerated by public opinion.
Although it has been set forth with perfect frankness by a succession of able political economists and professors of jurisprudence,
notably (in point of uncompromising lucidity) by De Quincey and
Austin, and justified as on the whole the best system human nature
is capable of, the only effect has been to make "political economy,"

as the demonstration was called, abhorred. The Capitalist system has not been preserved by its merits as an economic system, but by a systematic glorification and idolization of the rich, and a vilification and debasement of the poor. Yet as it gives to every poor man a gambling chance, at odds of a million to one or thereabouts, of becoming a rich one (as Napoleon said, the careers are open to the talents, and every soldier has a field marshal's baton in his knapsack), no one is condemned by it to utter despair. In England especially, where the system of primogeniture, and the descent of the younger son into the commonalty with a family standard of expenditure so far beyond his income that his progeny follow him rapidly into chronic pecuniary embarrassment and finally into wretched poverty, a sense of belonging to the privileged class is to be found in all ranks; and a docker who does not regard himself as a gentleman under a cloud rather than as one of the proletariat is likely to be a man with too little selfrespect to be of any use as a revolutionary recruit. Ferocious laws are made against those who steal in any but the legalized Capitalist way; so that though a woman may have the produce of sixteen hours of her work sold for ten shillings and receive only a shilling of it, and no man may buy anything without paying in addition to its cost of production a tribute for the landlord and capitalist, yet any attempt on the part of the proletarian to perform an operation of the same character on a proprietor is suppressed by the prison, the lash, the rifle, the gallows, and the whole moral armory of ostracism and loss of reputation and employment.

But it is not by its hypocrisies and its coercions, potent as these are, that Capitalism retains its main grip on the proletariat. After all, few of the hypocrisies impose on those who do not wish to be imposed on by them; and the coercions are applied by the proletarians themselves. The really effective lure is the defiance of Nature in the name of liberty: the apparent freedom to be idle. It is useless to demonstrate that no such freedom is possible for all: that if Adolphus survives in idleness, Bill and Jack and the rest must be doing his share and having their liberty correspondingly curtailed. What does that matter to Adolphus? And who does not hope to be Adolphus, if only for a day or a week occasionally? The moment Socialism comes to the point and hints at compulsory industrial and civil service for all, the difference between Dean Inge[4] and the Labor Party vanishes: they will stand anything, even Capitalism at its worst, rather than give up the right to down tools and amuse themselves at any moment. Thus their devotion to liberty keeps them in slavery; and after the most formidable combinations to better their condition they go back to defeat and drudgery under the unofficial but irresistible compulsion of starvation.

There is ghastly comedy in the fact that this right to idle which keeps the proletarians enslaved is cherished by them, not only as a privilege, but actually as a weapon. They call it the right to strike, and do not perceive that it is only a form of the right to commit suicide or to starve on their enemy's doorstep. This folly reaches its climax in the panacea of the general strike, the only sort of strike that could not possibly succeed even temporarily, because just in proportion to its completeness would be the suddenness and ig-nominy of its collapse. The ideal strike is a lightning strike of the waiters in a fashionable restaurant, hurting nobody but the enemy, and putting him for the moment in a corner from which he will extricate himself by any reasonable sacrifice. A general strike is a general suicide. A Napoleon who proposed to take his commis-sariat out of the kitchens and throw them into the trenches would be sent to a lunatic asylum. But the French General Confederation of Labor, though torn by dissensions between Communists, Syn-dicalists, Trade Unionists and heaven knows what other Ists, is solid adhesion to an idiotic welter of phrases called the Charter of Amiens, out of which nothing intelligible emerges except the proc-lamation that the salvation of labor is to be achieved by the general strike.[5]

A Socialist State would not tolerate such an attack on the com-munity as a strike for a moment. If a Trade Union attempted such a thing, the old Capitalist law against Trade Unions as conspiracies would be re-enacted within twentyfour hours and put ruthlessly into execution. Such a monstrosity as the recent coal strike, during which the coal-miners spent all their savings in damaging their neighbors and wrecking the national industries, would be impossi-ble under Socialism. It was miserably defeated, as it deserved to be. But if it had been conducted from the Socialist point of view in-stead of from the Trade Union point of view (which is essentially a commercial point of view) the strike might have been worth while. In that case, the leaders of Labor in Parliament would simply have challenged the Government to stop the strike by introducing com-pulsory service, and promised to vote for it themselves. This would have at once put them right with public opinion, and effected an epoch-making advance in Labor policy. And it would have put the Government into a very difficult position. All the Coalitionists of the extreme right, understanding their own Capitalism as little as they understand Socialism, and having no other idea but to smash these damned Trade Unions and bring the working class to heel, would have rallied to the proposal with enthusiasm. But the Government would have seen, or would soon have been shewn, that if the right to strike—that is, the right to be idle—were abolished, the Capitalist system would go with it. It is one thing to take a coal-miner by the scruff of the neck and thrust him down a mine with an intimation that if he does not hew his regulation number of tons in the week he will be handled as the conscientious objectors were handled during the war. It is quite another to lay violent hands on the Honorable Reginald Highcastle and his friend Tommy Briggs, the son of the Bradford wool millionaire, and yank them out of their hotel in Monte Carlo or their flat in St James's in the same uncompromising manner, with no ladies to taunt them into consenting to the operation by presenting them with white feathers and calling them slackers. To exempt Reggie and Tommy, even if any satisfactory line could be drawn between them and their fellow creatures, would be a revolution of the proprietary classes against free contract and a return to open slavery. To conscribe them would be to attempt to carry on the Capitalist system without the lure that has hitherto persuaded its victims to tolerate it, and with its boasted Incentive to Labor sidetracked. In such a dilemma the Government, instead of encouraging the owners to fight, would probably have told them that they must settle with the men at any cost.

The opportunity was lost, and lost solely because Trade Unionism, instead of leading to the solution of the problem, led nowhere. As the leaders were either not willing to face compulsory service or were convinced that their followers would desert them at once if they hinted at such a thing, they had nothing to say except that the men objected to have their wages reduced. The coal-owners replied that they could not and would not pay the same wages as before; and as the owners were in a position to starve the miners into submission, they did so, leaving Labor in a condition of humiliation and servitude, and Labor policy in a condition of exposed futility which has given Capitalism all the courage of success without giving Labor any of the courage of despair.

Labor won its way into Parliament as an independent party fifteen years ago; and its leaders made their way into the Cabinet. And this is the result. The Anarchists and Syndicalists smile, and say "We told you so." But they take care to add that however disillusioned they may be with Parliament and Government and Thrones and Churches and all the other superstitions of the bourgeoisie, they remain unalterably devoted to the Charter of Amiens and the general strike. Is it to be wondered at that prosaic men cry "A plague on your rights and lefts, your Reds and Whites and Pale Pinks, your first and second and third Internationals, your phrases that only differ from Lloyd George's in being translated from foreign languages: we shall vote for the Anti-Waste candidate, whom we can at least understand, and who has not sold us yet"?

There is nothing more to be said at present. There is nothing more to be done until Labor recognizes that there can be no life until the task imposed by Nature is performed, and no freedom until the burden of that task is impartially distributed and sternly enforced. The debt to Nature must cease to be regarded as a commercial debt which one man can accept for another like a bill of exchange. It is a personal debt which must be defrayed by the individual who has incurred it. If he says "My grandfather worked for six," the reply must be "Then go one better than your grandfather, and work for seven. In that way the world will be the better for your having lived, as it is for your grandfather having lived; and you shall not undo the good he did by wasting it in idleness." And as to the man who should say "My grandfather owned for a thousand," it is difficult to say what could be done with so hopeless a fool except to lead him to the nearest wall and ask him to look carefully down the barrels of half-a-dozen levelled rifles and consider whether he seriously proposed to follow his grandfather's example. At all events that is something like what will happen to him if the so-called Dictatorship of the Proletariat ever becomes an accomplished fact here as it is in Russia.

With compulsory social service imposed on every one, the resistance to the other measures involved with Socialism would not only become pointless but injurious to the resisters. Just as a poor landlord is a bad landlord, and a poor employer the worst of employers, an embarrassed, imperfect, poorly financed, struggling Socialist State would make things far less pleasant for its members than a powerful and prosperous one. At present the position of a rich proprietor is by no means free from care: his servants, his houses, his investments, his tenants all worry him a good deal; but he puts up with it, partly because he can no more help his riches than a poor man can help his poverty, but largely, of course, because he has luxury and attendance and sports and fashionable society, and can, up to a certain point, do what he likes, even if what he likes is doing nothing. But if his servants were conscribed for social service, and himself with them, of what use to him would his title deeds and his share certificates be? The possibility of keeping a big establishment vanishes with the servants; and even if the State employed him to manage his own estate, as it probably would if he had managed it capably before and not handed it over to bailiffs, stewards, agents and solicitors, he would be no better off as its legal owner than as a commissioner of Woods and Forests or any other state official of the managing grade. It would not be worth his while to offer a moment's resistance to the transfer of his property rights to the State: on the contrary, as the richer the State was the larger would be the income to be distributed to its members, and the shorter that part of his life compulsorily devoted to its service, he would regard individual property rights as an attempt to fix on him responsibilities and duties from which his fellow workers were happily exempt, without any equivalent advantage. Under such circumstances men would cling to and covet title, rank, renown, and any sort of immaterial distinction, as well as cherished personal possessions; but they certainly would not cling to property; and as the Socialist State would be liberal in the matter of moral distinctions and the glorification of good citizenship, and would enable its citizens to multiply choice personal possessions, their ambition and acquisitiveness would have ample satisfaction. There would still be a privilege for gentility. A man overpaying his debt to Nature, and thereby making his country better by every hour of his activity, would be distinguished as a gentleman, being thus exactly the opposite of the so-called gentleman of Capitalism, who leaves his country poorer than he found it, and is proud of the depredation.

Such a change as this, however little its full scope may be understood at first, is far too revolutionary to make itself effective by a simple majority of votes in a Parliamentary division under normal circumstances. The civil service would not administer it in good faith; the tribunals would not enforce it; the citizens would not obey it in the present state of the public conscience. The press would strain all its powers of comminatory rhetoric to make it infamous. Therefore, if circumstances remain normal, several years of explicit propaganda will be necessary to create even a nuclear social conscience in its favor; and the first step must be to convert the leaders of Labor and the official Socialists themselves. Trade Unionism must be turned inside out, and must deny, instead of affirming, that right to idle and slack and ca' canny, which makes the social parasitism of the proprietariat legal. The "weapon of the strike" must be discarded as the charter of the idle rich, who are on permanent strike, and are the real Weary Willies and ablebodied paupers of our society. The Marxists must cease their intolerable swallowings and regurgitations of Marxian phrases which they do not understand (not having read Marx), and cease boring and disgusting the public with orations at pompously quarrelsome Congresses ending in Amiens Charters calling for that quintessence of anti-Socialism, the general strike. If they have nothing better than that to recommend, they had better go home to bed, where they will bore and mislead nobody but themselves. They must at last begin to tell the public precisely what Socialism means in practice.

But the circumstances may not remain normal. The proprietary class, when it sees that the normal course of events is leading to the abolition of property, can and will produce abnormal conditions favorable to itself by Catherine the Second's expedient of a little war to amuse the people. The Labor movement may itself upset the apple cart by further attempts at a general strike by Triple Alliances and the like. It is important to remember that it was in Russia, the most backward first class Power in Europe, that the ground was cleared for Communism, not by the Communists, but by the Imperialists, who, in mere thriftless ignorance and incompetence, ditched their car, and left themselves at the mercy of an energetic section of Realist Communists, who no sooner took the country in hand than they were led by the irresistible logic of facts and of real responsibility to compulsory social service on pain of death as the first condition, not merely of Communism, but of bare survival. They shot men not only for shirking and slacking, but for drinking at their work. Now it is clear that in point of ignorance, incompetence, social myopia, class prejudice, and everything that can disqualify statesmen and wreck their countries, the sort of people who can get returned to Parliament at khaki elections in the west of Europe and in the United States of America can hold their own with anybody the Tsardom ever put into power in Russia. Capitalism is much stronger in the west than in Russia, where it was relatively undeveloped; but though it had not reached its climax there and was in its infancy, it has passed its climax here, and is getting unsteady on its feet of clay. It also may ditch its car, and leave the most capable realists to save the situation.

In that case, we may have the Dictatorship of the Proletariat in the sense in which the phrase is being used by the Russian Communist statesmen. To them dictatorship means overriding democracy. For example, though there are elected Soviets everywhere in Russia, and it sometimes happens that on some vital question the voting is 20 for the Government and 22 against it (the opposition consisting of Social Revolutionaries, Mensheviks, Syndicalists, and other persons quite as abhorrent to the Morning Post as the reigning Communists), the Government does not thereupon say "Your will be done: the voice of the majority is the voice of God." It very promptly dissolves that Soviet, and intimates to its constituents that until they elect a preponderantly Bolshevik Soviet they shall have no Soviet at all. It may even treat the majority as rebels. The British democrat is scandalized by this; and even those who are too cynical or indifferent to be scandalized say "What is the use of having a Soviet at all under such conditions?" But the rulers of Russia reply that the use of it is that they know where they are. They find out from it how public opinion is tending, and what districts are backward and need to be educated. The British democrat, dazed, asks whether it is cricket to exclude the Opposition from the governing bodies. The Russian Statesmen reply that they are fighting a class war, and that during a war an Opposition is the enemy. They are asked further whether they have any right to impose new institutions on their country until they have persuaded a majority of the inhabitants to demand it. They reply that if no political measure had ever been passed until the majority of the inhabitants understood it and demanded it, no political measure would ever have been passed at all. They add that any party, however revolutionary in theory, which refuses in a highminded manner to take any action until it is supported by a constitutional majority, is clearly led by *fainéants* (not to say cowards and incapables) who are making their democratic principles an excuse for keeping out of trouble.

Now I am not here concerned to refute or justify these retorts. I simply point out that they have been made, and always will be made, by Governments when they are accused of acting without democratic constitutional mandates, or of excluding from the franchise persons and classes on whose support they cannot rely. If what is quite incorrectly called the class struggle (for a large section of the proletariat is as parasitic as its propertied employers, and will vote and fight for them) is brought to a head in England by the mismanagement of the Government or by some catastrophe beyond its control, let no one imagine that either side will have any more regard for democracy than the Russian Communists, the Irish Republican Army, the British occupation of Egypt, Dublin Castle, or any Government in time of war. The democrats, as in Europe, will be inert: they will hold meetings and denounce both combatants as tyrants and murderers; and both sides will imprison or kill them when they are too troublesome to be ignored. They will have to console themselves as best they may by the reflection that in the long run no Government can stand without a certain minimum of public approval, were it only a melancholy admission that all the available alternatives are worse.

It must not be supposed that Capitalism has any more advocates than Communism if an advocate means one who understands his case. People are accustomed to it: that is all; and so it has plenty of adherents. When Capitalism is forgotten, and people have become accustomed to Communism, it, too, will have plenty of adherents. Meanwhile, the groups who do understand, and who desire the change with sufficient intensity to devote themselves to its accomplishment, will do what such men have always done: that is, strive for power to impose the realization of their desire on the world. But their craving will include a need for sympathy and countenance: there is little satisfaction in imposing what you conceive to be a millennial boon on the reluctant body of a neighbor who loathes you and your detested Communism. Until you can impose it on his soul by persuading him to desire it as ardently as you do yourself, you are not only not happy, but not secure. That is why the Russian Communists are insistent in their propaganda and inculcation of Communism, although the military forces and civil persecution which they employ against the counter-revolution are objectively undistinguishable from the forcible imposition of Communism on the bodies of their subjects, whether their subjects like it or not. Just as the English officer will tell you that if England gave back India to the Indians India would instantly be devastated by civil wars ending in chaos, so the Red officers of Russia will tell you that if Russia were abandoned by the Bolsheviks to the hardfisted doers of the counter-revolution and the futile doctrinaire phrasemongers of the Constitutional Democrats, she would relapse into the Tsarism (so deeply regretted by the Grand Duchesses and Princesses in Constantinople and London), under which women spent years in dungeons for teaching children to read (lest they should read Marx), laborers lived in cellars and earned one pound four a month, and the dear princesses could hire a droschky to take them to the Opera for fourpence. They can drive their lesson home by pointing to counter-revolutionary Vladivostock in the far east, and to the great republic of Capitalist freedom in the far west, both of them sentencing girls of eighteen to fifteen years' imprisonment for distributing leaflets uncomplimentary to Capitalism. I do not here pass judgment either on the White British officer or on the Red Russian officer: I merely say that when the so-called class war comes to blows in England (and I am afraid our proprietary Whites will not give in without a fight even if the Labor Party in Parliament comes in 600 strong) the Whites and the Reds will argue in exactly the same way; and the muddled man in the street, without knowledge or conviction either way, will cast his reactionary ballot in vain.

However, the Capitalists may very well take heart for the present. They have on their side the colossal inertia of established institutions; and the souls of the children in the schools are in their hands. They have the *soi-disant* brain workers on their side: has not Trotsky, when foolishly reproached for employing them handsomely (as if Communism meant organizing industry without brains or training), replied "Yes; but we had to give them a good hiding first." Even our university engineers, receiving less than the wage of a common fitter, dread the Communism that would raise their incomes to the level of a common fitter's. This straightforward exposition of mine, which might be dangerous (except that it would be superfluous) if men were politically intelligent and the working classes had not been commercialized to the bone by two centuries of wage slavery, will drop into the sea of Labor politics as a pebble drops into the sea when a boy throws it from the cliff. Labor leaders will still brandish the weapon of the strike: indeed already the Trade Unions, having found the Triple Alliance a failure, are organizing alliances of still higher numerical powers, so as to achieve the nearest possible approximation to the general strike and make failure quite certain. Many of them believe that the Triple Alliance might have succeeded if its organizers had dared to fire the gun they had so carefully loaded. A word in favor of compulsory service, or of any compulsion except the compulsion of starvation and the miserable eyes of hungry children, would send any Labor leader back to the bench or down the mine, a cashiered and never-to-be-pardoned traitor to freedom. Our rulers do not sing "Curzon's at the Foreign Office; and there's lots of money for somebody in the coming war with America for the command of the seas";[6] but that is what they mean when they sing, as they occasionally do, "God's in his heaven: all's right with the world." Perhaps it is. It may be that the reason our civilizations always break down and send us back to the fields is that we were never meant to be civilized animals, and that the collapses of empires are not catastrophes but triumphs of sanity, blessed awakenings from fevered dreams. If so, it looks as if we were in for another triumph presently; and then we—or at any rate, the handful of survivors—will enjoy a respite from both Capitalism and Communism until the fever breaks out again. But personally I am no Arcadian; and I should very much like to see Communism tried for awhile before we give up civilization as a purely pathological phenomenon. At any rate, it can hardly produce worse results than Capitalism.

Portions of a lecture delivered before the Fabian Society at Kingsway Hall, London, on Thursday, 26 November 1925. Published in the New York Times on 20 December 1925 under the title "Shaw Foresees a Four-Hour Working Day."

The Impossibilities
of Freedom

I do not think I shall give you a definition by way of formula; but I will make, I think, perfectly clear what I mean by freedom.

I ask you to imagine a man standing between 8 and 9 o'clock on a Saturday morning on Hammersmith Broadway. He has to catch a train and to be, by 9 o'clock, perhaps half-past nine, possibly 10 o'clock, in some shop or office. He has to remain there until 1 o'clock. There is no use in your telling me that the man is free. He may be whistling Rule Britannia as loudly as he possibly can; but he is not free, in any sense of the word that any ordinary sensible person will understand.

Even if he is not going into an ordinary shop or office; even if he is going to the Post Office, into the service of the community, although he is metaphysically free (from Mr Sidney Webb's point of view), from my practical and non-metaphysical point of view, which I am using for the moment, he is not free. If you ask him whether he can come with you to the National Gallery, say at half-past nine o'clock, he will tell you at once: "Oh, I am not free until 1 o'clock."

Imagine that when it is half-past nine that man is standing on Hammersmith Broadway again. His position is entirely altered. Now he is not bound to be in any particular place at any particular time. He considers what he will do. He can go to the Regent

Theatre matinee [where Shaw's plays were being performed]; he
can go off through Surrey on his motor bicycle and spend the
afternoon there; he can go on the river; he can go home and foozle
about with wireless, or he can dig in the garden, or he can sit down
and read, or he can do nothing. That man is free for that Saturday
afternoon. He is, for all ordinary purposes—and a fact in the only
sense you can give to the word without getting into a terrific
mess—free.

He says: "I am free until 6 o'clock," or something of that sort;
and we all perfectly understand what he means. It does not, of
course, mean that he can do exactly what he likes. There are certain
things that he has to go on doing. For example, he is not free to
stop growing older; and if you are a person of a litigious, argumen-
tative sort you may say that a man who is not free to stop growing
older is not really quite free at all.

He calls himself free, and I call him free, and in any practical
discussion of the affairs of life you will have to call him free, to that
extent. His freedom, we will say, lasts until 6 o'clock. Then there
comes a further compulsion on him. He begins to get hungry. As a
matter of fact, sometimes he gets hungry at 4:30.

The horrible habit of afternoon tea, which is destroying the nation, may come upon him. At any rate, he gets hungry. Also, to a
certain extent, he gets dirty, especially if he is in London. Therefore he finds that he is no longer free. He must go somewhere and
get a meal, and he must wash himself—unless he prefers to remain
dirty.

When he has got through his meal he may have another little
free time. But then he finds he wants to go to sleep; and, as a
matter of fact, he must go to sleep. He goes to sleep, we will say, for
eight hours, during which, if his digestion is good, you may say he
ceases to exist.

Now I suggest to you that what one may call the standard day,
the standard working day, under socialism, will probably be something like that. Four hours work, eight hours sleep (which comes to
twelve hours), and say four hours for eating, drinking, dressing,
undressing, and a little resting that is not included in your sleep,
and a certain amount of time for getting about.

So far as socialism goes it will give people the possibility of being
free for eight hours; and it would seem that, having shewn how
that may be secured, the Socialist has nothing more to say on the
subject of freedom than anybody else has. He may say: "Having

gained this leisure, which we never had before, if you like to use it to enslave yourselves (which would be very likely what you would do, judging by what you do at the present time) well, that is not the fault of socialism."

Partly through the domestic enthusiasm of Rosslyn Mitchell we have become very much interested in the question of marriage.[1] How will marriage be affected by this extension of freedom? It will be affected, not only by the mere question of leisure (which in itself would not affect it) but that condition of socialism, that condition of the working day, of equal income, and so on, will involve the almost entire abolition of what we call vested interests.

Anybody who has tried in our present society to get any change made knows that he always comes up against a vested interest some time. You will see that the entire disappearance of these vested interests would make political change very much easier than it is at present; that is to say would make political progress, would make social progress—which is essentially a matter of change—easier.

But when you come to domestic freedom, then it is not so much a case of vested interests; it is a case of economic independence. A tremendous difference will necessarily be made if you bring about a state of society in which every individual is absolutely economically independent.

We are all, I suppose, happily married men—but more or less. Some of us are really so unhappily married that we allow ourselves to recognize the fact that we are unhappily married; but a very great many of us would recognize that we were not very happily married if we could escape from the marriage.

You know there is an extraordinary practicability about the human mind, men's and women's. Somehow or other the ordinary man or woman who has got what is called good sense—they do not allow themselves to worry about things that cannot be helped. Accordingly, if you have a man and woman married together, and if the woman cannot break up her household and go, because she has no means of existence (she cant go out into the street and practically starve, and she does not see that she can support herself), and if the man is really in the same position—if the man cannot extricate himself without ruining himself or without embarrassing himself tremendously—then those two people will never allow their minds to dwell on the fact that they are not well suited to each other and might do better elsewhere.

I think you will see that in a state of things where a wife could leave her husband without experiencing the slightest pecuniary embarrassment: where she would be perfectly self-supporting; where she would have an income quite independent of whether she was with her husband or not, and where the husband would be in exactly the same position in regard to himself—naturally, under those circumstances, the social pressure that keeps very many households together being completely relaxed in that direction, a great many households would break up. That is to say, a great many that do not now break up would break up under socialism, because there would be a great deal of trial and error before the perfect union was formed.

I also very much doubt whether the union would be of that extremely close nature that it is at present—I mean, the way in which married people, even under existing circumstances, interfere with oneanother's lives to an entirely unnecessary extent. When the economic pressure was removed, then, I think, on the whole, that the marriage tie would really literally be a looser tie. And that, I think, makes for greater freedom, and probably would make for greater happiness, in marriage.

People under socialism are happily married—well, there they are. Nobody suggests that socialism is going to interfere with them. The only question is: Is socialism going to interfere at all? I think it is, because I do not think that any Government in any well-ordered State is likely to allow two people to get together and to produce children without asking them to register that bond in some way. One does not see, beyond the fact of registration, that socialism is going to interfere with them, except at one very important point, and that point is birth control.

It is difficult to conceive of a Socialist State which does not control birth. I do not want to pretend to know what I do not know about this question. It is an extremely obscure question. The question of birth control at present, and in our present society, has been prematurely forced on us. The present agitation for it is an entirely artificial thing, owing to the bad construction of our society.

If you take the world as a whole, to hear some of our Malthusian birth controllers dealing with the question, they really declare that the world is, and they imply always has been, under what is called by economists the law of diminishing returns. Which means, if you take it all through, that two men produce less per head than one man; that three men produce less per head than one man, and so on.

We all know, of course, that that is entirely untrue. Two men, if they co-operate with oneanother, instead of competing or trying to enslave oneanother, or fighting or squabbling (that is to say, if they are not normal Englishmen, brought up under our system)—those two men, by co-operating, will produce more per head than does one man, and three men co-operating will produce much more than three times one. When you come to the question of the relations between what a million men co-operating can produce, and what a hundred men co-operating can produce—well, the figures, if we could arrive at anything like exactitude in them, would sound fabulous.

A great many of our friends are very fond of talking about the class war. What they really imagine—what is at the back of their minds—is the idea that if they could organize the whole working class then they would be able to sweep away the proprietary class. They say that the war is between the proprietary class and the proletariat: "Proletarians of all lands, unite, and you sweep away the proprietors!"

Yes, but the proletarians of all lands will not unite, for the excellent reason that one-half of them, instead of being productive, are hanging on to the proprietors; they are the servants of the proprietors; they are the retainers of the proprietors; they are the tradesmen of the proprietors. When the proprietors rob the real productive proletariat, then the parasitic proletariat proceed to rob the proprietors as best they can.

If we project ourselves into the remote future, when socialism has placed us all under the law of increasing returns in food, then, for many reasons, it may be desirable to limit the population—for a number of reasons that we do not at present think of. If you ask me how that is to be done, I do not know. I do not know what the real consequences of the artificial means that are used at present are. They are forced upon us, as I say, by our existing capitalist civilization. There are no visible bad results which are as bad as the results of the over-population which would be produced if they were neglected. The consequence is that they are practised by practically all cultivated and educated people.

I suggest to you—I cannot, of course, hold out any hope as regards birth control at the present moment; birth control is a fact and a necessity at the present moment created by capitalism—if you want to get rid of that immediate necessity, you can bring about socialism.

My subject would not be complete if I simply dealt, as I have done, with marriage and politics and Parliament (which I have referred to in the matter of vested interests)—if I left out the very important subject of religion, and, what is necessarily associated with that, the subject of education.

Grown-up people must find their own religion. You cannot control their religion.

You can make them go to church; you can make them repeat a certain creed; you can say: "If you do not repeat the creed we will burn you." Under such circumstances you say: "Thank you, I will repeat the creed." That does not make people believe the creed, and it finally cannot make them behave as if the creed meant anything. But when you come to the question of children, then, of course, socialism will necessarily bring about a very great change.

If there is one lesson which we ought to have learned from the history of the last two centuries, it is the lesson taught us quite early in them by the German poet Goethe, who said that the man who wanted life and freedom had got to fight for them every day. Socialism has not only to be set going, but it has to be kept going— and it never can be kept going unless every child is educated as a Communist.

I remember devoting one of these lectures to this question of education. I pointed out how utterly disheartening it was to us all to find that when we had educated those people in our own generation who were live wires, who were capable of education; that when one generation of men had had, say, free trade knocked into them, then had socialism knocked into them, then a few years passed and the whole thing was gone, a new generation had come up in the hands of the parson, in the hands of the squire, being taught in the old ways and taught the old things; being given the Bible as a rule of conduct, and being given the Catechism and Prayer Book, and so on.

These people grew up knowing nothing whatever about free trade, nothing whatever about socialism, about utilitarianism, about any of these things that had so definitely been taught by Fabian societies, by utilitarians, by free-traders and all the rest. It was rolling a stone up a hill.

It is clear to me that a Socialist Government will say of the Bible: This literature is very interesting from an artistic point of view; people who want to become cultivated, people who for instance want to get an artistic literary cultivation, certainly must read the Bible. But we are not going to allow any person to put that Bible into the hands of a child and tell the child either that it is true as a statement of fact in every particular, or that it is a desirable guide to conduct.

Socialism will say: We will have our own religion. We will not have an Oriental religion which is completely out-of-date and is getting out-of-date even in the East. We will have an Occidental, a Western, religion, that belongs to our own time and that touches the morality of our own time.

You will have, of course, many people who will say: "We told you so. Socialism wants to abolish religion." If the sort of thing that they teach in the schools is religion, we are going to abolish it. But genuine religion is not quite so easily killed. Even the Bible cannot kill it, no matter how unscrupulously you use it.

You may take it that on the whole there will be a tolerably stiff State religion which will be taught to children; and anybody endeavoring to teach the children anything else will probably be treated exactly as we should treat a person like Fagin in Oliver Twist, who deliberately taught children how to pick pockets. A great deal of the morality which is taught at the present time, and which children are taught to regard as very sacred, and as being the quintessence of honesty, you must remember, is, from the Socialist point of view, nothing but picking pockets and trying to cover up the fact with fine phrases.

My own opinion is that the burden of what is at present called religion has become so intolerable that people are unable to conceive freedom without getting rid of a great deal of it at least. You need not be afraid of killing what are called the eternal elements in it, and you will have to be rather careful in dealing with it, because it is very hard to say exactly where people find their natural religious food.

I hope that a Socialist Government will deal very carefully and not too rationalistically with religion. There are people who call themselves ethical people, and very good people they are. Our ethical societies contain a great many admirable people; but they have produced some of the most horrible literature of modern times. They have produced books on morality for the use of children, and I solemnly declare that if I had a child I would give it ten Bibles—the Bible, and the Koran, and all the books that belong to the remotest past ages—and I would say: "Read these to nourish your soul, and to give you lofty ideals; but for God's sake dont read the works of the Ethical Society!"

I do not want to sit down without hoping that some of you will be able to let your minds play over the sort of future which comes down to the eight hours leisure a day; the tremendous fruits of leisure; the fact that leisure might become by far the busiest and the most fruitful part of the days that we should live.

I believe that we should probably do with less bread and butter. I am certain we should do with less clothes. I am not at all certain Mr Wells is not right in looking forward to the time when, at least in the middle of the summer, we might do almost without them. You see there is a large movement that way among women.

But that leisure will become an extraordinarily fruitful leisure. The freedom that it brings will lead to invention; will lead to all sorts of things. And it is that leisure, it is that freedom, which will transform the world far more than the mere economic side of socialism.

Abridged verbatim report of a lecture delivered before the Fabian Society at Kingsway Hall, London, on Wednesday, 24 November 1926. Published in the New York Times on 12 December 1926 under the title "Shaw Expounds Socialism as World Panacea."

Cultural Internationalism

I have one advantage tonight, I am addressing the last meeting of the series. The last shilling we can hope to take has been taken, and therefore, unlike the other lecturers, I am in a position to give away the show. The series of lectures has had for its general title The Shrinking World. Now I do now know how you interpreted that. If you interpreted it as meaning that the world was shrinking from the lectures, you may have been right; but I believe that the meaning of whomever invented that title was that the world is getting small. We all say that the means of communication have become so rapid, the distances between places have become so small in terms of time, that the world is getting smaller and smaller. That is the shrinking world. I put it to you, as sensible people, did you ever hear such nonsense in the whole course of your life?

The world is not shrinking, meaning the inhabited world, which is what we are dealing with; that is getting larger and larger. The cities are getting larger, and there are a great many more of them. The battles are getting larger. The cities nowadays are no longer cities, they are provinces. If you go to the Birmingham district or the Manchester district you will find that there are still a number of names of towns left scattered about, but they have all grown into one town. In military matters you will find that the battles have become campaigns; and that they never settle anything. All you can say is that they are enormously larger than the old battles and that the casualty lists are much larger.

If it is true that the inhabitants of the world can get at one-another more easily, that simply facilitates their cutting oneanother's throats. It may make certain operations more manageable, but that does not mean that the scene of the operations or the subject of the operations is getting smaller: on the contrary, it is getting larger and larger and more difficult. What we have got to understand is that we are not facing a shrinking world, we are facing a colossally expanding world, with its difficulties enormously increased by the fact that all the diverse people in the world have been put within reach of oneanother in a way that they never had been before.

Now, how are we facing that problem, that enormously increased world? We are facing it with the moral and legislative equipment of a medieval village, tempered by the regulations of a tribe of wandering Jews, made at a time when Moses, although he was within a few miles of his objective, had to keep them wandering in the desert round and round for forty years, until all the people who had come from Egyptian slavery had died out. Even then the results of getting them into the Promised Land at last, after all that toil, were not too encouraging from the point of view of the historian.

My special heading tonight is International Culture. What is a culture? A culture, I take it, is a body of thought common to a large number of people. As a result of that, it is a body of moral institutions, common beliefs; and the ideal culture would of course be a body of thought founded on a body of knowledge, real, scientific, genuine knowledge and resulting in certain common standards of conduct. It is true that a culture could be founded on a body of thought, a body of knowledge, but unfortunately it can also be founded on a common body of superstition, folly, romance, ignorance, and error. I am afraid that that is the description that applies in a greater or less degree to almost all the cultures that we have in the world today.

However, no matter; we say culture is founded on genuine knowledge. I said, by the way, a moment ago, scientific knowledge, but as the scientific knowledge of today is about the most romantic thing that human credulity has ever imposed on the human race, I prefer genuine knowledge, and knowledge which has some remote kind of correspondence to the facts of life. In any community, whatever its culture may be, you have to have government, order, and organization. As a result of that, you have to have a dogma, a good deal of dogma, and you have finally to have a dogma of infallibility.

The Roman Catholic Church has, as you know, got a dogma of infallibility about which we who do not belong to that church are occasionally very superior; but I really do not see that our own dogma of infallibility is any more plausible. The Roman Catholic says the Pope is infallible; we say the King can do no wrong. If you come to the common sense of the matter as it appeals to the ordinary man, there is nothing whatever to choose between the two statements, except that the Papacy is a little more venerable institution, and is better stage-managed, if I may put it that way, than the constitutional monarchy is. I am not sure that the dogma of infallibility, if you understand it as it should be understood, is not a little more imposing as applied to the Pope than it is as applied to the King. * * *

Now let us get a little closer to the question of culture as I have defined it. Let us take some historical examples of culture. There are two great religious cultures very familiar to us—the culture of Christendom, and the culture of Islam—Mohammedanism, as we call it. These cultures you may contrast with two other cultures— Feudalism and Capitalism. We are looking forward to what our friend Trotsky advocates so strongly, feeling as he does so strongly the need of it, and that is a new culture which he calls a proletarian culture. * * *

When you come to feudalism you have had large bodies of people, at one time a very large body, practising feudalism and really believing and acting on all the assumptions of feudalism. It is astonishing how many of those people still exist among us. You will find them even in Parliament, and even in the Government, and that peculiar stratification of society which is called feudalism is the one on which they habitually act and in the terms of which they habitually think.

When you come to capitalism you are still harder down on the facts. Capitalism got away from the theologic man and invented the economic man; and you know he is really a fact. The economic man, crudely conceived, is a man who will pursue his own advantage, who will make as much money as he can. Evidently that is not true of all. You will find men, for instance, who have had to choose between making a great deal of money, say, by stockbroking, promoting, underwriting, shall I say; and making hardly any money at all as poets. Nevertheless, they refuse to become stockbrokers on any terms, and they insist on being poets at all hazards.

Nevertheless, they do not cease to be economic men, because, once they have made a decision, once a man has become a stockbroker or a poet, he will make as much money by his stockbroking as he can or as much money by his poetry as he can. There are occasionally startling exceptions. At the last meeting of the Fabian Society I had to sit in a state of great confusion, not knowing exactly what to do, whilst the whole audience congratulated me on having received a large sum of money, which, as it happened, I had just handed back and had not got at all. I was not precisely acting as the economic man on that occasion, but you may regard that as being a very transient aberration.

I make as much money as I possibly can habitually out of my plays and novels. I insist on doing that rather than pursuing what may be called an honest trade; but there it is. You have this fact, as I say, that these economic cultures do come down very much more on the actual facts of human nature.

The consequence is that curious hopes are arising of an economic culture. All the time that we have been in this room studying these questions in a very large way, a sort of running accompaniment of our meetings has been kept up by Mr H. G. Wells in the shape of a number of volumes about a gentleman named Clissold. Clissold is a man who believes that, after all, the capitalists—or, rather, the men of Big Business, the financiers, the big employers, the organizers—are the men who are going practically to thrust Parliament and the churches and all that sort of rubbish to one side; and they are going to take the world in hand and organize it.

* * *

I think there is no doubt that this Clissoldism, as it were, is getting into the air. Already you find in fiction people like the gentleman in one of my plays called Undershaft. You find this idea of the great millionaire, the great organizer. Mr Wells thinks it is possible to educate them. I was particularly careful to shew in my play that Mr Undershaft would have nothing to do with any partner who was educated; he insisted on getting somebody who had escaped that process.

Since that is really the international culture which is in the air at present, and which is exciting some people, I want just to go a little this evening into its difficulties. My business tonight will be very largely to raise difficulties. That is all the use I am really in this world. Culture, in the sense in which I have been using the word—bodies of thought founded on bodies of knowledge or on bodies of superstition or on bodies of romance, or bodies of anything you like that possesses men's minds—there are several of them in the world; but when you get a perfectly genuine definition of culture, such as I have given you, you begin to perceive that the boundaries between these cultures are not vertical boundaries like war.

Cultures exist in strata. You have a top stratum and then you have one underneath that. If you take the ocean, for example, you have a stratum of water at a certain depth, a certain pressure of water; then you have another stratum under that, and another under that, and another under that. The fish that can live in one stratum cannot live in another. If you get hold of a fish in the lower strata and bring it up to the top, it bursts promptly; and that is exactly the case with a culture. If you take a man from a low culture and bring him up to the top culture, he bursts, more or less, figuratively; mentally and intellectually he does burst, or bodily occasionally.

You will see that I am now getting to the question of internationalism, because these strata are international. Let us borrow from the military gentlemen their classification—C-1, C-2, C-3. You have heard a lot of these, and it is a very good way. You can take C as meaning culture; C-1 is the top stratum; C-2 is the one underneath it, C-3 is the one underneath that. These are all international in the sense that, no matter where you go in the world, you will find C-1 people, C-2 people, and C-3 people. That is the way you must think of the matter. You must not think that there is an English culture, and a French culture, and a Chinese culture, and begin to consider how you can bring them all together. As a matter of fact, you will find in China the C-1 man and you will find in France the C-1 man; and you will find that these cultures really correspond to grades of human ability. * * *

The C-1 people are all right. *Les beaux esprits se rencontrent*, which means, the choice spirits find one another out. Therefore, if the C-1 people were left in control of the world, the world might get on pretty well. But before I go into that question I just want to point out to you, that when you envisage these strata, C-1, C-2, C-3, and so on, you must not think of that as being always a fixed thing. You must not think of men as being always the same, a man having a certain character and keeping it under all conditions. * * *

We are all C-1 people—at least we had better pretend we think oneanother so—but we have not a very powerful and commanding share in the affairs of the country. When you have a Signor Mussolini firing cannons at little children in Corfu, because he said the Italians wanted a striking gesture; when you think of the sort of things that happened in my own country, that really you did not manage to make Ireland what they call the Free State until you had done a frightful lot of murdering and burning.

I remember, when I went out to Flanders during the War, and they showed me Ypres, and I looked at it, and they said: "What do you think of it?" I said: "It is nothing to Dublin. You should see Dublin, the city where I was born. The walls of Ypres are standing." I remember telling Commander Haig at that time: "What you want is an explosive that will act laterally. Your explosives leave the walls standing." But they did not leave the walls standing in Dublin. They took the whole center of Dublin, and practically there was hardly a wall left standing; and that was only a part of a campaign of fire and murder of the most horrible description, quite equaling the sort of things that Alva used to do in the Netherlands.[1]

Remember, the man who was mainly responsible for what was done in Ireland was a minister, Sir Hamar Greenwood.[2] Do you look on him with anything of the sort of horror that, if you are a good Protestant, you are supposed to look back at Alva with? ("Yes"). A gentleman says yes; I assure that gentleman that Sir Hamar Greenwood got 1800 votes up in Sunderland without the slightest difficulty. There was no reaction against him politically whatever, as far as I could make out, but his electoral chances were rather improved.

I need not remind you of the atrocity of Denshawai—one of those hideous blots on the face of history but which never shook the credit of Lord Grey in the slightest degree.[3] Nobody ever bothered particularly about it, and the people who did not bother about it I dare say really thought they were C-1 people; but they were not. On the whole, when you look at that kind of thing, and then when you look at what—this was all done under the war strain—when you come to consider what is done under the religious strain, things do not get in the least better. * * *

All these cultures, which are represented by these religious movements, are really very fiercely nationalist and imperialist cultures—hatred of the foreigner, rivalry with the foreigner; hatred of the man who disagrees with you in religion; hatred of the man who has got £20 a year perhaps more than you, which is a very strong feeling—the refusal to allow your children to play with him, to allow your daughter to marry his son and so on. All these class feelings are very strong. It is only the C-1 man who gets out of them.

The question comes, What is the remedy, if you want to make a move, since the C-3 people and the C-2 people are an obstacle to real international union and culture of any kind? There is the eugenic remedy, the first one which suggests itself to some people. They say, breed out the C-2 and all the lower strains, and breed in C-1. Let us have a population, not of C-3 or C-2 people, but consisting exclusively of C-1 people. Unfortunately, we have not got the remotest idea of how to set about it or how to get it—not the slightest.

You go to your eugenics societies and all that. I once went to address the Eugenic Society, and I unfortunately began my address by saying that the object of the Eugenic Society was to breed a better class of human beings, and I nearly wrecked the society. They went into hysterics; they said that such an infamous idea had never entered their head. Why they joined the society I do not know; perhaps on the off-chance of hearing a speech from Dean Inge. I grant you that that is a very good reason; still, it was not a eugenic reason. It still remains the only step that we dare take. We know nothing about the subject. If you want to get better people the only thing to do is to extend the field of sexual selection, and the only way you can do that is by giving everybody the same income; and we are not very close to that as yet.

When you give up eugenics you say, What is to be done? Admitting that the C-1 man is a happy accident, not like myself, and that the C-1 men and women will be in a small minority, then comes your remedy. Why not entrust the government of the world and the management of diplomacy and international affairs—why not hand that over to the C-1 people? Some such idea as that always has been a little in the minds of men. There has been always a sort of habit, when you have got a government, or a priesthood, or a communion of saints, or any other sort of people, to look up to and obey them. People always do their best to persuade themselves that these persons are C-1, but we who look a little more closely at politics and know how things are done, know that they are not C-1, that that thing has not come about, that somehow or another the C-1's are on the whole much more likely to get crucified than to get into the Cabinet.

You find that Demos—that is a convenient term to describe C-2, 3, 4, 5, and so on—Demos does not like C-1's, C-2 never does. He fears them in some way. It is a curious thing, but remember that we are speaking of grades of ability, and higher grades of ability have something rather terrifying about them; and when you fear a thing you hate it. Almost all hatred in the world comes from fear. C-1 people have to spend half their time in intimidating people without in the slightest degree meaning to do so, and during the other half they are trying to get out of the mess that they have got into by intimidating them, not knowing exactly what is wrong. But, at any rate, it is out of the question at present to entrust international relations to C-1's, for the simple reason that the C-2 and C-3 people will not allow it. * * *

So that really you are driven out of this idea. Democracy wont let you carry it out. What would be a third thing? I think the third leads us back on our tracks. Why not go back to *laisser-faire* and trust to Clissold? Well, there is a movement, as I said, in that direction. There is this idea that Mr Wells is not really advocating but is only putting it as the point of view of a man who is handling affairs on the big scale.

One of the things that shews you how it has been in the air is that quite a large society has grown up in our midst of late years, a body called Rotarians. Their object is to raise the employer, the business man, who is a mere vulgar tradesman, to raise him to professional rank, to make him an idealist, seeing that so much of the government of the world has passed into his hands, to try and make him worthy of his destiny; in fact, the ideal that is put forward in Clissold. It is, at any rate, worth teaching to the employers, trying to raise them to this particular height.

I myself on two occasions addressed the Rotarians. You know the way they meet. They have a midday lunch all together in the various cities. There is supposed to be one representative of each business and that is how the club is made up. As a matter of fact, I found in them a great many representatives of a particular business. In the printing business, for instance, you had the machine

represented, and the printing represented, and the paper represented, and I do not know what else; at any rate, it is perfectly easy
to get as many men who are virtually printers into clubs as you like.

That does not matter; the more the merrier. I, in my eloquent
manner, the manner in which I am at present addressing you, and
in my lucid manner, I put the ideal before them; and I never saw
men more astonished in the whole course of my life. I tried first in
Liverpool, and then I tried in Edinburgh. It is quite true that these
men came together, and that they lunched, and told oneanother
funny stories, but I really could not see that any of them had any
idea in their heads that the Rotarians had any other object or purpose; and I am afraid that the ideal with which the thing was
formed never really has succeeded well in getting into the heads of
the business men. * * *

Sometimes, of course, you have a great employer of labor, an
organizer of labor, who is an idealist—Mr Ford, for instance. Mr
Ford's books are full of wisdom and his practice is very interesting.
He has cut out the eight hour day by introducing the five day week,
which is distinctly a new stunt, taking it, not as a fact perhaps, but
purely as a stunt.

But, somehow or other, when you are thinking always of the
international culture, a culture that will bind the people together, I
seem to remember the attempt that Mr Ford made to interfere in
the war, and it did credit to his heart, if we may say so, but it was not
very promising with regard to his head.[4] Somehow or other you felt
that government by gentlemen like Mr Ford would do a great deal
of good in various directions, but internationally, as a means of
preventing wars and preserving the peace of the world, there he
did not distinguish himself in the way that he distinguished himself
when introducing the Ford car and high wages in his factories. * * *

Capital at the present time is running away with the whole world,
and these gentlemen are very much in the position of a chauffeur
whose car has run away and he does not know how to stop it and
does not know how to steer it and, accordingly, all he can do is to
try to look wise and hold on to the wheel and hope he wont get into
the ditch or over the precipice; and, as we are all in the car, it is not
at all reassuring and we begin to suspect from time to time that he
does not in the least know what he is doing.

The fact that these wonderful extensions, these wonderful crea-
tions of what my friend Sidney Webb calls new social tissue in their

hands—the fact that this is taking place does not in the least prove that they are managing the whole thing. They are gripping on today and they are making money, but they are not making an international culture of it and I do not believe they will. You see, they represent a particular kind of ability. There are people of special ability in the world. Some of them are very nice; you dont bother about them at all. They may be able to make very large fortunes, and quite possibly, even if we introduce socialism, they might make a great lot of money, and it would be extremely unpopular to interfere with them. * * *

But the talent that is represented by the Clissold people is a quite different sort of thing. It is not an individual talent, exercised by the possessor of the talent; it is the art of exploiting other people's talent. It is the art of taking advantage of the business ignorance or incapacity of the individual man of talent, getting hold of him and practically enslaving him, giving him enough to live on and taking all the rest for yourself.

There are two sorts there; there is the organizing talent, and there is the disciplining talent. There are some people who, either from force of character or from a complete indifference to making themselves very disagreeable, are able to intimidate other people, able to keep discipline and get orders obeyed. They do not get quite such high prices because they are a little commoner than the organizers. But these organizing people, simply because they have a monopoly of this particular kind of talent that you call business talent—which does not really imply great moral qualities or great political qualities—a man has it in such a degree that he can pile millions on millions—you may infer that that man has an intellect and conscience like that of Mr Wells.

That is a tremendous mistake. Mr Clissold, in the book, was a little like Mr Wells occasionally; I think you will admit that; but, some way or other, the actual Clissold with whom you meet in the general theatre of life is rather deficient in that way. To be quite frank, one of the tasks we have before us is to rescue ourselves from the tyranny of the monopoly that these people have got of that particular kind of talent.

There is another great difficulty in doing that. Very much abler men than they are, serve their country in the army and the navy, in the civil service and in the Government. But these gentlemen are practically insatiable. What is more, they do not understand their own silly business in a political sense.

Take now, for example, the man who is really master of the modern situation, and that is the financier. In the nineteenth century, the American economic man, John Walker,[5] wrote a study of the industrial situation, and he said the employer was unquestionably the master of it; and that was so. The employer was the man who organized labor, without whom all the other classes were entirely helpless. The employer turned to the landlord, on the one hand, the helpless landlord; he turned to the helpless capitalist, on the other, and he said to the landlord: "You have got a lot of land, and you do not know how to make a farthing out of it; hand your land over to me, and I will pay you so much." He said to the capitalist: "You do not know how to employ that capital industriously"; and the capitalist said: "Certainly not. I am a gentleman. I am not a trader." The employer said: "Very well, give me your capital, I will use it, and pay you so much." In the same way he said to the laborer: "I will pay for your labor, I will pay you a living wage, and organize your labor so that plenty of money can be made out of it."

The employer was undoubtedly the cock of the walk. Now he is a proletarian. There has been a complete change. Not only have all the secrets of employment been so largely found out; it was a new thing, remember, in the nineteenth century, this organization of labor on the modern scale, but now it can be acquired by everybody; education has spread, so that people are not cut off now through want of education from it as they were before.

But there is another thing. The sums that are required to finance business are enormously larger than they used to be. My father, after being a civil servant, went into business, without the slightest knowledge of business; but he went into business. I do not know what his capital was. I dare say, between him and his partner, they may have had a couple of thousand pounds, or something like that; and that was quite common. Well, look at the latest reports of the merger, as they call it, of which Sir Alfred Mond appears to be chief.[6] I forget if it is fifty millions or fifty thousand millions: it does not matter much. The main thing is that these colossal sums are sums which are utterly beyond the capacity of an ordinary employer to collect. He cannot get them from his friends, they are too large, and his banker will not allow him to overdraw to that extent. He finds himself quite helpless.

He discovers that he has to go to a special, a new class of men, whose business it is to collect large sums of money, promoters. He has to go to these men, and he says: "I want a large capital, or I cannot go on; I want twenty thousand pounds." They kick him out of the office, saying: "Do you suppose we would dirty our fingers with things of that kind? Go to your own broker. Get out!" If smarting under that treatment, he says: "Will you get me seventy thousand pounds?" they say: "Well, it is not much, but if you will take seventy thousand pounds and call it a hundred thousand pounds and pay interest on a hundred thousand pounds and assume the responsibility of having borrowed a hundred thousand pounds, perhaps we will give you the seventy thousand pounds." That is really the sort of thing that goes on, and the result is that the financiers and the bankers are the men who really now are masters of the industrial situation, and the employer has practically gone.

* * *

On the whole I must dismiss, I think, the Clissold gentleman, the financier and the employer and the organizer of business. I do not say that he has not ideals. I do not like his ideals. As far as he has any ideals at all, they appear to me on the whole to be mischief. They may be excellent in the money market, but the money market is only a corner of the world, and it is the rest of the world we have to deal with.

After all, it comes back to the old Fabian solution. There is no use in imagining that you are going to have a great international culture in which all people will think alike. In our time and for some time to come you will do a great deal if you can bring all the different peoples to think alike even on one point, and I suggest to you that there is some reasonable chance of their getting to think alike on the great question of the distribution of wealth, or getting them to think that the present distribution of wealth is extraordinarily unsatisfactory, that it is ridiculous, that it is gross, that it is absurd, that it has gone beyond all endurance, that it has become simply a bad joke and a very mischievous one. Everybody knows that.

Indeed, if we stick at our Fabian work of advocating socialism, which really means advocating redistribution, I think a great many people who differ from us in the ordinary sense collaterally will be coming with us.

I have been extraordinarily amused of late by my friend Gilbert Chesterton. I have been lying low for Mr Chesterton for many years. He scorns socialism. Unlike his brother, Cecil Chesterton, he would not join the Fabian Society; he was disgusted with the whole thing, the whole conception of bureaucracy, the loss of liberty and all the rest of it. He invented a new thing himself, and, curiously enough, the first thing I smiled at was that he called this new thing not socialism but distributism, which, by the way, is rather a better name for socialism than socialism, because it describes it, and after preaching that what you want is a redistribution of property and doing it in a rather vague way, never coming down to tin tacks, giving you a sort of vision of Chesterton under his own vine and fig tree, with a nice little rivulet going through his garden and he digging the soil and producing wheat and that kind of thing—the sort of life that would make him commit suicide if he had ten days of it.

But he never came nearer to it than that until the other day, when he was suddenly plunged into practical politics by the coal strike. He settled the coal strike and his remedy is nationalization of the coal. He begins absolutely with a measure which sweeps away all his little private property plans—they are all gone, and behold Mr Chesterton a full-blown Socialist, although he has adopted a coal culture which many of us cannot dissent from. What does that matter if he agrees with us on that side?

If we find that all over the world people are being driven by mere pressure of circumstances to apply their minds to this, then I think there is some hope, as I say, in our time of getting a sort of common belief that may unite the peoples of the world in a movement which is the only possible solution, and that solution is equal distribution, because you have nothing to do but try any other solution that can be proposed, and you will find that it wont work, that it is impossible. That would rid us of over-population, it would rid us of poverty, it would rid us of that moral evil which Mr Wells has very rightly called attention to, the resentment complex, which is so very general. All that would be worth trying. * * *

I suggest that our old panacea, the redistribution of wealth, the introduction of socialism, is the one thing in which I see any hope of a union for the whole proletarian world. Accordingly, my advice to you Fabians is not to let yourselves run away on Clissoldism or on international cultures or anything of the kind, but to learn the old game, the old Socialist game, and peg away at it.

Extract from a lecture delivered before the Fabian Society at Kingsway Hall, London, on Thursday, 22 November 1928, and published in the Newcastle Daily Journal and North Star *on 19 January 1929 under the title "Civilizations." A different extract from this same lecture appeared earlier in the* New York Times *on 9 December 1928 under the title "Shaw Peers Deeply into the Future."*

The Future
of Western Civilization

Civilization is not a thing that you must consider as something single that is going to grow and grow and grow. Of course, most English people have a conception that civilization is English civilization, and that it is going to broaden down from precedent to precedent and going on getting grander and more enlightened until it reaches—well, until it practically grows up to the heavens. But that is not what happens. Civilizations are like men and women, in respect of the fact that they die. They begin, they grow, and when they have reached a certain point they decay and they perish. But, unlike men and women, they do not die outright. They do what gardeners call dying-down; they die down, and then they begin again. I am by no means convinced that the next growth of civilization will be an English growth, or even a Western European growth. It might possibly be a Negro growth, it might be a Chinese growth, not perhaps in the old sense, but the next great civilization might be a civilization of persons of different color to ourselves, and we will have reason to be extremely thankful if that is the only difference. Because, as I have very often stated, the powers that created us give us no reason to suppose they are as yet exhausted, and they might produce a civilization of men and women who would be sufficiently enlightened to see that their first duty was to exterminate us. Perhaps it would be just as well if we remembered that occasionally, and were correspondingly a little careful in our conduct, at least a little more careful than we are at present.

Our consciousness of our civilization is very much hampered by the fact that it really has to be created by people who write books and make Constitutions and things of that kind. You can hardly say that a civilization exists in our consciousness until it exists on paper somewhere. Some literary man invents it for us. If we go on without a body of literature, without a body of Scripture, we go on knowing really no more about civilization than, for instance, a single hero in the late war knew about the war. After going through that, and perhaps suffering horribly in going through with it, when he came home and people asked him, "Well, what was the war like?" he was perfectly unable to tell them; he had to go and find a book written by somebody who was not at the war before he was really conscious of what the war was about. This involves what mathematicians and scientific men call a lag; that is to say, the book always has to come after the event. Consequently, our consciousness of civilization is always out-of-date. You may observe that very conspicuously in our governing classes, because they make very conspicuous mistakes. But with most people who have any general consciousness at all of history and civilization—you will find that it stops, it does not come up to the present moment; it stops at a more or less considerable distance behind the present moment.

I have recently written an extremely good book called The Intelligent Woman's Guide to Socialism. The only difficulty about it is that it ought to have been written at least 70 years ago, and then it would have been of some use. But you have this continual lag, this literature lag, which keeps our consciousness always behind the point which we have reached. The result is that we are always marching forward in the dark. It is quite true that a few miles behind us the country is brilliantly lit, and we begin to realize the sort of country that we march through, but the part that we are actually marching through is dark. We are in the position of drunken men who, when they wake up in the morning and see the precipices that they have skirted, think that they are very lucky that they are not smashed to pieces. That is the sort of matter that we very often have to congratulate ourselves upon.

We are hampered a great deal with this literature lag. Take, for instance, the most obvious example. Take the case of Karl Marx. Karl Marx is extraordinarily out-of-date in many points, and yet he is quite a recent discovery, not with old men but with young men.

Young men who call themselves Communist nowadays believe not only that Karl Marx is up-to-date but that he is a prophet whose vision extends right into the next two or three centuries. The only consolation is that Marx is rather stiff to read, and that as a matter of fact very few of his disciples have read him or ever will read him. But still there you are.

Now, in considering our conduct, as I say, we cannot depend very much on books; but there is another thing you have to take into account, a theory of human conduct. It is not really a new theory, but it has the delightful and very appropriate name of Behaviorism. That means that a man is what he does. Usually it is considered polite and ladylike and gentleman-like to assume that a man or a woman is what he or she professes to be; that, for instance, his belief is his creed, the creed that he utters; that his politics are the principles of the Party that he belongs to; and so on. Now Behaviorism is merely giving a name to something that I as usual have been saying ever since I began to say anything of particular importance. I have always said that if you want to find out what a man believes you must observe what are the assumptions on which he habitually acts; and those assumptions are what he really believes. If, for example, you find that on asking a man what his beliefs are, he tells you that this world is a vale of tears and sorrow, that it is only a brief, transitory dwellingplace on his way to a condition of eternal bliss, which he hopes to attain by observing certain very simple formulas and so on, and that it is the next life, the eternal life, the life of glory and heaven, and so on, that is the main thing with him, and that this life is comparatively nothing—

Well, if the man says he believes it, it is not polite to contradict him; but if you observe the behavior of that man when a mad bull comes along, for example, you will immediately perceive that he instantly acts in the hastiest and most violent and most desperate manner, on the assumption that death, instead of being the gate of a better life, is the greatest possible misfortune that could befall him. He regards it as the greatest evil that he can inflict on his fellow creatures, as the worst punishment that he can inflict on a criminal. Therefore, in making speculation and observations on the present civilization, I shall assume this creed of Behaviorism, I shall assume that people's beliefs are not the creeds they repeat, but the assumptions on which they habitually act. I dont know that I mean that to lead up to anything in particular, but I am just dodging about for an opening on one or two disconnected things I want to say. One of them is that a man's beliefs, that is to say, the assumptions on which he habitually acts, these make him the man he is. But it follows from that that if you change the assumptions on which he acts, he becomes a different man.

People are always telling you that you cannot change human nature, by which they mean that a man will always be the same. As a matter of fact, a man is continually changing. You do not find, for example, that our politicians effect any very great change in the character of the people, because they never tell the people anything that they did not know before. That is the secret of their popularity.

If I were seeking your votes, if I wanted to become a popular statesman, I should stand on a platform, I should make a collection of the grossest platitudes I know, things that no person could possibly have avoided thinking for themselves, and I should repeat those with an air of conviction, I should deliver every one of them as an ultimatum; and at the end of a very short time I would have the crowd madly cheering on that account. But I should not have changed them in the least, I should only have excited them. If you tell people something that they had not thought of before, it might make you popular, it might make them dislike you most intensely, but it really does not change them. A man who has learned something new is not the man he was before he knew it. Therefore, do not be too much overwhelmed by the unchangeability of human nature, by the apparently enormous inertia of the mass that you are confronted with. As a matter of fact, people really are very changeable, and what you call educating the people is a very important thing, because, as I say, a man is changed by everything that he knows.

That is cheering. But I want to remind you of something else— that the man is changing not only by the things that he knows but by the things that he thinks he knows. If you tell a man something that he has never thought of before and it is true, you change the man; but if you tell him something that he never thought of before, and it is false, and he accepts it, then you change him too. Our process of education consists, very largely, particularly among the upper classes, of putting them into certain institutions where they are told things most of which are not true but which they are led to believe, and they effect the most extraordinary change in them.

You discover that the man who has been to his preparatory school and to his public school and to his university, and has been going to church the whole time, is a quite special product. You find if you take a man who has never been through any of those particular processes, you have got an absolutely different kind of man. There is no use in pretending that you have not. The two kinds of men cannot associate together; they form almost a different species.

So now all these rambling remarks of mine are made to produce a frame of mind on your part in which you will see that the man who wants to produce social change has every prospect—in fact, rather an alarmingly promising prospect—of being able to do it. There will be a great deal of change in men as they come to know things that they do not know now, and the process of teaching them will be continually accompanied by the process of teaching them not only things that are true but the things that interested parties want them to believe.

An extensively revised text of a lecture entitled "A Cure for Democracy" delivered before the Fabian Society at Kingsway Hall, London, on Thursday, 27 November 1930, and published in The Clarion, *February 1931. Unrevised extracts were earlier published in the* New York Times, *21 December 1930, under the title "Shaw Finds Democracy Dying from 'Fallacies and Follies.'"*

Follies, Fallacies, and Facts

I am not an alarmist. The difference between an old Socialist and an old Conservative or Liberal is very much the difference between a man who lives on Vesuvius or Etna and a man camped on Primrose Hill. The Socialist knows that Capitalism sets up strains in society which may at any moment cause a fiery convulsion which may ruin anything, himself included. The other gentleman lives placidly on, expecting the world to go on as it has been, without anything particular happening, except motor accidents.

What we have to make now, and this is very urgent, is not Socialism, but the means of arriving at it.

We want to make a statue, but we have no chisel, and are trying to make it with a poker. There are social symptoms which shew that if we do not find some better means than the poker, it is quite possible that the poker may be laid rather roughly about our own heads, about the head of modern civilization.

Capitalism is a thing that came into existence as a theory of society very much as Fabianism did. There is quite a remarkable likeness between the two events. Both were introduced by a clique of very clever writers and lecturers. Capitalism was a Utopia, much more a Utopia than Fabianism. It was introduced as a theory of social organization, and it was written up, lectured up, by men who were thinkers and theorists and economists, and also historians.

What was the doctrine they taught? Simply this. If you made the sources of production in the country, in the first place the land, private property, and then enforced strictly by law all contracts made voluntarily in the community between the citizens generally and the proprietors of the sources of production, leaving nothing to the Government but the enforcement of the contracts and the suppression of ordinary crime, the effect would be to solve the tremendous problem which confronts every Government as the very first condition of the existence of the country, that is to provide a satisfactory answer to the daily prayer, "Give us this day our daily bread."

All you had to do was to adhere unflinchingly to these conditions and by the mere operation of human nature, on the assumption that every man would pursue his own obvious interests by buying in the cheapest market and selling in the dearest, every citizen in the country who was willing to work would be offered a subsistence wage, and, in addition to that, a rich and leisured class would arise who would be the repositories of culture and good manners and fine art and all the rest of it, besides being saturated with money to such an extent that they would provide the necessary accumulation of capital, because they would have enough money to save without enduring the slightest privation. This is the sort of thing that has been taught at the Universities to men like the late Lord Oxford and Dean Inge.[1] The social mischief that has been done through these two gentlemen having swallowed it with their mouths open and their eyes shut is incalculable.

In some respects the system has been an extraordinary success. In the department of production it has produced miracles which quite eclipse the old miracles of the Church. It has also produced such colossal private incomes that, whereas in the seventeenth and eighteenth centuries whenever anyone wanted to instance a very rich man he thought of the King, at the present time kings rank as comparatively poor men.

But in the final and crucial social department, the department of distribution—"Give us this day our daily bread"—the capitalist system was and is one of the most grotesque failures that has ever occurred on the face of the earth. The industrial agents of the capitalists have had to confess that not only must there be unemployment under Capitalism, but that you cannot conduct the capitalist system without unemployment.

It was to solve the problem of a satisfactory distribution that the Fabian Society was founded.

The distinctive characteristic of the Fabian Society was that it was constitutional. The Fabian Society found Socialism soaked in the Liberal tradition of barricades and revolutions. The greatest man in the Socialist movement was William Morris, and in the eighteen-eighties William Morris said to the working classes, from his own observation of life, "I tell you that there is no hope for you, except in revolution." Well we, God forgive us, converted him from this view, or if we did not absolutely convert him in the depths of his soul, at any rate drove him to say, "Well, well! I dare say it will come about as Mr Sidney Webb thinks it will come about. It is a process that does not interest me. I shall go back to my art and my day's work, and leave Socialism to Mr Webb and the Fabian Society."

We were then quite sure that Socialism would come through Parliament, by organizing the vote; by extending the franchise to all adult workers, male and female; and by making Socialism entirely respectable. Our success was apparently prodigious. To illustrate this I shall have to quote figures.

In the nineteenth century the continent of Europe, leaving out these islands, was governed and politically organized in four Empires, eleven Kingdoms and two Republics. Taking republicanism as the farthest march towards democracy, that seemed pretty bad for democracy. At the present time you have in Europe no Empires: the four Empires are gone right bang away. There are twelve kings, but they are very apologetic for their existence and are in an obvious and confessed minority. And there are sixteen republics. The number of persons transferred from monarchical to republican rule exceeds three hundred millions. Such a stupendous conquest of Europe by democracy was beyond our wildest hopes. But it occurred. And the famous Fabian Plan of Campaign for Labor succeeded so completely that we have at the present time a Socialist Government in power, not for the first time, and most certainly not for the last. Glorious, you will say. But wait a bit. There is a snag. In fact there are two snags. Under that big transfer to Republican rule how many of the three hundred millions have been transferred from constitutional rule to dictatorship? 257,303,952. That rubs a very great deal of the gilt off the gingerbread.

All the Parliamentarism that we supposed would be the instrument of the change has practically been discarded. This was not a case of barbarous countries jumping straight from one despotism into another. The unfortunate fact is that almost all of them tried our parliamentary system, and found it so inefficient that they were forced to substitute dictatorships. Parliamentary institutions have not been discarded politely. They have been kicked out; and though the dictators who have assumed command have not been exactly popular (rulers who govern capably never are popular), nevertheless the people have seen the futility, the delay, the impossibilities of the parliamentary system, and have said anything is better than that. *Viva il Duce!*

Evidently there is something wrong with what we call democracy: that is, giving votes to everybody. We were clearly mistaken in supposing that when we got our majority of votes everything would go smoothly and rapidly. Why did we make that mistake? The explanation lies in our history. Democracy had been one of the most wonderful forces in politics. Looking back over its history in the eighteenth and nineteenth centuries, you are amazed to see this curious force making its irresistible way, breaking down old institutions, becoming an incentive to statesmen, an inspiration to poets. My memory goes back to the palmy parliamentary days of Gladstone and Disraeli, and of John Bright, that great tribune of the people, whose magnitude you can hardly imagine. To these men democracy was a real thing. They said and believed that public opinion in England would never stand any interference with the liberties of the British people. Their pet phrase was that any statesman who proposed such an interference would be out of power in a fortnight. This belief and these phrases made Democracy a living force, a great and beneficent force, and we threw it away by giving the people votes.

Public opinion is a great power so long as you take good care that the public has no opportunity of expressing it. We Fabians came into political life with our Socialism carefully overhauled and brought up-to-date, and our Democracy an old ready-made reach-me-down of shibboleths and superstitions. We did not recast our history. We were led to believe by history that the advance towards democracy was an advance towards liberty. We were taught that England had led the advance. We were proud of the bad things in it and reviled all the good things. We were particularly trained up to admire parliamentary life and public election, the vote, and the constitution broadening down from precedent to precedent, and never faced the glaring fact that the whole growth of a power outside Parliament had been built up in order to destroy the power of Parliament. Finally, when the British Parliament had become the perfect instrument we all boasted of we overlooked the fact that it was an instrument of inhibition, of prevention, of negation.

Now the Labor Party did make very large promises to the people. It was necessary. You must give people hope. But with a parliamentary machine which works most efficiently against it and most inefficiently for it the Labor Party cannot fulfil its promises. It is unable to form the national labor corps which Mr G. D. H. Cole has suggested, and which is the most obvious thing to do with the unemployed until we are ready to face compulsory service for all with a working day of four hours, which is the final and real remedy. The coal industry is going to the devil. The obvious remedy is to nationalize the mines. The Labor Party is committed to it by its principles, and it would cheapen coal for everybody; but nobody dares even mention it. Nationalization of banking would be quite simple, and would benefit every small industrialist and tradesman in the country; but seen through our parliamentary spectacles it seems as far off as the moon. No wonder the disappointed electors ask where the difference is between Mr Baldwin's Cabinet and Mr MacDonald's.

What can the Labor Party do to avert the defeat which must follow repeated disappointments? For one thing they can tackle the reform of the constitution. The English public will always rise with wild enthusiasm to a Reform Bill. If the Labor Party goes to the country on such a Bill it will play a card that Mr Baldwin and Mr Lloyd George will find it hard to trump.

An unpublished verbatim report of a lecture by Bernard Shaw, delivered before the Fabian Society at Kingsway Hall, London, on 26 November 1931.

What Indeed?

The last time I addressed you from this platform, I appeared more or less in the character of a political prophet. Now you may have noticed that when gentlemen, especially old gentlemen, make political prophecies, when they happen to be fulfilled they are just as much astonished as anybody else, just as much taken aback. That, of course, is very natural because after all the gentleman who told you yesterday over the wireless that this was going to be a wet night will get just as wet himself as anybody else.

My prophecy was that unless the Labor Party did something more than those sort of activities that the public know nothing about, unless it put some really striking measures into its shop window—and I proceeded to suggest various measures, particularly a large measure of political reform—I said that the result at the next election would be that the electorate would be so disgusted and disillusioned by the failure of all the hopes, the millenial hopes that had been held out before the last election, that the Labor Party would be disastrously routed. That prophecy of mine has been, to say the very least of it, fulfilled, fulfilled with the most extraordinary completeness.

It has not only put me on the top of the wall but has thrown me clean over to the other side. The only statesmen who seemed to have taken it thoroughly to heart were Mr MacDonald and Viscount Snowden,[1] and their method of taking it to heart was to clear out before the catastrophe occurred and go frankly over to the enemy. I confess that I did not quite anticipate that. I had always given my friends MacDonald and Snowden credit for not only occasionally declaring themselves Socialists, but really knowing what Socialism was and really meaning it. It was a little bit of a shock to find that when it came to the point, they discovered they were not Socialists at all.

However, that has put us now on perfectly easy terms with them. I feel just as comfortable now with my old friend MacDonald as I do with my somewhat newer friend or acquaintance Mr Baldwin, or my friend Lord Londonderry.[2] I know now where to have Mac-Donald and Snowden, and they know, I hope, where to have me.

I cannot say I was very much pleased with the way that we conducted our campaign. I will just take one specimen. Mr Runciman[3] in the course of his electioneering got in one deadly shot at us, and that was the shot about the Savings Bank, and instead of immediately saying, "That is a perfectly fair and sound solution, and what are you going to do about it?" we declared it was a monstrous calumny, and that the savings of the people in the Savings Banks are perfectly safe, which is not true. The only excuse we made was the fatal excuse that Mr Winston Churchill got up and defended us and said, "I did that too when I was Chancellor of the Exchequer." That was about the last knock-out blow for us at that particular election.

The question is, where are we now? I want tonight to point to some of the changes in the situation, especially those that have been produced in the country where there has been a real change, and that is Russia. I want to make you aware, if you are not so already, that with the success of the Russian experiment has occurred a sort of revaluation which we must recognize in our terminology, in the words that we are going to use.

Up to the present you have had Fabianism, Social-Democracy, Collectivism, Socialism and so on. All that has gone. There is now nothing but Communism, and in future it is quite futile to go about calling yourselves Fabians. They will merely think, "Oh, this is an old bird from the nineteenth century. We did not know that there were any of them left." From henceforward, owing to what has happened in Russia, you are either a Communist, or what Mac-Donald and Snowden are, whatever that exactly may be.

Of course, that brings about the question that you have to consider what Communism is going to mean in future, and what I am going to try and do tonight—I shall have to do it very imperfectly because it would take me several hours to do it at all exhaustively except to myself—but what I am going to try and put in order for you is the fact that the Russians having adopted Communism as being the name of their particular sort of Socialism, and having made so far a success of it, their process of making that a success has been a process of turning what used to be called Communism gradually and under pressure of experience into Fabianism.

By the way I am bound to remark that as long ago, I believe, as 1917 or 1918 Mr Philips Price himself made that remark even at that early stage.[4] He visited Russia and wrote a book at that time, at that very early stage of affairs, it was apparent to him that under pressure of practice that Russian Communism would become Fabianism. But you see we cannot, this little Society that I am now addressing, cannot turn round and say to the Russians, "Ha, Ha, now you have got to call your system Fabianism." They would laugh at you. They always made fun of the Fabians. We have our revenge in the fact that they have come round to our opinions and to the ways that we suggest, but they will not come round to the name. And as they are an enormous European power and we are an extraordinarily insignificant little knot of people in London, although we have called the tune, they will give the tune its name. They have given it the name of Communism, and I repeat Communism is the name that it will go by from henceforth, and Communism will be the power which will be set up against Capitalism. You will have a definite confrontation of that kind.

I want now to trace that evolution of Bolshevism which was the beginning, as you know, of the Russian Marxian Communism. I want to trace the steps by which Bolshevism became Fabianism, called Communism.

I would just like here parenthetically to say that the change in the name is one which will be quite welcome to me. I have always liked to call myself a Communist. The name Socialist is not very good English, in fact it is very bad English, and it is not very expressive. My friend Mr Chesterton hit on a very much better name Distributism, but he has not yet succeeded in associating that name with a sufficiently powerful body of doctrine to impose the word on a world which, as I say, is now thinking of Communism. But I like the name just as William Morris liked the name. I think every person who was really a Socialist through and through, as far as you can be in existing society, liked the word Communism better; but Communism had not attained any very strong intellectual self-consciousness, or self-knowledge perhaps I had better put it, and Bolshevism therefore began as Social-Democracy plus Anarchism plus Syndicalism, plus Heaven-knows-what, plus certainly Anarchism, and that Anarchism, although the people who called themselves Anarchists did not know it, was simply Liberalism in its last ditch, and I might almost say in its most uneducated phase.

That enormous stress on liberty, on individual liberty, the thing which has kept us the slaves that we are up to the present moment, the dislike of an Englishman to be ordered about, the fact that he would not stand being ordered about and kept himself entirely unconscious of the fact that mostly from nine till six and sometimes much later than that, he was being ordered about and paid very little for it, but still there was this clinging to liberty. Bolshevism was very strongly flavored with that, a great part of it was.

What I want to do is, I want to take these constituents of the old Bolshevism, which are by the way very largely the constituents of what calls itself the Communist party in this country, and I want rapidly to trace the steps by which those things gradually got pushed out or reduced to a practical form.

I think the first thing that I will shew you under the refiner's fire of actual practice is Syndicalism, because Syndicalism is a thing of which I am very much afraid. I am inclined to think that if a revolution were to break out in this or any other country, the first thing that would embarrass and hamper it would be an outburst of practical Syndicalism.

Syndicalism means that the persons who are actually occupied in a particular industry should lay hold of that industry, should seize its instruments and proceed to work it themselves. Syndicalism means the railways for the railway workers, the mines for the miners, the pawnbrokers for the pledgers—you see the idea. And, of course, when you apply it to agriculture, it takes the very important form of the land for the individual cultivator, i.e. the land for the peasant.

Let us take first the agricultural part of it, because that was practicable for some time in Russia and it occurred in Russia. Lenin was brought up—I do not believe he was brought up as a peasant, I have seen his hands, and they were not a peasant's hands—but at any rate he was brought up in the country and he knew the peasantry. Trotsky was the son of a successful farmer, a man whom today he would call a kulak, and he also knew the peasants. They knew that in a country of 160,000,000 inhabitants—it was not quite so much then—with an overwhelming majority of agriculturists, they knew that unless they could get these men at the back of the revolution, the revolution would have no chance. Accordingly they took the Syndicalist's line. The peasants were to seize the land, and the peasants did seize the land. They laid hold of the land in all directions, and the result was that the peasantry became the bulwark of the revolution.

Now this is a remarkable thing. Litvinoff[5] said to me in Russia, "There is a thing which is very difficult for us to understand. We read of travellers in the heart of Africa, and something happens in the very heart of Africa; when they manage to reach the coast of Africa, they find that for some time past the things that happened to them in the heart of Africa are known to the people at the coast." That is to say, that the intelligence travels from mouth to ear quicker than the newspaper press can spread it. They will tell you in Russia, as Litvinoff told me, that nothing is more curious than the fact that when a Russian landlord, a great noble, or a large landed proprietor or even a small one who has had tenants, when that man dies, after an honorable career as a taxidriver in Paris or a waiter in Monte Carlo or whatever it may be, whenever and however he dies, his old tenants immediately know all about it, and feel greatly reassured and comforted by the fact. The one thing that gives the counterrevolution no chance in Russia is that the peasants are afraid that the landlord would be brought back on them.

What happened when the land was syndicalized? Immediately a peasant proprietorship was established, and there you had the peasant, so much admired by Mr Belloc and Mr Chesterton, in fact by almost all real Cockneys, they always idealize the peasant: and there the peasant is. I myself have seen him. There is a tremendous lot of him still, and there he lives in a horrible dog kennel, I cannot call it anything else. It is a large dog kennel, made of unpainted brown wood of a very ugly color. In this enormous dog kennel there are two main objects. There is a sort of kiln, which he calls a stove, a thing made of cement and you can sleep on the top of it when you want to go to sleep. A Russian is not a man who goes to bed for so many hours and then gets up. The Russian goes to sleep whenever he wants to. He eats whenever he is hungry. If you ask him what is the dinner hour, he does not understand what you mean. If you said, "What hour do you go to bed?" he would say, "When I want to sleep," and very often he will lie down and go to sleep then and there.

There is the stove and there is the bed. The bed is an indescribable thing, a cupboard which has everything in the house in it in the daytime, and a great many other things which you cannot see but which you feel are there. The rest of the space is devoted to anything, cows, pigs, very little furniture apparently.

There this man lives, and he cultivates a strip of land. As you pass along the railway you see them in Poland and parts of Russia, these strips of land; the country looks as if it were simply a lot of ribbons spread on a counter. They work with an intolerably intensive industry to get a better living out of these little strips. All these little strips have ridges between, so that you cannot use tractors or machinery of any kind.

The peasant, the moujik, is rather a pleasant sort of chap in his way. I felt I rather liked him. I felt he would be got rid of somehow, that he was not a species which really could be kept up in a civilized country society. But as he stood there, very jolly, with his great big beard, and on my showing him some civility, he would seize my hand and jam it into the beard and kiss it enthusiastically and repeatedly, and address the most affectionate expressions to me, and Lady Astor was his darling and his "Little Mother," and all that sort of thing, I felt what a pity to turn this rather picturesque, jolly, easy-going chap into a regular industrial fellow, getting up when there is a hooter going, and having his meals regularly.

But I knew it had to come, and after some time it became apparent to the Soviet Government that he had to go. You see, to begin with, some of these moujik gentlemen were very much cleverer than others, very much harder-hearted, more business-like, and presently you got the prosperous proprietor beginning to appear again. He had several horses and cows and was getting rich, and beginning to employ other men to work for him instead of doing all the work himself, paying them wages and so on. What was more, with that system of strip cultivation, not enough food was being produced to feed the emancipated Russians decently. Accordingly the Soviet had to begin to consider what it was going to do. The present system was breaking down and rich men were beginning to appear.

They tried various things that I need not trouble you with. They tried getting more grain out of the peasants, but the peasant would not produce anything that he was likely to give up, and the only effect was to make him produce even less than before.

Then they went for the prosperous, respectable man with two or three horses and threw him out into the street and said, "We do not want rich men like you. We do not want men who want to get rich themselves. We want men who want to make Russia rich and the Russian people rich."

The only effect of that was that there was still less food going, and accordingly they had to take a great many of those gentlemen by the collar again and throw them back into their farms and say, "You go on. We detest you and scorn you, but go on producing food. Later on we will be able to deal with you perhaps." They left the kulak enjoying the pleasurable anticipation of that happy time coming, in which he himself did not believe.

Then they began to turn to America, and now this is a thing that we have got to take to heart, because in the old days, under the Tsardom, Russia turned for its industrial management and its industrial enterprise and for any novelty that it had in hand to Germany, Belgium, France, and to some extent to England for it. But it is something, as I say, that we had better take to heart that this time it never dreamed of going to those places; it kept an eye on Germany, but it seriously and really went to America.

In America there was something that was called the Seattle community. The Seattle community suggests to you a lot of really 100% Americans.[6] There is something in the name Seattle that is 100% American. I think you will acknowledge that. But, lest the Americans should get an intolerably swelled head by giving a lead to Russia as they did, I wish to insist on the fact that the Seattle community did not consist of Americans but of Finns, persons from Finland who had, of course, become Americans. They, being a community with a religion,—I forget exactly what the religion was, but at any rate it kept them together working really as Communists—when they discovered that instead of being knocked about by the police and imprisoned for eighteen years and that kind of thing, as they did with Communists in a land of freedom in the West, when they discovered that there was a Communist Government in the world, they in the simplicity of their souls came over to Russia and said to the Russians, "Will you give us some land?" The Russians gave them, I think, 150 acres or something of that kind.

There is plenty of land in Russia. You can be open-handed with it—I forget whether it is eighteen or eighty million square miles. At any rate they gave these Finn gentlemen the land.

These men worked it as a collective farm, and they worked it with such extraordinary success that they not only greatly increased the crop, multiplied the ordinary crop that was got by the other peasant cultivators from the land, but for their wheat they got eight times as much as the ordinary wheat produced under the peasant proprietorship system. I believe to this day they produce nothing but seed wheat, which has to be very specially good to be distributed.

The Soviet Government took the hint. They said, "These fellows have shewn us the way to do it." They then established the collective farming, which is now such an extraordinary success.

So, you see, by a perfectly natural process, Syndicalism vanished except in so far as you have to have peasant proprietorship. But the peasant proprietorship they are gradually pushing on to collective farming. The moujik holds out against it as long as he can, but when the collective farm comes, and his children see it, and see the children in the collective farm, and see the food that they get and see all the nice films that they get and all the rest of it, and the houses they live in, which are all the houses of the old gentry except new houses built on the same scale, the end of it is that not only do the children insist on going for the collective but they begin to abuse their parents. And they can do so in Russia, because in Russia to strike a child is a crime. If you box your child's ears, the child hails you before the magistrate and charges you with assault, so that the old remedy of the moujik to keep his child in order has gone.

In the end the moujik consents to go into the farm, to go to work at a fixed hour, and the moment they get the moujiks out of their dog kennels, they immediately burn the dog kennels. They burn his boats, if I may put it in that poetic way.

I am not putting this before you as being an ideal way of proceeding. You may have your own opinion about it. I want simply to point out that by a purely natural process, Syndicalism was driven by the mere weight of experience out of the Bolshevist program, and the Communist program became one of collective farming.

Let us go back to Syndicalism as applied to industry. Syndicalism as applied to industry cannot be practised at all. You must always remember that whereas you can make shift with Syndicalism in agriculture by peasant proprietorship until you are ready to shove it out, that cannot be done in industry.

A friend of mine, a Russian gentleman—this was in Italy, by the way—was a marine engineer and had a factory which he hated, being a person of an artistic turn. One day his workmen, who had been listening to Syndicalist orators, came to him and said, "You clear out, Guv'ner. This factory belongs to us." He was only too glad to do it. He only wanted to have an excuse for his family to become an artist, at which he was likely to starve.

Nothing very dreadful happened. At the end of a week the workmen came back to him and said, "You have to come back. We cannot run this show." Accordingly he came back until he was able to wind it up.

No harm was done there, but imagine a big revolution taking place, in which all the factory hands and the men in the factories suddenly seized the factories, and the managers ran away and did not remain in the neighborhood, what would happen? The factories would simply collapse. Nothing would be done.

That was what the Bolshevists found. There was a great deal of Syndicalism. There was a great deal of seizure of factories. Lenin saw that the thing was impossible. He saw that the Syndicalist seizure of the factory simply went on, that the factory went out of business, and consequently the country was going to be starved.

Being an amiable sort of man, Lenin made speeches and issued proclamations and begged and implored. It was no good. The thing went on. So then Lenin shot them on a very large scale. I do not know how many Syndicalists he shot, but he did shoot enough of them to convince the rest that the Syndicalist game was up.

Then he also was driven by that experience into the thing that you see called the N.E.P., the New Economic Policy, over which our press was so triumphant. You see what happened. What Lenin saw was absolutely necessary was that until they were ready to take over the factories and socialize them bit by bit, private enterprise must be left running the factories, just as they had left the kulak on the farms.

So you see Communism did spread from factory to factory. They organized it as fast as they could, but they left under the New Economic Policy the manager in possession of the factories they could not reach. That is to say, Lenin was by the pressure of practical and immediate and imperative experience converted to what we call gradualism.

I may mention that Lenin owes quite a great deal of his eminence to the fact that he was clever enough at an early stage of his career to study the works of Lord Passfield. It is quite interesting to me who knows Mr Sidney Webb's work very well to say that I can see in Lenin's utterances and actions quite clearly that he was influenced by Mr Webb. At any rate he became a gradualist. I said to them when I was in Moscow, "You have no inscription over his great tomb. Why not put up, 'The inevitability of gradualism.'"

What did they do? I told you before that they turned to America, and this time too, when they began running their collectivist factories, they suddenly discovered that they did not know how to do it. An acquaintance with the works of Marx, even of Sidney Webb, does not qualify a number of amateurs immediately to run a factory, and they very soon realized that they were turning out nothing like the things the Americans were turning out. Curiously enough, they never came to see what we were turning out. America had got hold of their imagination.

They said, "What we have to achieve is the American industrialization of our industry here, and accordingly they sent over a Commission, the Stalingrad Commission, to America. There was also the Seattle community, as I told you, but there was something else. They asked a firm, whose name I have got a note of here, a firm of consulting engineers, Messrs Stuart, James & Cooke[7]—they are quite real, I have spoken to Mr Stuart—for advice. They said, "You are consulting engineers. We wish to consult you. Will you come over to Moscow and tell us what the dickens is wrong with us, because we find that with out peasant proprietorship so very largely spread, and with factories managed as we are managing them, it is utterly impossible to feed our people. We are extremely hard up and we shall get into debt and go bankrupt."

Messrs Stuart & Cooke went over and they drew up a report on Russia, and that report practically skinned the Soviet Government in the way of criticism. The engineers submitted the report to some English people, who, to their credit, added a good deal of criticism which was very useful. The American engineers admitted that. The English people, having made the suggestions, said, "Now, you are criticizing these Russian people. Nobody will ever hear a word of that report again, and you will not be six weeks in Russia before they hoof you out, and jolly glad you may be to get out with your skins whole."

That was a nice encouraging thing, but they sent in their report, and within two days of the delivery of that report—it was a scathing criticism of management in Russia and the way Communism was managing its factories—within two days of it there were 10,000 copies of that report in circulation. You try and get out any report within two days, 10,000 copies, and you will see what a feat it was. I do not know whether the American engineers immediately wrote to their English friends and pointed out that that was the celebrated way the Russians suppressed criticism. Of course they sought criticism and were very glad to get it and gave it the very widest publicity. If an American press reporter had happened to come along and begun to criticize in his entirely unhelpful and mendacious fashion, I do not say what would have happened to that gentleman. Whatever had happened to him, probably it would have served him right.

But you see now my point. They set to work. I cannot give you all the details, but they began to organize in the way that the American engineers told them to organize, and some of the results were amazing. There was one Russian who had learnt his business in America. He started, and he started with everything against him in the way of the people in the industry that he was working in being very reluctant to be stirred out of their old ways, but he managed to increase the output in a very short time by 400%.

The most important industry for the Russians, of course, is the making of tractors, because their whole future depends on agriculture by machinery. Therefore they want more tractors than anything else. They got American machinery which was guaranteed to turn out 154 tractors every day in the enormous factory they put up in Stalingrad. They turned ten thousand peasants in to go to work, and they started to turn out 154 tractors a day.

They turned out eight. I cannot tell you how many of those tractors tracted, but most of them did not, and in the process of turning out those eight, they pretty well smashed up most of the machinery.

They had to learn from Mr Ford what was called the moving assembly. Their idea of making a tractor or motorcar was, they got all the component parts which constitute a tractor or a motorcar and heaped them up in a shed, then started trying to put the thing together, picking the bits out of the various heaps. You can see how long it takes to make a tractor under those conditions, particularly when the people doing it have not the least idea what any part is for. Even if they were American engineers who knew all the parts, you can imagine the waste and loss of time involved in going to all those heaps and picking out this and that, and bringing them to the middle of the room and fixing them in position. Of course, the modern method of Mr Ford is the moving assembly. The tractor never stops. It comes in and moves along, and as it passes a particular place, a man who deals with that particular part, takes up that part and shoves it on to the tractor and so on.

Those were the things that they had to learn, and, of course, with the assistance of the American engineers they learnt them very rapidly. They went on from 8 to 12, then 16 a day and so on, and at last they have now arrived at a point at which the increase in the output of tractors in the year is 149%.

Every day in Russia things are changing. You must always remember that. They are learning, taking advice. They are bringing in Americans in large quantities. They would be very glad to get Englishmen if they could get intelligent Englishmen who knew their jobs but had not been hardened into doing as little as possible of it in the time. I think I can recommend any man who is the master of a trade, and who can direct other people a little, and who is entirely indifferent to personal comfort, if he has an ideal before him—it is not perhaps easy to find gentlemen of that kind—and who will accept the Russian regime wholeheartedly, and their aims in with it, and adopt the Communist will-to-succeed, I think he will probably do much better in Russia than here. At any rate they are getting in plenty of them.

The point I am arguing is this, that Syndicalism had to go, finally crushed out by the mere force of experience. So Syndicalism went in industry even more suddenly and catastrophically than it could possibly do in agriculture, where it still survives in peasant proprietorship in a very large part of Russia.

I now come to the collapse of some of the other constituents. You will remember that I mentioned Syndicalism as being a large ingredient in original Bolshevism, as it is in British Communism so-called at the present day.

Now the class war. There was a great deal to be said for the practical application of the class war. I myself, if I were at the head of a revolution here, should be very much tempted to begin by saying, "Well now, the important thing is that no person who has ever been at an English Public School or University, or any establishment of that nature, inspired by the ideals of the Public School or University, I should be inclined to say, I not only will not allow any person of that kind ever to get near a child and educate it in any way, but I would never let him get into a factory or a workshop."

That is really a good practical form of the class war. In 1917 practically the whole professional class, the whole managing class had got what education they had got in establishments of that kind, and they were ostracized. They were deprived of the rights of citizenship, of votes, and were classed with monks, with ex-policemen from the Tsarsist regime, ex-officers from the Tsarist regime, and as professional men they were deprived of the full franchise. Their rations were cut short, and their children were deprived not absolutely of education, but only allowed to get what was left after the children of the manual workers had been educated as much as they could hold.

That was the practical form that the class war took. I may say that this whole body of professional men, managing men, private traders and the rest of them, and former officials, they were all lumped under the general term Intelligentsia, a term with which you are familiar. At any rate we all heard, and with some dismay, of the fact that to belong to the Intelligentsia, to be what we call a real lady and gentleman, Public School, University and all that sort of thing, to be that in Russia was to be persecuted, to be trampled on, to be oppressed, to be insulted, to be regarded as a criminal class. That was really going in for the class war, and there was a great deal to be said for it.

But the first snag came in the war of 1920 and thereabouts. As you will remember, England always makes war on revolution, having made two herself and boasted immediately of them afterwards, but she did what she could to destroy the French Revolution, and she began to do what she could to destroy the Russian Revolution. Mr Winston Churchill took advantage of all the military stores from the Great War and continued the war as a war against Russia, and was not stopped until he found there was a "Hands off Russia" movement going on in England, and then he had to drop it.

Unfortunately Mr Stalin has a very vivid remembrance of that time when we spent a hundred millions of our money to destroy the Soviet Government. He explained to me personally that that was one of the reasons for keeping a strong army, because he thought Mr Winston Churchill was still going very strong. The results of the recent election have not weakened his conviction on that.

When the war had been going for some time—the war, of course, was the triumph of Trotsky. Trotsky performed astonishing things as an organizer of war. Two years he spent in a railway carriage, conducting the war and raising out of Russia an army apparently out of nothing, because he began with a few young men with Browning pistols, which are not ideal war instruments. A revolver is very much better, particularly with a flat-nosed bullet in it. But with these few people he had to fight Europe, you may say. He had to fight our soldiers, fully equipped, and all the soldiers that could be got from reactionary Europe, and he threw back all those enemies and beat them all.

But, you know, Trotsky very soon discovered that if you are going to have an army, you must have professional officers who know their business. Accordingly matters had not gone very far when Lenin suddenly discovered to his unspeakable horror that Trotsky was employing men in the army who had been members of the Tsar's army and the Imperial Army. He immediately communicated with Trotsky. He said, "This must be put a stop to. These men are dangerous. You must get rid of them." Trotsky said, "Do you know how many I have?" Lenin said, "No matter how few, they must go. They are dangerous." Trotsky said, "I have thirtythree thousand." Lenin shut up. There was nothing else for it.

So you see the ostracism of the professional classes broke down at once under the strain of war.

But it was equally breaking down under the strain of industry. You had to have a professional class. You had to have managing men. You had for the matter of that to have men who could read and write, and very soon two things began to happen. A certain number of men turned up and managed, and when you asked them who they were, they did not say, "My father was Prince so-and-so," but they said, "My father was a peasant."

I met the most charming, plucky young ladies. I could see that none in their family had done a stroke of work for two or three centuries. I used to say, "You have a very lady-like appearance. Who was your father?" They always replied, "My father was a peasant." So you see you had your professional class at once by simply going through the formula of saying, that your father was a peasant.

Another thing happened. You had a very elaborate system of education being carried on. Everybody was getting opportunities of education. The result was that the proletariat themselves began to develop naturally a professional class, people whose fathers really were peasants. Finally there came a time when all this business about ostracizing the intelligentsia was not working, it was ridiculous.

When I went to Russia, I was received at Moscow by a large delegation of authors. To begin with they always planted authors on me in all directions. They were the very last people I wanted to see. There were also men of science, artists, and the rest of it. They all came. I noticed they looked uncommonly jolly and prosperous and so on.

I said to the authors, "I am glad to see you looking so prosperous and so on." Not a single author in Russia tried to borrow a single shilling from me. That is an absolute record for the earth. I said to them, "Are you not the intelligentsia?" They replied, "Certainly not. We are not the intelligentsia."

I said, "I knew that, of course, but I thought it was more or less of a family secret between ourselves. How did the Russian Government find it out, and if you are not the intelligentsia, what are you?"

They answered, "We are the intellectual proletariat."

So in spite of all this ostracism and outlawing and depriving of citizenship of the monk, the private trader and the ex-police official, at this present moment 99% of the Russian population have full rights of citizenship, and you have an intellectual proletariat just as you have a manual proletariat. In other words, the class war has gone the way of Syndicalism.

You may remember that I talked about Anarchism. Anarchism did constitute a serious danger at one time. That was during the war.

Trotsky was organizing the war, but throughout the country there were a great many men with, I will not call it a Russian spirit because it was almost an English spirit; it was a spirit of liberal independence, and every one of those chaps thought himself just as good a general as Trotsky. Accordingly they said, "You want such and such things done. We do not hold with that. We have our own ideas." Many of them were men with strong pacific ideas. They were not quite certain that they ought to use their forces for warlike purposes at all. They believed in peace.

You cannot fight a country that way. Trotsky said that orders had to be obeyed, and the gentlemen who would not work with them got "liquidated." You know that expression. They had to go, and they did go. As a matter of fact, if you are carrying on a war, you cannot carry it on anarchically. You cannot have these old-fashioned liberals springing up, imagining they were Bolshevists and Socialists and all that, and saying they did not hold with this and that. They had to put one man there—Trotsky—and his tactics and his strategy had to be carried out, or rather his strategy leaving the tactics to the other responsible people.

So, under the pressure of a war, anarchy got swept out.

You see what I have been putting before you is a Bolshevism which, like our own Communism here, was started with Syndicalism, class war, and Anarchism, and all that. The mere pressure of events squeezed that quite out of the Soviet system, and the residue, of course, was Fabianism. All the other things went, all these things which have prevented many of our Communist friends from joining the Fabian Society, all these things have now vanished from practical Communism. There you have the sort of thing that happened.

I now come to something which really ought, I think, to have had this whole course of lectures devoted to it. I pointed out that one of the constituents of the original Bolshevism was Social-Democracy, and I want now to come to what happened to democracy under the Bolshevist system. You will remember that I am using the word Bolshevist to signify the Soviet Government at its beginning. At the present time they call themselves a Communist Government. You must be careful, when you go to Russia, to use the word Communist, not Bolshevist.

If you want a little compensation in the other way, I may mention to you that you need not be so particular about calling the capital city Leningrad. I took a great deal of trouble to do that until I found it was generally called Petrograd.

Quite early, of course, you understand that the system began as what we would call a democratic system, that is to say all power was to go to the returned soldiers and to the workers, to the Committees they formed. They elected little bodies which were called Soviets, and the whole structure began with all these Soviets supposed to be working together in any sort of hierarchy that presented itself.

Before it had been going on very long, Lenin found that in one Soviet the result of a division on the question at issue was that twentytwo members voted against what Lenin wanted done and twenty voted in favor. That brought Lenin up against democracy. Lenin knew perfectly well that these fortytwo gentlemen had not the slightest idea of what they were doing or anything about it, that they were entirely unfitted to deal with an important question of state. So he immediately removed the twentytwo persons from the Soviet and told the Soviet to go on with the twenty.

Having had that object lesson as to the desirability of agreeing with him when there was a crucial division going on, things went more smoothly.

That is one little incident, but it illustrates what happens when you are in a community where everything has got to be done more or less by the public and by the State. Here it does not matter of what fools a village council may consist, or a borough council or an urban district council. And there is not much voting in a factory of a big industrial establishment about what is to be done. What the boss says goes. When Russia began to organize itself like one great industrial institution, Lenin very soon understood that it could only be done on the principle—what the boss says goes.

Well, it is very interesting to follow the ways in which they managed to cure the shortcomings of democracy. They still have a voting system. Everybody votes. But the first difference that you have to note is the difference from our system: that whereas our system is a geographical system, a local system, in which you give the vote to the house and take your chance what sort of man or woman lives in the house, in Russia there is nothing of that kind.

In Russia the vote is a vocational vote. You vote as a worker, and you vote with the group of workers with whom you work, and it is they who meet together and elect their Committees. They elect their governing bodies. It has a certain advantage because many of the election meetings are often extremely interesting. My friend,

Mr Maurice Hindus, has given us some very interesting accounts of these.[8] If you have one of those meetings of electors, and some man gets up and proposes himself as being one of the Committee, one of the governing body, immediately somebody gets up and says, "I do not approve of this gentleman. I happen to know something about his mother-in-law, and she told me this, that, or the other, and Jim so-and-so saw that man going to the races on some day when he ought to have been at his work."

I should mention that when I am talking of races, I am not speaking ignorantly, because to my intense horror they celebrated my seventyfifth birthday in Russia partly by a horserace. The principal race of the day was for a Bernard Shaw prize, and I had to present that prize to the winning jockey. It was in a small envelope, and I suppose it was perhaps a rouble or something of the sort. At any rate I did so. But at first, when they spoke of this race, I said, "Race! But as you have eliminated competition, I presume there will only be one horse." Curiously enough that was the one point of real Communism that I could not make the Russians understand. I almost said, "After all, scratch a Russian and you find an Englishman, when there is a horse-racing question."

However, I must get back to my theme, which is the fact that there is a great deal in these meetings which have these elections. It is extremely hard for a man who has anything against him whatever to get through without his being thoroughly shewn up. His wife can shew him up. At any rate on this vocational franchise there are Committees elected, and then from that up it is a system of indirect election. These elementarily elected Committees elect other Committees; these come into Congress, and they elect the higher Committees and so on, and you get right up to the top, and at the top there is what we would call a Cabinet, consisting of a Minister, a Foreign Minister, a Minister for this and that. It is called the Sovnakum. Above that there is a body called the Presidium, consisting of about twenty men. These men control the Cabinet and can turn the men out of the Cabinet if they like. That body is the top, and the top of that body is Stalin. That, of course, is how he officially gets there.

I asked what Stalin was. If you go to America and if you ask "What is Mr Hoover, he is President." There is no doubt about it. What is Mr MacDonald? He is Prime Minister, and he is going to be Prime Minister no matter what party is in. You ask, who is the gentleman

in Buckingham Palace who with Bernard Shaw keeps up the fashion of wearing a beard? Oh, that is the King. You have something
to get hold of there.

If you ask what Stalin is, nobody can tell you. I was once asked. I
had left Russia at the time. I did not say it while I was there. I think
it was on the platform either at Warsaw or Berlin the question was
put to me. I said, "Stalin is the Secretary of a General Committee,
chosen by himself, mostly for the purpose of electing him as General Secretary. That is as near as I can approach to it."

But the real truth about Stalin is this. He is at the head because
he is really the ablest man. He is two things that none of the others
can get to.

In the first place, he is a complete opportunist, not in our sense
of a man who drifts with any wind and is nothing, like some of the
gentlemen I have already referred to too often; but by that I mean
a man who has an object, namely the establishment of the Soviet
State as a perfect State. That is his object, but he does not care how
he gets there; he will take every method. He will not allow any
doctrinaire consideration to stop him. He will change his policy
from one day to another without any hesitation.

He tries one thing, tries another, and just exactly in that temper
which got rid of Syndicalism, the class war and so on, he goes on in
that way, and in that way he has beaten some very able men who
thought certain methods were not socialistic. Stalin does not care as
long as they lead to Communism.

The second thing is this: he is a Nationalist. He, of course, even
as all the Russians, believes that in the long run Russia will convert
the rest of the world to Communism. The Russians are fanatically
religious people, not like us. They really have a faith. They are
quite willing to suffer and work for it, and they believe that Russia
is going to save the soul of the world, but whereas it was part of the
Marxian doctrine and part of Trotsky's doctrine that you could not
have a successful change over from capitalism to Communism in
one country unless it simultaneously occurred in the other countries, unless there was not merely a Russian or English or German
revolution but a European, a world revolution, Stalin says, "I dare
say, but I am not going to wait. I have these eight million, or eighty
thousand million"—or whatever they have—"and I am going to do
it here, and if the rest of the world is foolish enough not to follow
my example, so much the worse for it. We will be able to do it here."

And being a very able man, and being, as I say, an opportunist, and Nationalist, that has put Stalin where he is.

But if Stalin made a mistake tomorrow, he would lose his position, if it were a mistake that were generally understood. Because, remember, there are no means by which a man can hold on to his post in Russia except by means of delivering the goods. No amount of influence in the Communist system can keep him there. On the contrary the tendency is to throw out the incompetent man, and the Communist party throws them out. I forget how many thousand a year they throw out of the Party, but about 13% per annum.

These are men who have got cold feet, got tired of doing managing work, and they retire into private life. Or if they have been corrupt, something worse may happen to them; in extreme cases liquidation may be resorted to. There are no family or economic interests that can protect a man if a man is doing his work badly. If he has been corrupt, if he has tried to favor his relatives, or put money in his own pocket, detection is almost certain and he goes.

That, of course, is the safeguard, because with this system I have described, by which the members of the trade, the vocational group, elects a Committee, what sort of people would get elected on that Committee? We have, of course, a typical Fabian. By a typical Fabian, I mean a man who instead of making money for himself and his family and then going home and enjoying himself, takes an interest in public affairs and the future of the world, who deserts his family in the evening and comes to public meetings like this to listen to me. They read elaborate and dry books like Marx, Shaw, and Webb; they stuff themselves with it; they try and educate themselves. Well, these are the people who will quite naturally get picked by the ordinary vocational man who does not want to go on a Committee.

So they manage to pick out men of public interest, and in that way you have to get that great body you call the Communist party. I forget how many there are: they say two million of them out of one hundred and sixty millions. People here make a lot of that and say the place is governed by a minority, the idea being that England is governed by the great majority.

But as a matter of fact, if you ask a man, "Is your wife a Communist?" I was puzzled by the fact that none of their wives were Communist. Then I found he understood me to mean, was his wife an official member of the Communist Party, taking a part in the government of the country. When she was simply taking a part in his government and that of the children, he did not call her a Communist. But when he understood me, he hastened to assure me that she was just as great a Communist as he was.

There you get a very good solution of the democratic problem. You get the men engaged in the government of the country who have a natural aptitude for it and the mental qualities to enable them to extend their interest beyond their own affairs to those of the nation.

There is only one snag in it. You really cannot tell what will happen to a man of that sort or a man of any sort when he suddenly becomes entrusted with power. You may get the famous phenomenon called a beggar on horseback. It may be the ruin of a man. Nero, I am sure, who was a very good violinist, would have been probably a very honest and pleasant violinist if he had remained a violinist, but making him Emperor of Rome simply drove him mad.

It is of the very greatest importance that we Fabians and all students of public affairs in this country should devote the most earnest study to the Russian system, because it is the Socialist system put under the test of practice. It is democracy brought to the test of how far it is compatible with a Communist system.

I can give you some fairly up-to-date information. There was a body in America called the National Convention of the Society of Industrial Engineers of the United States. On the 14th October 1931—that is recent enough for you—they held this Convention of theirs, and they got a report from the American firm, from Mr Stuart, as to the working of the Soviet system. They got a report from Polakov, who multiplied production by 400% when he went from America back to Russia. There is also a Mr Carmody who is an authority on the Soviet.[9] They said that Russia was going to get through, but that the terrible thing was that the Russians were a nation of very imaginative, very clever, very intelligent, idealistic amateurs, and that they had not got what they called factory instinct.

One of them described it to me personally. He said, "When I was a boy, I was brought up near Pittsburg, and there the factories are not all fenced in. There are no fences. The result is that all the boys of the town make for the factory. They all like looking at workmen working, and machines, and they infest the factory. Sometimes the workmen chivvy them out, but they also make them run errands and do little odd jobs of work, and they often get hold of bits of disused machinery." The man who spoke to me had an old corner of the foundry, and he and the other boys used to melt the metal and so on.[10] He said, "In that way you absorb a sort of curious disposition and taste and sense of how things are actually done. You get factory sense, and that is what the Russians have not got."

"The most encouraging thing," he said "that I saw in Russia was that in one place the young ladies of the town, girls of fourteen and sixteen, who had their day off from school, instead of going and amusing themselves in the usual way, went carrying bricks about at the factory. Instead of going and looking at tennis matches at Wimbledon and that kind of thing, they, like the boys, thought it good fun to look at the workmen working and the machinery."

As those factories grow and as the children play about, you are getting a generation of Russians growing up, and they are beginning to get factory sense.

In the meantime the place is crowded with Americans, but there is still a great shortage of men who can act as foremen and managers. What they lack is managerial technique. That is the only rock on which we think they might possibly split, but nature is remedying this.

They all say that the really awful thing about it is that when you do teach them managerial technique, you find that they are always going off to attend meetings and attend discussions and make speeches. That is the last relic of the old-fashioned democracy.

Only a month or two ago the Conference of Industrial Managers, meeting in Moscow, came to this conclusion: "It is impossible to conduct industry continuously in this way." They meant men going off to meetings and having long discussions. So you may take it that that sort of thing is going to be put a stop to.

A young English gentleman went to Russia to study land surveying. What put him rather out of countenance was that there were about two hundred students there and they made him feel very small. Their reading was extraordinary. Their knowledge of history was magnificent. They had a superb knowledge of the theory of land surveying. He felt like a worm. But when they had to go out and actually survey some land, he was the only person who could do it.

The fact is there are too many people in Russia like Shaw and

Webb and so on. We are magnificent parasites. We grasp the whole thing. We know the history of it, but we cannot do it. When they have put a stop to all this meeting and discussion, when they have grown factory sense, the advantages of their system are overwhelming and nothing can stop them.

Verbatim report of lecture delivered before the Fabian Society at Kingsway Hall, London, on Thursday, 23 November 1933. Published in The Lecture Recorder, *December 1933.*

The Politics
of Unpolitical Animals

Tonight, I should like to take a look at the new world in which the Fabian Society is living—or dying. Fifty years ago, I was a remarkable young man of twentyeight, and the Chairman was a rather more remarkable young man of twentysix, and we became convinced of the validity of Socialism. We found ourselves in a world of strong Liberal tradition, which was largely the barricade tradition, and the work that we set ourselves to do was to make Socialism constitutional and respectable.

In turning the movement over, from the barricade tradition to the constitutional tradition, we made, what I suppose now appears to be, our big mistake. That is to say, we proposed to bring about Socialism through Parliament, and ultimately we had elections, at which the candidates were professed Socialists and the programs were Socialist. We had not discovered, what we have now discovered, that you cannot bring about Socialism through Parliament, because you cannot bring about anything through Parliament! Parliament has grown up historically, as an instrument for preventing the country from being governed, and in that, of course, it is an entirely representative institution. As the Chairman says, every Englishman is an island in which he is a Robinson Crusoe, who is not to be governed by anybody. But, unfortunately, when all the islands come together and coalesce into dry land, you must have an active, positive Government which must be carried out as any other business undertaking is carried out. With the exception of the Party system of government, I know of no business establishment, in which one man is sent in to do a job and another man is sent in to prevent him doing it, and in which, from precedent to precedent, there has grown up a quite extraordinary machinery of procedure, which makes the opposition of the Opposition completely ineffective, unless the two parties can agree on something that will not make very much difference to either of them.

We were so busy getting rid of the barricades, that we did not scrutinize, too closely, what we were putting up in their place, and we created the Labor party—God forgive us!—because the Labor party drew away all the effective men in the movement into Parliament and made an end of them.

Not only did our Parliament extinguish every effort towards Socialism, but out of it there grew the Parliament at Geneva—the League of Nations—where, because it is supposed to be a democratic institution, all the delegates prevent oneanother from doing anything, a typical instance being over disarmament. Nevertheless, you will observe, that they do not give it up in disgust because, being practically all Parliamentarians, they are naturally too delighted to find themselves on a Disarmament Committee with the absolute guarantee that nothing will be done. They all know perfectly well, that not one of the great Powers has the slightest intention of disarming. In a vague way, they say that they would like to reduce the cost of armaments a little, and they say to oneanother, "A sixteen-inch shell is much more expensive than a ten-inch shell; would you mind if I shot you with a ten-inch shell?"

Now, there are springing up, here and there, throughout the world, a number of gentlemen who want to get something done, and they have taken steps which have resulted to some extent in things being done. I want now to carry my survey into personalities and to look at the different countries.

First of all, let us take Herr Hitler—a very remarkable, very able man. For some time I, myself, was very much puzzled about Herr Hitler as to whether he was merely another Titus Oates, or whether he really was an able statesman. But Hitler suddenly made a great stroke, and to understand it, you must take a look at the way Germany was treated after the War. We went on the assumption that, since Germany had been defeated, she could be treated as a defeated person, could be kicked vigorously and continuously and, as Hitler said, the assumption was that this was to go on until the end of the world. Now, to any of us who had any real political intelligence, it was quite evident in 1918 that the treatment of Germany as a vanquished power could not last very long. I remember that, at a luncheon which, I think, Mr Ramsay MacDonald gave to the late Herr Stahmer (the first German Ambassador here after the War), I was sitting near the German Ambassador and, on the other side of the table, there was an Englishman—an "island" of extraordinary insularity. We were talking about one thing and another, and I happened to say, "If only Germany discovered some weapon of war, which made military coercion absolutely impossible, and put her on a level militarily at once with all the Powers, do you suppose that she would ever pay another penny of reparations?" The "island," on the other side of the table, suddenly went into eruption and said, "Herr Stahmer, do you confirm what this gentleman has said?" And the German Ambassador smiled and said, "I am always glad to meet my friend, Mr Shaw, he is always so entertaining." Now what Hitler grasped was the fact that the Treaty of Versailles had to be repudiated and, as a statesman, he knew that the time had come when the repudiation could be made with impunity, because the only thing that the Allies could do was immediately to levy a distraint and put in the man in possession—in other words, to send their armies into Germany and make a partition of Germany, like the old partition of Poland. He knew they would not do it, because they would be afraid and they could not afford it.

He saw, clearly enough, that if anything was to be done, he had got to get rid of the Parliamentary system. We did not see what Hitler saw that, with the rest of the world not being prepared to go through with the partition of Germany, he might repudiate the Treaty of Versailles and also re-arm, and I daresay he buys a gun or two, even from this country, because there are still a few English firms who have that sort of broad international outlook, which will sell guns to anybody.

One of Hitler's aims is to get an absolutely solid German block in the middle of Europe, and I do not know what is going to come of it, because it may bring him into conflict with Mussolini. He was against the Austrian Empire, because it was broken up into Germans and Slavs, and he was against the old Empire, because that was developing on the Slav side and not on the German side. When the War suddenly took Austria, and cut off all the Slav parties, and separated and left Vienna as a German Austria, then immediately it was quite clear (although he is not saying much about it now) that one of the things Hitler was going to work for, was a combination of Austria and Germany and, in my opinion, that combination is inevitable. But Signor Mussolini does not want this very powerful state there, on Italy's northern front. However, we will not go into that tonight because Hitler is really a good statesman and is, for the moment, waiving that question.

There is one thing about Hitler which recommended him to me from the very first, and that is his face—it has an expression of intense resentment. That is the expression that every statesman ought to have in the world, more particularly the statesman who knows what it is to have been a poor man and who has known the real state of things in Europe. It is because our statesmen never have an expression of resentment on their faces, but are always in a state of entirely good humor and good fellowship, in surroundings which ought to make them mad with fury, if they really had any social sympathy, that nothing is done.

But I cannot agree with Hitler on every point. In the first place, I think he is the victim of bad biology and of a bogus ethnology. He seems to believe in the division of mankind into an Aryan race and a Latin race. That is all nonsense. We are an extraordinarily mixed lot, and not only is it impossible to divide the sheep from the goats, in that particular way, because they are not sheep and goats but a sort of animal that is half sheep and half goat but, I think the evidence is irresistible that, unless a stock is crossed, and that pretty frequently, the stock degenerates. Look at the English. In our older hereditary classes, the people who have kept themselves English, the aristocracy, you have a type of Englishman who is very handsome, very pleasant to meet, often skilled in all sorts of sports, but it is the beauty of a Borzoi dog. Those who have Borzoi dogs know that although they are irresistibly attractive, they have absolutely no brain, and that is the kind of Englishman we have got from inbreeding.

Now let us look at Signor Mussolini. What has he built up? He is trying to build up in Italy what he calls a corporate state. He wants to put all the different industries into the hands of corporations, as he calls them, and then, finally, to create a Council of Corporations to succeed Parliament. I approve of that, because it is precisely what the Fabian Society wants, and it is clearly a necessary part of Socialism, no matter what you call it.

I do not know whether Signor Mussolini really believes that he can get through to his ideal without Socialism, but I know that he cannot, because he may form his corporations, but they will have no real power whatever, unless every corporation owns the means of production which it is supposed to supervise. For instance, you go to the corporations and ask them to organize the coal and iron industries, but if the mines and land are owned by private land-lords, the corporations will be able to do nothing, except organize the industries for the benefit of those private proprietors, who will finally take everything that they produce, except the bare subsist-ence of the people who are doing it.

Now let us come to another interesting gentleman, whose per-sonal acquaintance I have had the pleasure of making—Stalin. Mussolini, particularly by virtue of his taking all the Cabinet posts, may not unfairly be described as a dictator, but when you turn to Stalin, you get something else. Stalin is not a dictator. The nearest comparison you can get to Stalin is the Pope. Their positions are very much the same. The Roman Catholic church grew out of a number of men, who were not elected by anybody, but they them-selves decided to be priests and joined together in a priesthood and, finally, elected their own hierarchy. They depended, of course, on the fact that most of the people looked to them and accepted them because of this particular religious conviction. Now, exactly the same system prevails in Russia, where a number of persons had a political conviction and, in the old days, these men faced all sorts of martyrdoms and imprisonments, and they gradu-ally formed what is now called the Communist Party. The Com-munist Party is more democratic than the Catholic Church is now because, in the latter, the people do not elect their priests, and in the Russian system, the men at the top are selected from below and the election is a real thing.

Now Stalin is a Nationalist exactly like Hitler. He does not fall back on the world revolution, but understands that he has to have Socialism in Russia, which is quite big enough for him to look after without him troubling himself about Socialism in Edinburgh, or anywhere else. Stalin is an opportunist; whatever is the shortest way to get a thing done, he tries that way, and when persons say to him, "This is against the principles of Marx," Stalin says, "I am going to try it. Marx was infallible. I will try it, and if it succeeds, it cannot be against the principles of Marx, because Marx cannot make mistakes," and if, under those circumstances, you say that Marx is against something that is a success, you will have to go to Siberia until you get a little more prudent.

Now I come to the real beginning of my lecture, and that is the question of extermination. When you are governing a country, a regiment, or anything else, the first thing you have to know is who you have to kill and who you have to leave alive. We have such a list. In Scotland, for instance, you can kill people who throw vitriol, in America, kidnappers and so on, but it must be evident to any thinking man that there is a much larger category of people who have to be exterminated, and the moment you become a Socialist you are committed to the opinion that private proprietors, speculators and profiteers have to be exterminated, and there must be no hesitation. For instance, Stalin has said that the peasant must be exterminated, and Mr Chesterton says that, on the contrary, the whole world ought to be put to death. Of course, Stalin cannot send out a body of executioners and hang them all, for the very excellent reason that you must not kill the goose that lays the golden eggs, and in Russia there would immediately be famine. In fact, Russia has very nearly been famine-stricken in consequence of going a little too fast with the peasant. The way to exterminate the peasant is not to bring him up as a peasant but as something else; bring him up to be a man with the collegiate habit, the educated habit, the habit of living in civilization with a number of other people and joining his interests with theirs. That, of course, is what Russia is trying to do. She is putting the sons and daughters of the peasants on to collective farms instead of letting them cultivate their own strip of land.

I think we shall have to build up our international state by nationalist states of some solidity. Although in the nineteenth century, we thanked heaven that we had passed through the old wicked wars of religion, I am not at all certain that we are not going to have wars of religion, and wars perhaps of a very fierce kind.

I agree with Mr de Valera, Mr Hitler, Mussolini and the rest of them that foreign trade is an evil thing in itself. The idea in production, exclusively and unchangeably is, I think, that the producer should as far as possible be on the same spot as the consumer, so that there may be less transport.

The papers are very full, at present, of the tremendous multiplication of the powers of production. I, myself, have seen a roll of
blank paper go down a room and, at the end, come out as a perfectly cloth-bound book in twenty minutes. That time could have
been reduced to five minutes, if only somebody could have made a
paste that would dry a little quicker! I think that is splendid, but I
want to know about the production of food, which is the one thing
we want. Have we progressed so tremendously in that? I have
heard of one helpful thing. Imperial Chemical Industries have
learned that, if you feed the dried grass grown from nitrogen-
treated ground to cows, they will produce a much more nutritious
sort of butter, a much more vital sort of milk, and if you eat that
butter and drink that milk you will never suffer from disease and
you will never die. In the same way, the Anthroposophical Society
points out that if you collect all the weeds which you now burn,
make a silo of them, and put in certain chemical constituents (which
the Society will supply for a consideration), you get a manure of
such virtue, that if you grow your food with that manure, you will
never suffer from any disease and you will never die. Of course,
these inventions immediately threaten us with overpopulation!

Devising Socialist constitutions for unpolitical animals in the Fabian manner is like composing symphonies for the deaf and painting pictures for the blind. Three-quarters of a century ago, Bulwer
Lytton anticipated the Fabians by a Utopia, called The Coming
Race, in which all our difficulties were vanquished, because Man
had been forced to become political by having developed a power
of killing at sight, which made oppression or even irritating rude-
ness too dangerous to be practised. Those who would not behave in
a civilized manner became neither conquerors nor pro-consuls, but
corpses. The attainment of this power, Bulwer Lytton saw, was the
only hope of human civilization.

The thrice-blessed invention of poison gases and high explosives
promises to realize Bulwer Lytton's dream. Our oppressors, with
their silly Disarmament Conferences, strive desperately to retain
their monopoly of the powers of life and death, and to perpetuate
war by Queensberry Rules. But they dare not cease to develop the
new powers of destruction to the utmost limit; and these powers
will force mankind into a real civilization, though probably not
before at least ninety per cent of them have exterminated each
other in driving the lesson home.

Meanwhile, let those of us who hate cruelty agitate with all our might for the discovery of a painless, but infallibly and instantaneously fatal, gas, capable of being manufactured by everybody. Our domestic gas supply, laid on from house to house, is an invaluable advance in this direction; and we owe a great deal to the disinterested experiments carried on daily by our suicides.

An article published in The Observer *(London) on 13 August 1944.*

How Much Money
Do We Need?

What is the amount of money everyone ought to have to keep civilization safe and steady? I have had to think this question out, because I am an absentee landlord, a capitalist, a "renter of ability," and by conviction a Communist, which is a combination much more frequent than that of Communist proletarian. In fact, the professed Communists know less about it—if possible—than the rest of our politicians, and, if left to themselves, will attempt to solve it by a plundering match between the rich and poor, which will end, not in there being no poor but in there being nobody else.

I shall state the case in 12 articles, premising only that the basic income must be equal for everybody, because, as it applies to newly born babes, centenarians, and families, it can have no regard to differences in personal qualities, talents, and deserts.

1. The political object of equality of income is the prevention of the ruptures and compound fractures, the internal strains, conflicts, and civil wars, caused by the division of society into financial classes, each struggling for the lion's share of the national income, and nobody being assured of getting any share at all except as a pauper. Every former civilization known to us (there are half a dozen) has been wrecked by these strains; and ours is going the same way.

2. This suggests that the best possible distribution of the national income is equal distribution.

3. It seems to follow that the basic figure can be ascertained by simply dividing the income figure by the population figure.

4. It does not follow immediately. The national income provides about four shillings per head per week. A family of two parents and three children would have £1 a week to live on, with no possibility of adding to it by their labor, already absorbed by its production.

5. The Cabinets, the executive public services, the judiciary, the Bar, the scientific institutions, the cultural institutions, the directors of business and finance, all of them necessary to high civilization, cannot be recruited from families living on a pound a week.

6. Nature (sometimes called Providence) produces the necessary percentage of specially capable people; but as this is a percentage, not of any class, but of the entire population, the basic income to be aimed at must be a family income sufficient to put within everyone's reach the cultural home atmosphere and schooling without which natural capacity cannot develop. Four shillings per head per week would mean cultural sterilization, ending in a relapse into primitive tribalism.

7. Equality of income must therefore begin with a basic income large enough to produce prime ministers, higher mathematicians, historians and philosophers, authors and artists, as well as ploughmen and dairymaids. They are necessities, not luxuries nor parasites.

8. Such an income has been estimated by Mr H. G. Wells at £4,000 a year in present terms. But from eight to twelve hundred would do to begin with. This, in a scientifically organized society, would command a handsomer life than £4,000 does now. Later on, with volcanic blow holes and our British tides harnessed to industry and agriculture, £800 a year would go farther than our £20,000.

9. For the present, however, so high a basic income as £800 puts equal division of the national income out of the question for the moment, as the national quotient falls so far short of it. In Communist Russia it has been found that to maintain the indispensable "intellectual proletariat," even with Communist secondary education and "centers of rest and culture" within everyone's reach, it is necessary to distribute income in wages and salaries at rates varying as widely as ten to one.

10. This means that the basic rate will be enjoyed at first by only 10 per cent of the population. Only what is left can be distributed

among the 90 per cent, who in the factories and mines, the ships and trains and city offices, have only to do what they are told and need not think about it.

11. From this point progress towards equality of income must depend on increased production. The thinkers and directors being sufficiently paid, and the rank and file underpaid, the increase must be used to raise the family incomes of the rank and file until they, too, can afford the privacy, the leisure, the culture, and all the other amenities and opportunities which the basic income commands, and which, applied to family life, supply the nurseries from which the thinking and directing functionaries are drawn.

12. During this process, all attempts and pretensions of the receivers of the basic income to keep their distance above the rest by having their incomes increased must be resisted. Those who have enough must be content with it until those with less than enough are raised to their level.

And now what is to be the test of sufficient equality to make a civilization stable and secure? Will it be achieved when for every two and sixpence allotted to the Astronomer Royal his housemaid is allotted half a crown? Theoretically yes, practically no, because with the spread of culture there will certainly be competition for the post of Astronomer Royal, and, what has already begun, a growing objection to the drudgeries of housemaiding, insuperable unless these are mitigated by electric fires, vacuum cleaners, luxurious kitchens, servants' bedrooms, bathrooms and the like, combined with higher wages, shorter hours, and the abandonment by the astronomer of all pretence to social superiority.

The test will be intermarriageability. When the astronomer's son can marry the housemaid without the slightest misalliance, the trick will be done as far as law or policy can or need do it.

At that point unequal incomes will cease to trouble us. At present, though a person with £50 a year cannot marry a person with £5,000 without not merely misalliance but downright miscegenation (for the two figures produce two different human species), a person with £5,000 a year can marry a person with £50,000 without the least difficulty: in fact, if the £50,000 person refused to marry anyone with less he or she would find it hard to get married at all. But when the basic income is secured to everybody, it will not matter a rap if here and there geniuses or freaks with lucrative talents or attractions earn ten times that figure. Like the late Andrew Carnegie or Lord Nuffield,[1] they could do nothing with their superfluous money but "do good" with it.

The directors of the equalization process must not be doctrinaire idealists beginning at the end instead of at the beginning and thereby becoming wreckers of the civilization they are bent on saving. The road to equality starts from inequality, not the haphazard inequality that now makes millionaires of a few children-in-arms, and paupers of multitudes of people worn out by toil that begins before they escape from their elementary school prisons into industrial slavery, but a scientific inequality based on the inexorable facts.

Great geniuses do not need more food, better clothes, a warmer fire or a more rainproof roof than the hewers of wood and drawers of water; in fact their clothes last longer and they eat less. But they cost more. They must be brought up in houses where there are not only tables and chairs, washstands and beds, but books and pictures and musical instruments and mothers and fathers to whom such things are necessities and whose manners and language differ accordingly from those of illiterate laborers who are barely kept alive until they reproduce themselves.

Here and there we may come on a peer who began as a farmer's boy or a millionaire who began as a bootblack; but there are not enough of these swallows to make a summer; and when neither the industries nor the professions can exist without from 5 to 10 per cent of intelligentsia we cannot depend on the 0.001 per cent who can break their way through all class barriers to the top. The Bolshevik revolution in Russia, beginning with a ruthless persecution of the existing Tsarist education and culture, not only half-starved itself, but when tested by war soon found that it could not organize its army without a majority of ex-Tsarist officers, nor its industry without bourgeois bosses, nor its Cabinets without ministers who had never in their lives handled hammer or sickle to earn their living.

The U.S.S.R. is really a Fabian Federation, forced into that mould by sheer pressure of hard facts on Marxian goodwill towards men. The same pressure will operate here on Primroses and Reds impartially. Progressive Conservatives are not lacking in goodwill. The struggle will be between the progressive Levellers-up and the catastrophic Levellers-down; and the Progressives will win if and when they learn their political business.

Notes

"Life, Literature, and Political Economy"

1. A character in the *Arabian Nights*. Alnaschar inherits one hundred pieces of silver and invests them in a basket of glassware. He then dreams of the riches he will acquire from successive trading adventures until finally he has enough money to marry a vizier's daughter. Becoming angry with his supposed wife, he kicks at her in his dream and upsets the basket, smashing all his ware.

2. Henry Fawcett (1833–84), English political economist, advocate of female suffrage and other reforms. He wrote *Manual of Political Economy*, which led to his election to the chair of political economy at Cambridge in 1863.

3. The works to which Shaw is alluding are Charles A. Fenn's *A Compendium of the English and Foreign Funds, and the Principal Joint-Stock Companies*, first published in 1838, and *Whitaker's Almanack*, an annual reference work, first published in 1869 by the great Victorian bookseller and publisher Joseph Whitaker (1820–95).

"The Solidarity of Social-Democracy"

1. August Ferdinand Bebel (1840–1913), German socialist. Became leader of the Social Democratic movement in 1871 and its chief spokesman in the Reichstag.

2. Karl Johann Kautsky (1854–1938), German socialist. Kautsky was an orthodox Marxist whose views clashed with those of other disciples of Marx including Nikolai Lenin and Eduard Bernstein.

3. Adolphe Thiers (1797–1877), leader of right-wing liberals in France. He was bitterly opposed to socialists and, as head of the provisional government of Bordeaux, ordered the troops to suppress the Commune of Paris of 1871.

4. Mikhail Bakunin (1814–76), Russian anarchist and opponent of Marx

in the Communist International. He was outvoted and expelled at the Hague Congress in 1872; he believed that Communism, with its withering away of the state, was an essential step towards anarchism.

5. Prince Bernhard Heinrich von Bülow (1849–1929), German states-man, Chancellor, 1900–1909. Eduard Bernstein (1850–1932), German socialist leader. From 1888 to 1901 he lived in England, where he as-sociated with the Fabians. Bernstein was an advocate of revisionism, an evolutionary form of Marxism.

6. Alexandre Millerand (1859–1943). A moderate and gradualist among French socialists. He caused a furor in 1899 when he accepted office in a Radical cabinet in the belief that socialism could best be achieved by cooperating with the necessary forces of social evolution. Jules Guesde (1845–1922), French socialist who advocated the rejection of any com-promise with capitalistic government. Paul Singer (1844–1911), German socialist and leader of the Social Democratic party. Singer was a practical politician and organizer rather than a theorist. Henry Mayers Hyndman (1842–1921), leader of the Social-Democratic Federation and the founder of *Justice*.

"The Bitter Cry of the Middle Classes"

1. William Thomas Stead (1849–1912), English journalist and reformer. Editor of the *Pall Mall Gazette* from 1883 to 1889; later founded the *Review of Reviews*.

2. Spencer Compton Cavendish, eighth Duke of Devonshire (1833–1908), Liberal politician. Lord President of the Council, 1895–1905.

3. John Burns (1858–1943), British labor leader and politician. Elected M.P. for Battersea in 1892; became president of the Local Government Board in 1905 and the Board of Trade in 1914. He was the first working-man cabinet minister in Britain.

4. Poplar is one of the East End districts of London.

5. Shaw is alluding to the differences in tone and perspicacity between several strident letters from middle-class "bittercriers" and a letter submit-ted by G. K. Chesterton in the 24 July 1906 issue of *The Tribune*. One writer invites readers to join the newly formed "Middle Class Defense Organiza-tion"; another maintains that socialistic legislation will only have a ten-dency to "increase that already large body of helpless, useless, idle, drunk-en, improvident class." Chesterton, meanwhile, declares that Sims "exagg-erates the determining power of economics." He defines the middle-class man, not in economic terms, but as someone who has a certain view of himself and goes on to point out that, having lost a common creed, the middle-class man is now indistinguishable from the workman.

"Socialism and the Artistic Professions"

1. Cyril Flower, first Baron Battersea (1843–1907), M.P. for Brecknock, 1880–85, and Luton, 1885–92. James Keir Hardie (1856–1915), Scottish labor leader and one of the founders of the Labour party. He worked in a coal pit as a boy. The first of all Labour candidates, he was defeated in his first try in 1888, then sat for West Ham, 1892–95, and Merthyr Tydfil, 1900–1915. Hardie started and edited the *Labour Leader*.

2. Andrew Fletcher (1655–1716) of Saltoun, Scottish patriot and writer.

"A Socialist Program"

1. Robert Blatchford (1851–1943), British socialist and journalist ("Nunquam"). Founded *The Clarion* in 1891.

2. Shaw is referring to George Jeffreys, first Baron Jeffreys (1648–89), an infamous English judge. A willing tool of the monarchy, he presided at the trial of Titus Oates and later was sent to the west to try the followers of Monmouth. There he came to be known as the "infamous Jeffreys," for he hanged, transported, whipped, and fined hundreds of the followers during the "bloody assize." William Laud (1573–1645), English churchman, Archbishop of Canterbury. Working closely with Charles I, Laud tried to enforce High Church forms of worship in the Church of England and to eliminate all Puritans from important positions in the Church. He persecuted and imprisoned many Nonconformists. He was impeached by the Long Parliament and condemned to death.

3. Evelyn Baring, first Earl of Cromer (1841–1917). A member of a great banking family, Baring was Administrator of Egypt from 1883 until he resigned in April 1907. In July 1907 Parliament granted him £50,000 out of public funds in recognition of his "eminent service" in Egypt.

The incident at Denshawai took place on 13 June 1907, when a party of uniformed British officers drove to the village of Denshawai to go pigeon shooting, a sport not too popular with the Egyptian farmers who kept the birds. The headman of the village was away; his deputy, intimidated by the officers, granted them permission to shoot pigeons if they did it some distance from the village. The local pigeon farmers became angry when the shooting began and attacked the officers, the youngest of whom accidentally discharged his gun in the scuffle, wounding three men and a woman. The woman was thought dead, and the young men of the village, led by Abd-el-Nebi, the woman's husband, then attacked the officers. Two officers ran for help: one got to the next village and died of sunstroke after giving his report; the other met a patrol, which came to the rescue of the party.

The judgments handed down by the British tribunal which tried the Egyptians were quite severe. Abd-el-Nebi and another young man were sentenced to penal servitude for life; eight men were flogged; and four men, including the principal pigeon farmer involved, were hanged. Sir Edward Grey, the Foreign Secretary, was informed of the sentences of the tribunal prior to their execution. Although he believed that they were startlingly severe, he determined, in consultation with the Prime Minister, Campbell-Bannerman, and the Chancellor of the Exchequer, H. H. Asquith, not to overrule the tribunal, fearing that disorder might break loose in Egypt.

4. Peter Curran (1860–1910), socialist and trade union leader. Organized the Gas Workers' Union and was a Labour M.P. from 1906 to 1910. First chairman of the General Federation of Trade Unions. Henry Campbell-Bannerman (1836–1908), Liberal English politician. Campbell-Bannerman became a Liberal leader in Commons in 1898 and identified himself with progressive causes. He became Prime Minister in 1905; bad health forced him to resign in 1908. Arthur James Balfour, first Earl of Balfour (1848–1930), Conservative English politician and philosopher. Balfour was Prime Minister from 1902 to 1905; his philosophical writings include *The Foundations of Belief* (1895).

5. Victor Grayson (b.1881). In 1907, as an independent socialist, Grayson won the seat at Colne Valley in Yorkshire. He caused trouble in Parliament by refusing to sign the "Party Pledge," which would have compelled him to vote as a majority of the parliamentary party decided, and defied the standing order of the House by making a scene when he demanded that priority should be given to considering the claims of the unemployed. He lost his seat in 1910.

6. Wilfrid Scawen Blunt (1840–1922), English poet and traveler. A violent opponent of British policies in Africa, India, and Ireland, he espoused the cause of Arabi Pasha and Egyptian nationalism.

7. Feargus Edward O'Connor (1794–1855), Irish Chartist who devoted himself to the cause of the working classes in England. His Leeds *Northern Star* did much to help the Chartist cause. He sat for Nottingham in 1847 and presented the huge Chartist petition in April 1848.

8. A character in Dickens's *Bleak House* who sacrifices her family to her concern for the African natives of Borrioboola Gha. Thavie's Inn is one of the nine Inns of Chancery.

9. Robert Bontine Cunninghame Graham (1852–1936), Scottish author and politician. Member of the Social-Democratic Federation. An M.P., 1886–92, he was imprisoned, along with John Burns, for breaking through the police cordon in Trafalgar Square on "Bloody Sunday," 1887. For information about H. M. Hyndman, see note 6, "The Solidarity of Social-Democracy," above.

10. Prince Peter Kropotkin (1842–1921), Russian geographer, savant,

revolutionary, and nihilist. In 1872, he associated himself with the extremist section of the International and was arrested and imprisoned in Russia. In 1876 he escaped to England; he returned to Russia in 1917. Walter Crane (1845–1915), painter, designer, and decorator. A friend and collaborator of William Morris, he worked with him in the Socialist League. For information about Keir Hardie, see note 1, "Socialism and the Artistic Profession," above.

11. Reginald John Campbell (1867–1956), Congregational minister and Fabian socialist. Pastor of the City Temple, London, from 1903 to 1915.

12. Will Thorne (1857–1946), trade union leader, member of the Social-Democratic Federation and M.P. member of the Parliamentary Committee of Trades Union Congress, 1894–1934.

13. In August 1907, in consequence of the murder of nine European workmen by Shawia tribesmen, the French bombarded and occupied the city of Casablanca. Engaged in improving the harbor works, the Europeans had been working close to a Moslem cemetery. The Shawias became excited by reports that the cemetery had been desecrated, and proceeded to pillage the city. The French responded in force and before order was restored, the dead in Casablanca numbered in the thousands.

"On Driving Capital Out of the Country"

1. William Albert Samuel Hewins (1865–1931), economist. He was the first director of the London School of Economics, and resigned in 1903 on his conversion to tariff reform.

2. Brunner, Mond and Company, a chemical firm founded in 1873 by Sir John Tomlinson (1842–1919) and Ludwig Mond (1839–1909).

3. Frederic Bastiat (1801–50), French economist. An acquaintance of Cobden and Bright, Bastiat wrote and lectured on behalf of free trade. In the revolution of February 1848, he spoke out vehemently against socialism, arguing that it involved protectionism.

4. For information about Keir Hardie, see note 1 to "Socialism and the Artistic Profession," above; and for Pete Curran, see note 4 to "A Socialist Program," above.

5. Sir George Thomas Livesey (1834–1908), promoter of labor copartnership. As a director of the South Metropolitan Gas Company (London), he admitted foremen (1886) and workmen (1889) to share in the profits of the firm.

6. Sir John Lubbock, Lord Avebury (1834–1913); known for his research on primitive man and on the habits of bees and ants. His works included *Prehistoric Times* (1865) and *Origins of Civilisation* (1870).

7. Inspector Bucket is a character in Dickens's *Bleak House.*

8. Albert Walter Gamage (1855–1930). In 1878, Gamage founded the famous drapery and department store in Holborn. It closed in 1972.

9. Shaw is referring to the department store founded by William Whiteley (1831–1907), who styled himself "The Universal Provider," and to the "Stores," established by the Civil Service Supply Association in 1865, and the Army and Navy Stores in 1872, both of which had a considerable effect on the development of the department store.

10. From 1906 to 1910 Philip H. Lockhart operated a chain of thirty to forty restaurants and dining rooms in London. The Aerated Bread Co. Ltd opened its first teashop in 1880. Soon there were over 220 branches. Both Lockhart restaurants and the Aerated Bread teashops served inexpensive meals to Londoners. Peel and Poole were two firms rather than one which Shaw joins together for alliterative purposes. Peel's was a bootmaking firm; Henry Poole and Co. was a firm of tailors located on Savile Row.

11. Jean Jaurès (1859–1914), French socialist leader, writer, and orator. He was perhaps the greatest leader the socialist movement produced. Socialism was for him the culmination of republicanism; and collectivism was the natural end of radical reform.

"Socialist Politics"

1. See note 11 to "A Socialist Program," above.

2. See note 4 to "A Socialist Program," above.

3. Burgh Canning Hubert George, second Marquess and fifteenth Earl of Clanricarde (1832–1916). English land proprietor. He resisted the movement to limit the Irish landlord's power. He never visited his property, but used the weapon of eviction to fight tenants who refused to pay. Following a number of disturbances and the murder of some of his bailiffs, he was supposed to have said of his Irish tenants, "Do they think they will intimidate me by shooting my bailiffs?"

4. Christopher Furness, first Baron Furness of Grantley (1852–1912), ship owner and industrialist, Liberal M.P. in 1891; was voted out with the liberals in 1895. He was not a popular man among his business competitors; his business methods were severely criticized.

5. Harry Quelch (1858–1913). A member of the Social-Democratic Federation and active in the Independent Labour party. For information about H. M. Hyndman, see note 6, "The Solidarity of Social-Democracy," above.

6. Frederick Sleigh Roberts, Earl of Kandahar, Pretoria, and Waterford (1832–1914), British military leader. He played an important role in operations in India, Afghanistan, and South Africa.

"What about the Middle Class?"

1. Stanislas Leszczynski (1677–1766). Elected king of Poland in 1704 but was driven from the throne in 1709 by Peter the Great. In 1736 he received the duchies of Lorraine and Bar, where he held a small but distinguished court at Lunéville. He was partly responsible for the embellishment of the city of Nancy.

"The Case for Socialism"

1. In 1894 Sir William Harcourt (1827–1904) imposed, as Liberal Chancellor of the Exchequer, the so-called death duty, which took a substantial toll of the capital wealth left by deceased persons. He brought all forms of property—landed and other—for the first time into one reckoning. In his momentous budget of 1909–10, David Lloyd George (1863–1945) introduced the supertax, or graduated income tax.
2. Bournville and Port Sunlight are both "model villages." Port Sunlight, founded by Lord Leverhulme, consists of the extensive soap works of Lever Brothers. Bournville, located south of Birmingham, is a garden suburb founded by George Cadbury in 1879.
3. Charles Gore, Bishop of Oxford (1853–1932), High Church leader, Christian Socialist, and social reformer.
4. Pooh-Bah is a character in Gilbert and Sullivan's opera *The Mikado*.

"The Case for Equality"

1. Barnett Barnato (1852–97), South African millionaire and speculator. After engineering the Kaffir boom (1895), he committed suicide at sea.
2. For information about the death duty and the supertax, see note 1, "The Case for Socialism," above.
3. Charles John Darling, first Baron Darling (1849–1936), Conservative M.P., 1888–97. His appointment as a judge of the King's Bench aroused widespread controversy and ill-founded misgivings. In his august office, his wit and humor tended to get the better of him as they enlivened his books of light verse.
4. Correctly, "The career open to talents."
5. Alfred Charles William Harmsworth, Viscount Northcliffe (1865–1922), the founder of modern popular journalism. He founded the *Daily Mirror*, published the *Daily Mail*, London *Evening News*, and, from 1908, was proprietor of the *Times*.
6. Robert Wiedemann Barrett Browning (1849–1912). His pet or familiar name was Penini—hence Peni and Pen. He was a sculptor as well as a painter.

"Socialism and the Labor Party"

1. A variation of the original verse by Jonathan Swift in his 1733 poem, "On Poetry, A Rhapsody." Swift's verse reads

> So naturalists observe a flea
> Has smaller fleas that prey on him
> And these have smaller still to bite 'em
> And so proceed *ad infinitum*.

2. Fourteen years later in 1934, Shaw dramatized this episode concerning Edward III and Queen Philippa in a short play, *The Six of Calais.*

3. For information about Karl Kautsky, see note 2, "The Solidarity of Social Democracy," above.

"The Dictatorship of the Proletariat"

1. Arthur Henderson (1863–1935). Entered Parliament as Labour M.P. in 1903. Largely responsible for the organization of the Labour party, he was its treasurer and then its secretary. He served as Home Secretary in the first Labour government and Foreign Secretary in the second. Joseph Robert Clynes (1869–1949), English Labour politician. Entered Parliament in 1910. Clynes was food controller in 1918 and Lord Privy Seal in Britain's first Labour cabinet in 1924.

2. Parolles is a character in Shakespeare's *All's Well That Ends Well.*

3. Whitley Councils were councils for joint consultation between employers and employees. The government committee that proposed them in 1917 was presided over by John Henry Whitley (1866–1935), Liberal M.P. for Halifax from 1900 to 1928.

4. William Ralph Inge (1860–1954), Dean of St. Paul's from 1911 until 1934.

5. The Confederation Generale du Travail adopted at its Amiens Congress in 1906 a charter which proclaimed the complete independence of the trade union movement and the movement's repudiation of all political party alliances. The charter commended the general strike as an instrument of political action and claimed that the class struggle was the basis for trade union action.

6. In 1920, Lloyd George called for the subjugation of Ireland in order to ensure the security of England. In a series of articles published in the *New York American* on 5, 12, 19, and 26 December 1920 under the general title "The New Terrorism," Shaw asked if national independence was to be the privilege of those possessing the biggest battalions, and then went on to point out that Lloyd George's new line of playing for absolute security would inevitably lead Britain into a Darwinian "survival of the mightiest" war with America.

"The Impossibilities of Freedom"

1. Edward Rosslyn Mitchell (1879–1965), solicitor and author. Shaw is alluding to the articles on family life by Mitchell which were appearing in *The Daily Record*, Glasgow. In 1932, a selection of these articles was published in book form under the title *Impressions*.

"Cultural Internationalism"

1. Ferdinand Alvarez de Toledo, Duke of Alva (1508–82), Spanish general and statesman. On the revolt of the Netherlands, Phillip II sent Alva there in 1567. Alva established the "Bloody Council" and boasted that he had executed eighteen thousand men.

2. Hamar Greenwood, first Viscount (1870–1948), British politician. Liberal M.P. for York, 1906–10, and Sunderland, 1910–22; chief secretary for Ireland from 1920 to 1922. He reinforced the Royal Irish Constabulary with the undisciplined Black and Tans, whose violence he defended.

3. For information about the Denshawai, see note 3, "A Socialist Program," above. For information about Dean Ralph Inge, see note 4, "The Dictatorship of the Proletariat," above.

4. Shaw is referring to Henry Ford's peace mission during World War I. In 1915 Ford was reported to have said that he would "get the boys out of the trenches" by Christmas. Ford established and financed a permanent peace delegation in Norway which remained in existence until the United States entered the war in 1917.

5. Shaw is probably thinking of the American economist Francis Amasa Walker (1840–97). Walker wrote opposing the wage fund and was interested in the question of the rent of ability. He was professor of political economy and history at Yale (1873–81) and president of the Massachusetts Institute of Technology, (1881–97). His published works include *The Wages Question* (1876), and *Money in Its Relation to Trade and Industry* (1879).

6. Alfred Moritz Mond, first Baron Melchett (1868–1930), British industrialist and politician. Son of Ludwig Mond, one of the founders of Brunner, Mond and Company. Liberal M.P., 1906, and first Commissioner of Works, 1916–21.

"Follies, Fallacies, and Facts"

1. Herbert Henry Asquith, Earl of Oxford and Asquith (1852–1928), Liberal Prime Minister, 1908–16. For information about Dean Inge, see note 4, "The Dictatorship of the Proletariat," above.

"What Indeed?"

1. Philip, Viscount Snowden (1864–1937), British Labour statesman. He was Chancellor of the Exchequer, 1924, 1929–31, and remained in the coalition National government under Prime Minister Ramsay MacDonald (1866–1937) without enthusiasm but from a strong sense of duty.

2. Charles Stewart Vane-Tempest-Stewart, sixth Marquess of Londonderry (1852–1915), English conservative politician, chairman of the London School Board, 1895–97, and president of the first Board of Education under the Balfour Act, 1902–1905.

3. Walter Runciman (1870–1949), shipowner and Liberal politician. Long-time M.P. and president of the Board of Trade, 1914–16, and again, 1931–37.

4. Morgan Philips Price (1885–1973), Russian correspondent of the *Manchester Guardian*, 1914–18. A socialist, he wrote several pamphlets and books on his experiences in Russia. Shaw errs when he claims that Price prophesied Communism gradually evolving into Fabianism as early as 1917 or 1918. The earliest date that Price makes that claim, and then only in a very general way, is in the concluding pages of *The Economic Problems of Europe, Pre-War and After*, written in 1928.

5. Maxim Litvinoff (1876–1951), Soviet commissar. Deputy People's Commissar for Foreign Affairs in 1921 and Commissar from 1930 to 1939.

6. The Seattle Community was a group of Finns who left Seattle in 1930 and settled in Karelia, a republic of the U.S.S.R. east of Finland. They were not a religious sect as Shaw suggests, but rather a socialistic community.

7. A firm of consulting engineers headed by Charles E. Stuart (1881–1943). In 1926, they were hired by the U.S.S.R. to prepare a study of projections for new coal, iron, and copper mines and the rehabilitation of old ones. They made a formal report to the Russian government in 1931.

8. Maurice Gerschon Hindus (b. 1891), American writer. His works deal with interpreting the political views and cultures of Eastern Europe to the people of the United States. *Humanity Uprooted* (1929) and *Red Bread* (1931) are his best-known books.

9. Walter N. Polakov was an American citizen, head of an engineering firm which bore his name, and author of technical books on power production. In 1929 he was appointed consulting management engineer to the Supreme Economic Council of the U.S.S.R. He held that post for approximately two years. In the 8 November 1931 issue of the *New York Times*, he urged the formation of a one-billion-dollar pool to finance American manufacturers in filling Soviet orders on a more liberal credit basis and argued that the U.S.S.R. represented a huge market for American tractors. John Michael Carmody (1881–1963) was president of the Society of Industrial Engineers and was named editor of *Coal Age* and *Factory and*

Industrial Management in 1927. In 1931 he made a survey of industrial developments in Russia for the McGraw Hill Company.

10. The sense of this passage seems to be that the boys, with metal cadged from the men, played with a piece of disused machinery, probably a casting mold, in some old corner of the foundry.

"How Much Money Do We Need?"

1. William Richard Morris, first Viscount Nuffield (1877–1963) British Motor magnate and philanthropist. He started in the cycle business and by 1910 was manufacturing prototypes of Morris Oxford cars. He used part of his vast fortune to benefit hospitals, charities, and Oxford University and in 1943 established the Nuffield Foundation for medical, scientific, and social research.

Acknowledgments

I wish to thank the National Endowment for the Humanities for awarding me a fellowship which started me on the road to gathering materials for this collection and Creighton University for the support which it has given me during the preparation of this collection. I wish also to thank the Society of Authors and the Shaw Estate for permission to publish the articles and lectures. I also wish to thank the Library Board of Cornell University for permission to publish Shaw's lecture "What Indeed?" from the Burgunder Collection.

I also owe a word of thanks to a number of individuals. I must thank the Finnish Community in Superior, Wisconsin, for their assistance in identifying the Seattle Community; Andreas Gommermann for a useful translation; William and Rita Paterson for several hours of research in the British Museum; Gordon Bergquist and James Karabatsos for reading my manuscript and advising me on it; and Mary Lynn Strecker, who typed the manuscript and helped enormously with the proofreading.

I wish finally to acknowledge a great indebtedness to my wife, Beverly, who never faltered in her support, and to Dan Laurence, who assisted me in so many ways that it is safe to say that this collection would not have been published without his generous help, his patience, his kindness, and his encouragement. For these reasons, I have dedicated the collection to him.

Index